*Administration and Supervision
of the
Modern Secondary School*

M. Dale Baughman
Wendell G. Anderson
Mark Smith
Earle W. Wiltse

Administration and Supervision of the Modern Secondary School

Parker Publishing Company, Inc.   West Nyack, N.Y.

© 1969, BY

PARKER PUBLISHING COMPANY, INC.

WEST NYACK, N.Y.

ALL RIGHTS RESERVED. NO PART OF THIS
BOOK MAY BE REPRODUCED IN ANY FORM OR
BY ANY MEANS, WITHOUT PERMISSION IN
WRITING FROM THE PUBLISHER.

LIBRARY OF CONGRESS
CATALOG CARD NUMBER: 77–80411

PRINTED IN THE UNITED STATES OF AMERICA
13-005256-6 B & P

Acknowledgments

The enterprise of bringing into existence a book such as this one is seldom a one-person endeavor. No exception, this book has required the resources of others, in addition to the team of four authors.

First, we credit Karl Plath, Superintendent of High Schools, Highland Park, Illinois, who contributed heavily to the writing of Chapter Seven and Assistant Professor William Wilkerson, Indiana State University, who assisted in preparing Chapter Ten. We acknowledge the assistance of Marjorie Jerry, Sister Antonita Duffy and James Skelton, Graduate Students, Indiana State University, who made major contributions to Chapter Fifteen. Mary Hawkins and Becky Zeller contributed heavily to the typing of the manuscript and to other mechanical details. Also recognized in this category are Dala Baughman, Mable Stroman, Cleo Anderson, Joanne Clement, Cindy Jones, and Carol Nelson, manuscript readers and typists.

It is both proper and desirable, perhaps even diplomatic, for the authors to express gratitude and simple thanks to their wives and families for their abundance of tolerance and patience. This we do happily.

A Word from the Authors About This Book . . . .

"The buck stops here" reads a sign on former President Harry S. Truman's desk. In a sense it was one executive's way of expressing belief in his own capacity to make final decisions. It is at the levels of administration and supervision where major decisions are made that profoundly affect the operations of an enterprise. The executive roles in education sometimes are very complicated ones. Organizations differ in size, purpose and functions and new positions are created and new appointments made. As schools grow bigger and more complex, school leaders move upward, laterally or downward according to their successes.

Under the direction of the superintendent and responsible to him, the principal runs his school. This means that he must make decisions and interact with people at varying levels and from diverse backgrounds. He directs some and guides others. To do so he must possess a sound philosophy, justifiable principles and use effective practices. That is what this book concerns.

Roles in educational administration are changing enough to warrant serious study and analysis by all persons involved. New demands require new skills and new approaches. Professors of educational administration, practitioners and future school administrators as never before find it necessary to keep abreast of modified roles through continuing study.

The authors' views stem from many years of experience as students and practitioners of educational administration and are based on the results of practice as well as on theoretical considerations. Yet their major contribution in the present book perhaps lies in their descriptions of successful practices.

Hardly a secondary school principal is now alive who can hope to avoid involvement in change. Indeed, today's and tomorrow's principal is expected to induce, perpetuate and weigh change as one of his obligations. Therefore, the nature of the principal's role in effecting change is included. The specific role of the principal at this level is delineated carefully. Since unique differences do exist in the junior high school principalship, they are sharply defined and emphasized as helpful guides to those who administer such schools. Certain specific competencies are required for outstanding leadership in secondary schools, and these are pointed out as significant factors in the nature and challenge of educational leadership.

Through simplicity of expression and clarity of style we seek to communicate *new ideas, new directions, tested procedures* and *reality-oriented guidelines* to those who seek such help. The material includes the results of research studies, but primarily, the results of actual experience form the basis for the book.

The message is intended primarily for experienced principals and assistant principals of junior and senior high schools, but will also be helpful to those in training. Because of its broad content, all professionals who work at this level of education will find portions of its content helpful and stimulating. Teachers of graduate courses in junior and senior high school administration, supervision, or curriculum will find the book especially appropriate as a textbook or as a major reference book.

Dealing expressly with the daily and projected work of the secondary school principal, we hope to reflect the broad and varied backgrounds of a combined authorship of four experienced secondary school principals.

We wish you success in your application of the material that follows.

M.D.B.
W.G.A.
M.S.
E.W.W.

Contents

Part 1
THE ADMINISTRATIVE STAFF IN THE MODERN SECONDARY SCHOOL

1. The Nature and Challenge of Educational Leadership 3

    NEW ROLES AND FUNCTIONS   3
        PROPOSAL WRITING   3
        COLLECTIVE NEGOTIATIONS   4
        REACTING TO PROTESTS, DEMONSTRATIONS AND POSSIBLE WALK-OUTS   5
    EXPECTATIONS OF ADMINISTRATIVE LEADERSHIP   5
        THE LEADER AND THE LED   6
        INCONGRUENCE IN PERCEPTIONS   6
    THEORY OF ROLES   8
    THE CHALLENGE OF CHANGE   9
    TRADITIONAL FUNCTIONS   12
    THE ROLE OF THE SECONDARY SCHOOL PRINCIPAL   16
    SELECTED READINGS   18

2. Fundamental Principles of Administration and Supervision 21

        ADMINISTRATION AND SUPERVISION IN PERSPECTIVE   21
        HUMAN SKILLS IN SUPERVISION   25
        TECHNICAL SKILLS IN SUPERVISION   28
        RESEARCH METHODOLOGY   28
        CREATIVE SUPERVISION   29
    BASIC TENETS FOR ADMINISTRATIVE AND SUPERVISORY LEADERSHIP   30
        SELF-REALIZATION FOR THE PRINCIPAL   30
    SELECTED READINGS   35

3. The Principal's Program of Self-Improvement 37

    PROFESSIONAL GROWTH   37
        GRADUATE WORK   38
        PROFESSIONAL LITERATURE   39

CONTENTS

3. THE PRINCIPAL'S PROGRAM OF SELF-IMPROVEMENT (*Continued*)

        INSTITUTES, WORKSHOPS, CONVENTIONS, AND CONFERENCES 40
        PROFESSIONAL ORGANIZATIONS 41
        WRITING—SPEAKING 41
GROWTH AS A PERSON 42
        READING 42
        COMMUNITY ACTIVITIES 43
        RELAXATION 44
SELECTED READINGS 45

Part 2

THE PROFESSIONAL STAFF

4. PERSONNEL REQUIREMENTS AND SELECTION 49

REQUIREMENTS 49
        QUALITATIVE 49
        QUANTITATIVE 50
SELECTION 51
        PROFESSIONAL POSITIONS 52
        THE SEARCH 52
INTERVIEWING 55
THE NOMINATION 60
SELECTED READINGS 60

5. STAFF UTILIZATION AND SUPERVISION 62

STAFF UTILIZATION 62
        REORGANIZATION OF INSTRUCTION 63
        CHANGES IN STAFFING PATTERNS 64
        INSTRUCTIONAL METHOD AND TEACHING AIDS 65
        FACILITIES 66
        SUPERVISORY FUNCTION OF THE PRINCIPAL 67
        A DESIGN FOR EFFECTIVE SUPERVISION OF INSTRUCTION 68
SELECTED READINGS 70

6. MORALE AND PROFESSIONAL GROWTH OF THE STAFF 72

MORALE 72
        HUMAN RELATIONSHIPS 72
        INSTITUTIONAL ELEMENTS 75
        PARTICIPATION 76
PROFESSIONAL GROWTH OF THE STAFF 77
        PROFESSIONAL STAFF MEETINGS 77
        AREAS FOR STUDY 79
        IN-SERVICE APPRAISAL 80
SELECTED READINGS 81

Part 3
THE PROGRAM OF STUDIES

7. REQUIREMENTS AND OPTIONAL SUBJECT OFFERINGS 85
    REQUIRED SUBJECTS—JUNIOR HIGH SCHOOL 85
    REQUIRED SUBJECTS—SENIOR HIGH SCHOOL 86
    CONSTANTS, VARIABLES, AND ELECTIVES 86
    GUIDANCE AND SUBJECT AREAS 87
        SUBJECT AREAS 87
        SPECIAL PROGRAMS 94
    SELECTED READINGS 99

8. TYPES OF CURRICULUM DESIGN 101
    PRINCIPLES UNDERLYING CURRICULUM DESIGN 101
    CURRICULUM DESIGNS AND RELATED ELEMENTS 102
        CORE AND BLOCK OF TIME PROGRAMS 102
        A LONGER SCHOOL YEAR 103
        EXTENDED SCHOOL DAY 104
        ACCELERATION AND ENRICHMENT 105
        THE ADVANCED PLACEMENT PROGRAM 106
        OUTDOOR EDUCATION 106
        TEAM TEACHING 107
        INDEPENDENT STUDY 108
        THE NON-GRADED SCHOOL 109
    TECHNOLOGY AND THE CURRICULUM 110
        MODULAR SCHEDULING 110
        FLEXIBLE SCHEDULING 111
        THE AUTOMATED SCHEDULE 113
    POSTSCRIPT 115
    SELECTED READINGS 116

9. SELECTION AND ORGANIZATION OF LEARNING MATERIALS 117
    RELATING MATERIALS TO OBJECTIVES 117
    GROWING IMPORTANCE OF TECHNOLOGY 118
        FILMS, FILMSTRIPS, AND SLIDES 118
        EDUCATIONAL TELEVISION 119
    PROGRAMMED LEARNING 121
        ELECTRONIC LABORATORIES 123
        OTHER MEDIA 123
    EDUCATIONAL COMBINES 124
    KEEPING THE MEDIA PICTURE IN FOCUS 125
    THE BUDGET FOR INSTRUCTIONAL MATERIALS 125
    A WORD OF CAUTION 126
    TEXTBOOKS 127
        METHOD OF SELECTION 128

CONTENTS

9. SELECTION AND ORGANIZATION OF LEARNING MATERIALS (*Continued*)

    LIBRARY   129
        LOCATION   130
        THE LIBRARIAN   130
        THE LIBRARY STAFF   131
    SELECTED READINGS   132

10. Planning for Innovations in Educational Facilities 134

    THE PLANNING ROLES   135
    ORGANIZING FOR PLANNING   137
    MAJOR CONSIDERATIONS IN PLANNING   138
    COMMUNICATING EDUCATIONAL NEEDS TO THE ARCHITECT   143
    SOURCES OF INFORMATION FOR PLANNERS   144
    INNOVATIONS IN PLANT AND EQUIPMENT   144
    SUGGESTIONS TO GUIDE INNOVATIONS IN BUILDING DESIGN   145
        INNOVATIONS AND ADAPTABLE IDEAS IN USE   146
        RATIONALE FOR INNOVATIONS IN SCHOOL BUILDING DESIGN FOR EARLY ADOLESCENTS   151
    NEW IDEAS IN EQUIPMENT AND OTHER FACILITIES   152
    EQUIPMENT FOR LABORATORY INSTRUCTION IN DRIVER EDUCATION   152
    CONCLUSIONS   153
    SELECTED READINGS   153

Part 4

THE STUDENT

11. Pupil Personnel Services 159

    ORGANIZING PUPIL PERSONNEL SERVICES   160
        CUMULATIVE RECORDS   160
        PERMANENT RECORDS   162
    RELATION OF GUIDANCE AND COUNSELING TO THE TOTAL PROGRAM   162
        HOME ROOM   162
        ACCOMMODATIONS   163
    THE NATURE AND EXTENT OF PUPIL PERSONNEL SERVICES   164
        PUBLIC LAW 85-864   165
        QUALIFICATIONS OF COUNSELORS   165
        ORGANIZING AND STAFFING PUPIL PERSONNEL SERVICES   166
        STAFF QUARTERS   166
        SOCIAL WORKER   166
        PSYCHOLOGICAL SERVICES   167
        SCHOOL HEALTH SERVICES   167
        THE PUPIL PERSONNEL COORDINATOR   169
    THE PRESENT STATUS OF PUPIL PERSONNEL SERVICES   169
    THE PRINCIPAL AND PUPIL PERSONNEL SERVICES   171
    SELECTED READINGS   171

CONTENTS

12. **Developing and Maintaining Effective Disciplinary Policies and Procedures** 173

    FOUNDATIONS OF GOOD DISCIPLINE   173
        CHARACTERISTICS OF THE ADOLESCENT   174
        GENERAL PRINCIPLES   176
        HELPING TEACHERS WITH DISCIPLINE PROBLEMS   178
    DISCIPLINE POLICIES   178
        ESTABLISHING POLICY   178
    DRUGS, SEX, AND RIOTS   181
    KEEPING THE PROBLEM IN PERSPECTIVE   183

13. **Pupil Activities** 185

    VALUES OF EXTRA-CLASS ACTIVITIES   186
        LEARNING BY DOING   186
        FEELING OF SECURITY   187
        SOCIAL VALUES   187
        LEADERSHIP   187
        CIVIC RESPONSIBILITIES   187
        EXTENSION OF KNOWLEDGE   187
    TYPES OF ORGANIZATIONS   188
        THE STUDENT COUNCIL   188
        STUDENT ASSEMBLIES   189
        CLUBS   190
    TYPES OF PUBLICATIONS   190
    THE PERFORMING ARTS   192
    INTERSCHOLASTIC ATHLETICS   193
    INTRAMURAL SPORTS   195
    FINANCING EXTRA-CLASS ACTIVITIES   195
        LEGAL STATUS   197
        ACTIVITIES BOARD   197
        STUDENT TREASURERS   198
    GUIDING PRINCIPLES FOR ADMINISTERING SCHOOL ACTIVITIES   198
    SUMMARY   201
    SELECTED READINGS   201

Part 5

SCHOOL-COMMUNITY RELATIONS

14. **Understanding the Problem** 205

    THE ROLE OF THE SCHOOL IN THE COMMUNITY   206
        A CORPORATE IMAGE OF EDUCATION IN THE JUNIOR HIGH SCHOOL   206
        THE TRINITY OF HOME-SCHOOL-COMMUNITY   209
        OBJECTIVES OF THE COOPERATIVE APPROACH   211
    SPECIFIC RECOMMENDATIONS   215

14. UNDERSTANDING THE PROBLEM (*Continued*)

        THE NEED FOR INFORMATION AND INTERPRETATION 216

  SELECTED READINGS 216

15. BASIC PRINCIPLES OF COMMUNICATION AND HUMAN RELATIONS 218

  HUMAN RELATIONS 219
  COMMUNICATION 222
  APPRAISAL, MARKING AND REPORTING OF PUPIL PROGRESS 225
  EFFECTIVE ADMINISTRATIVE PRACTICES IN SCHOOL-COMMUNITY RELATIONS 227
  SELECTED READINGS 229

INDEX 230

Part 1

THE ADMINISTRATIVE STAFF IN THE MODERN SECONDARY SCHOOL

ONE

The Nature and Challenge of Educational Leadership

In the last decade social and technological changes have wrought results which affect all areas of living. Education is no exception, and as a consequence secondary school principals are now facing new and distinct challenges. Few such leaders can avoid confrontation with such raw reality as extreme diversity in student background, aspiration and potential; drug addiction and drug peddling; and greater permissiveness in all matters pertaining to sex.

Perhaps the greatest of the new challenges are problems centered in new roles and functions arising from (1) increasing federal involvement in education, (2) mounting teacher assertiveness and (3) tendencies of secondary school students to emulate college students in insisting on being heard. Therefore, the secondary school principal of today and tomorrow is involved in proposal writing, collective negotiations and strategic maneuvers to forestall and/or react effectively to protests, demonstrations and walkouts.

NEW ROLES AND FUNCTIONS

PROPOSAL WRITING

Today's secondary school principal is expected to have many ideas about educational improvement; implementation of the most productive ones is also expected by boards of education, superintendents and citizens; ideas have to be "hitched" as well as "hatched." For the former to occur, funds in generous amounts are usually necessary. Fortunately, opportunities for securing financial assistance to initiate and sustain projects abound, but one must first submit a worthy proposal.

Preparation of research proposals has become one way to prevent the escape of ideas. It is both an art and a science, and some of the latter can be learned through planned effort. Intrinsic merit and superior presentation do much to guarantee acceptance of an idea by a funding body. Principals, therefore, are urged to consider a self-improvement program in presenting ideas in need of funded implementation. One very helpful source is a 50-page pamphlet, *How to Prepare a Research Proposal,* by David R. Krathwohl. It is available from the Syracuse University Bookstore, Syracuse, New York.

COLLECTIVE NEGOTIATIONS

Teachers are demanding the right to negotiate what should be taught, how it should be taught, who should teach it and who should supervise teachers in their work. Naturally, it is an understatement to say that teacher successes in the bargaining movement will profoundly affect the principal's sphere of authority. Is he being disinherited? One thing is certain; the negotiations rumble is pulling principals and teachers apart in some situations. Whatever happens in the conflict, if a schism becomes permanent and widespread, eventually children will suffer.

There is good reason to believe that principals can be found among the most effective leaders of teacher organizations, and it is possible that negotiating units which include principals can be effective. Obviously, in some conflict situations, marked by long-standing disharmony of staff and administration, it may be desirable to restrict the negotiating unit to non-supervisory personnel. Realities of some situations will prevent the teamwork philosophy, but all things considered, unity, not divisiveness, will make the greater contribution to quality education.

We don't accept the notion that partial eclipse of principals should occur. It is hoped that even the most militant teachers will recognize and support the need for effective supervision and administration, whatever its source and nature. It is incumbent upon the principal always to recognize that teachers have an ethical right to discuss matters pertaining to their own welfare. The principal's leadership role will change, but it is not likely to disintegrate.

Readers are directed to the following appropriate and specialized references for further study of the problem of collective negotiations:

American Association of School Administrators, *The School Administrator and Negotiation.* Washington, D.C.: the Association, 1968.

Epstein, Benjamin, *The Principal's Role in Collective Negotiations.* Washington, D.C.: National Association of Secondary School Principals, 1965.

Markus, Frank W., *Negotiations Bibliography.* Kansas City: Metropolitan School Study Group of Greater Kansas City and the School of Education, University of Missouri, 1968.

Schmidt, Charles T., Jr., Parker, Hyman and Repas, Bob, *A Guide to Collective Negotiations in Education.* East Lansing, Michigan: Social Science Research Bureau, Michigan State University, 1967.

REACTING TO PROTESTS, DEMONSTRATIONS AND POSSIBLE WALKOUTS

At a recent pre-school workshop for teachers in a suburban Chicago school system, a bold and imaginative young director of instruction added to the program what was billed as a "Youthquake." Through song, poem, narration, discussion and new experience, secondary school youth quite effectively communicated their side of the story. The author heard one 17-year-old girl calmly describe her role in organizing a student walkout in a Chicago High School. Objectively, assuredly and without passion she justified the action and her contribution to it. It was a protest against inappropriate, outmoded and even hazardous facilities and equipment. This is merely one example of how secondary school youth are moving ever nearer the scene of decision making and action. Under urban conditions the trend may first develop, but it will likely spread to suburban, small town and rural areas in succession.

The principal is compelled to think deeply on these likely events and, with teachers, other administrators and interested parents and citizens, identify some alternative courses of action designed to recognize youth's ideas and help them to direct their contributions toward constructive experiences and for noble purposes. Through any conflict and adversity he must remain firm but flexible, for best judgment suggests that adults, especially those in leadership positions, must listen to youth with perception beyond the tympanum and must view youth with perception beyond the retina. The secondary school principal is admonished, "Anticipate or Acquiesce."

EXPECTATIONS OF ADMINISTRATIVE LEADERSHIP

Editorials, magazine articles, and radio-TV commentators continually deplore the lack of leadership in almost every phase of the contemporary scene, schools included. Most, if not all, school administrative positions developed out of the function of teaching. For this reason holders of administrative positions, especially principals, traditionally are expected to have served as a classroom teacher and to retain a primary interest in instruction. This expectation plus others arising from the demands of educational programs of schools in diverse communities adds up to a multiple functioning which requires that administrators possess unique preparation, skill and vision if they are to meet successfully the expectations of their workers.

A brief historical account of authority figure-worker relationships will be presented prior to considering the question, "What should be the relationship between the leader and the led?" In the dominant rural economy of our early history we first saw the boss-worker relationship, that of the father-son shepherd team. Next came the feudal system where the lord commanded the serf, which in turn was followed by the master-apprentice kinship in the guilds. The worker probably first came into his own with the opening up of frontiers in America and elsewhere. In this era individuals found freedom to acquire land, create their own jobs and manage their own affairs. Bringing with it mass production, the industrial revolution altered the leader-led situation considerably. Now the employee is held responsible for the execution of no more than a small segment of a larger task. Subsequently, large corporations instituted the military-like line and staff organization, essentially a personal power structure. The follower's image of himself throughout these various work relationships has been molded by certain aspirations: (1) to achieve and justify self-direction and self-discipline, (2) to preserve his personal dignity and integrity by modifying the command-over-people concept into a command-over-work situation, and (3) to be permitted to participate in the whole job through planning and checking results rather than simply performing specific tasks in isolation.[1]

THE LEADER AND THE LED

The leadership role is determined by the perceptions held by the leader and the led. A person assigned to a position of leadership is said to be a status leader; he may or may not be the real leader. If he is more than a status leader, he will meet most of the expectations of leadership held by those affected by his actions. In any social situation where leadership is involved it is obvious that followers are likely to hold many, differing kinds of expectations for leadership. When the leader finds it impossible to conform to many different kinds of expectations, role conflict is said to exist. Such a dilemma should not be surprising for it is related to the conflict of the individual and the organization, and of work and authority. To strengthen the leader-led relationship the former must keep uppermost in his mind the need-dispositions of worker-followers. According to Ohmann, as we have earlier indicated, these are the search for meaning, self-fulfillment, and self-realization.

At least three findings from social science seem to have implications for the administrative leader who desires to build and maintain effective relationships with his subordinates. First, small face-to-face groups are essential in planning and communicating. Second, decentralization of authority and encouraging staff participation in decision making are acknowledgment of one fundamental aspiration of the led. Finally, the leader will be sufficiently person-oriented to engender supportive relationships, and he in turn will be supportive of his followers' motivations.

INCONGRUENCE IN PERCEPTIONS

Evidence that teachers and administrators are not congruent in the manner in which they regard administration and its role in the school was revealed in a pilot study by the Council for Administrative Leadership in New York State.[2] Using the problem census approach in eight sections of the state, the Council reported a possible growing gap between points of view held by teachers and administrators. Simply stated, it is very

---

[1] O.A. Ohmann, "The Leader and the Led," *Personnel Magazine,* Nov.-Dec., 1958.
[2] Council for Administrative Leadership in New York State, *How Teachers View School Administration,* January, 1959.

probable that the principal estimates incorrectly how his staff members view administration, how they expect to work with administration, and what they expect principals to know.

The instrument used was aimed at aspects of the school administrator's job which are important to teachers, bases on which they accept his authority, and the relationships they expect to have with him as well as what knowledge or information they expect him to possess. The following general outcomes derive from 1009 responses from teachers in eight sections of New York State: teachers have firm convictions about administration, they possess insights into it, they differentiate among the positions, they accept administration on a personalistic rather than on a legalistic basis, they expect administration to facilitate their teaching and they expect an administrator to possess a vast amount of knowledge.

These results of teacher perceptions of the administrative role were then presented to 430 school administrators whose responses indicate how well they had perceived their jobs and themselves from the vantage point of the teacher's desk. Although a few administrators responded in a manner which failed to indicate a gap in points of view, many more were surprised and puzzled that teachers rated the items as they did. The implication should be clear to school administrators: take steps to determine if the teacher view of administration deviates markedly from the administrator's perception of his role; if it does, the alert school leader will seek ways to close the gap or he will choose to perform his administrative functions in a more compatible setting.

Another investigation on teacher-principal agreement was conducted by Campbell [3] who studied the relative perceptions of 284 teachers and 15 principals on the teacher role. On a sixty-item form each principal indicated his expectations of teachers; also he rated the effectiveness of his teachers. The same form was given to each teacher who was asked to express what he most wanted in his teaching position, rate his own satisfaction and effectiveness and express his confidence in the principal's leadership. At the outset three hypotheses were established: (1) that those teachers whose wants and needs were more congruent with their principal's expectations would express significantly higher job satisfaction than would those teachers whose needs were in conflict with the principal's view of the teacher's role; (2) that teachers whose expectations were nearly the same as those held by the principal would be rated as more effective; (3) that teachers whose wants and needs agreed with expectations of the principal would express more confidence in leadership than would teachers whose desires conflicted with expectations of the principal. Hypotheses (1) and (2) were confirmed. Substantial agreement between teacher and principal on the teacher role tends to result in greater teacher satisfaction, and the degree of congruence in values between teachers and principals is directly related to the teacher's confidence in the principal's leadership.

From this study we may infer that the principal, to achieve maximum goal achievement, must bring as closely together as possible his definition of the teacher role and the teachers' perspective of their roles. Although he may attempt to accomplish this

---

[3] M.V. Campbell, *Teacher-Principal Agreement on the Teacher Role,* Administrator's Notebook, February, 1959.

objective through selective staffing or through appropriate in-service "manipulation," a more ethical and desirable method is advised—that of compromise wherein he seeks staff members who to a degree meet his expectations, modifies their wants and desires within reason, and then submits his own concepts of the teaching role to reevaluation.

A task of primacy in bridging the gap of principal-teacher understanding is that of effective communication of the expectations of the former to his staff members. In all likelihood many situations exist where individual teachers are unaware of exactly what the principal expects of them in the teaching situation. Reasonable expectations communicated with clarity and precision to teachers contribute much to confidence in leadership, an ingredient essential to purpose achievement.

THEORY OF ROLES

One fruitful approach to the study of school administration is through analysis of the theory of roles. It was within such a framework that Willower [4] studied the leadership styles of principals in western New York State. Two styles of leadership were used: the nomothetic and the idiographic. The first style is authority centered, task- and institution-oriented and motivated by conformity to regulations. In the idiographic style the leader is just as eager to achieve his goals, but he does it through the independence and unique requirements of the individual. Willower's hypothesis was formulated: "Principals employing an idiographic leadership style will tend to regard teachers as professionals to a greater extent than will principals employing a nomothetic leadership style." Forty-one chief school administrators identified for the sample 66 idiographic and 43 nomothetic principals who responded to a 40-item teacher professionalism form. The results showed clearly that idiographic principals tend to regard teachers as more professional than do nomothetic principals.

For these administrators who choose the idiographic alternative, the authors suggest that the key to closing the gap lies in the principle that "adequate administrators and teachers nurture adequacy in each other." [5] Adherence to such a basic premise means that the school administrator will behave with dignity and self-trust in establishing an "open" environment where teachers eventually will be professionals with dignity and integrity. This climate of trust and self-other appreciation perhaps is best described in the 1962 A.S.C.D. Yearbook: "Supervisors and principals working in such settings come alive! Their self-trust leads them to see themselves and to see the school and its opportunities in the larger context of society. Professional work is not a daily chore, stifling and rigid, but a service which is satisfying because it is at once self-fulfilling and creative." [6]

---

[4] D.J. Willower, *Leadership Styles and Administrator Perceptions* (Albany, N.Y.: Council for Administrative Leadership, April, 1961).

[5] Association for Supervision and Curriculum Development, *Perceiving, Behaving, Becoming*, 1962 Yearbook, p. 219.

[6] Association for Supervision and Curriculum Development, p. 219.

THE CHALLENGE OF CHANGE

When a school leader such as a junior or senior high school principal discovers that his definition of the leadership role is far out of tune with teachers' concepts of how he should perform, he has two major alternatives for resolving the conflict. He may consider re-evaluation and modification of his own values to harmonize with teachers' expectations. This is not a likely solution generally if teacher perceptions of the leadership role are unsound. The second alternative is that of step-by-step modification of the values and expectations of the members of the social system, in this case the staff.

Although the second alternative is the more promising for lasting results, it is also considerably more difficult to accomplish. In fact the alternative of changing staff expectations can be implemented by the leader only through diligent and perceptive attention to the processes of group interaction. The leader's ultimate goal is to gain the confidence of the group, a necessary condition for his role of change agent.

Change is a rather simple process if it merely involves minor alterations in present conditions; yet, the authors prefer to view the term in this text as more complex in meaning. Here it means a sequential, gradual movement toward improvement. The foregoing discussion of change as it relates to role concepts is basic to further changes in the form and content of educational programs.

The premise for change arises perhaps from the dimension of quality in the educational enterprise. It may be safe to say that all professional school leaders desire quality in education. The question of greatest import seems to be not one of the value of change to achieve quality but rather one of the degree or extent of change. One of the authors interviewed scores of principals for purposes of possible career advancement. Almost without exception the interviewees spoke of change. Probing by the interviewer usually elicited that the change was caused either by addition or subtraction of form or content. The change agent, however, is responsible for careful study and evaluation leading to *basic* alterations of existing materials and methods.

These basic changes are urgent for such obvious reasons as the great increase in the number to be educated, pressing demands for conceptual and specialistic skills, the growing necessity for flexibly educated citizens, as well as society's need for citizens with sound democratic values.

In discussing the anatomy of change, Smith [7] pointed out the dimension of modes of influence. In general he has observed the use of four different influencing factors which are as follows: (1) the influence of scientific information, (2) legislative prescription, (3) modifying instructional materials, and (4) changing instruction through modification of teacher behavior. Smith believes that in practice legislative and material modes have been more successful than other types of influence.

Reformers of educational practices must also be aware of the ingredients of change. Ten such elements suggested and elaborated by Trump [8] are the following:

---

[7] B.O. Smith, "The Anatomy of Change," *The Bulletin,* NASSP, 47 (May 1963), pp. 4–10.
[8] J.L. Trump, "R/ Ingredients of Change," *The Bulletin,* NASSP, 47 (May 1963), pp. 11–20.

1. Planned relationships among curriculum content, instructional technology, and institutional arrangements.
2. Clear analysis of all the forces that stabilize the present condition.
3. Experimental studies.
4. Preparing and distributing brochures.
5. Speeches by knowledgeable people.
6. Demonstrations by teachers and students.
7. Using mass media.
8. Issuing summary reports of changes.
9. Keeping staff members informed.
10. Encouraging experimental approaches.

Ideas related to the first of these ingredients are fully detailed in *Focus on Change—Guide to Better Schools*.[9]

Lest the reader interpret in error that the local school can function successfully in all facets of the change process, it is appropriate to suggest what can feasibly be done by the building principal. If, as Brickell[10] points out, there are three discrete phases of educational innovation—design, evaluation and dissemination—at what point does the educational leader take hold? From Brickell's point of view the secondary school is basically concerned with educating people, not with producing new truths for the educational institutions of the nation. It follows, therefore, that the secondary school principal should be primarily interested in improving his own program through adopting new findings which are judged to be superior. Evaluation is confined to the simple question, "How has our own program improved?" Therefore, it is the dissemination stage in which the local school can best participate. Although design and/or evaluation for use in educational institutions in general are more appropriately the work of campus laboratory schools, some junior and senior high school principals may justifiably involve their staff in designing, evaluating and disseminating educational innovations for use in other schools in other communities.

Specifically, what is the principal's role in change? In an earlier publication Brickell[11] indicated that it is the principal who should initiate changes in instructional programs. How to fulfill this function of leadership perplexes many principals. Though it is not an easy process, some techniques for implementation are known and can be learned by most principals.

In the first place it is recommended that principals and teachers observe the results of change in schools similar to their own. Assuming that such observations are convincing to a majority of staff members, then how does the principal go about introducing change into his school? Involving at first those who are most amenable to modification,

---

[9] J.L. Trump and D. Bayham, *Focus on Change—Guide to Better Schools* (Chicago: Rand McNally & Co., 1961), p. 147.

[10] Henry M. Brickell, "Dynamics of Change," *The Bulletin*, NASSP, 47 (May, 1965), pp. 21–28.

[11] Henry M. Brickell, *Organizing New York State for Educational Change* (Albany, N.Y.: The University of the State of New York, 1961), p. 22.

he plans the new approach, providing continuing leadership in assisting those who are directly concerned.

In most schools the chief evaluative measure, though not the only one, is likely to be observations of student reaction. Since success in promoting a new program is largely the result of its being in the spotlight, the wise principal will avoid excessive publicity to the new idea. Rather, equal attention must be given to the traditional or comparison situation.

Let's take an example of change as it fits our definition expressed earlier and see how a principal might perform the role of leavening agent. Since reading, basic to any kind of curriculum innovation, is the most important subject of all, it shall be the example. The first insight of leadership is the principal's acceptance of the fact that reading instruction is not something apart from his front office responsibilities. Next, he perceives and appreciates the difficulties any secondary school teacher faces in significantly improving the reading skills of a large number of very different learners. The real test of his leadership ability comes as he organizes and utilizes his staff for the proposed improvement. Can he identify those teachers with leadership potential who can rally the cooperation and interest of less potent staff members? Assuming that he is able to call into play the unique talents, experiences and skills of individual staff members, what are the next steps?

Implementing the twin strategies of appraisal and action, the principal more or less simultaneously involves the staff in probing for reading blights and in developing materials and resources for treatment. Although appropriate action is the necessary result, the principal who fails in the evaluation phase may fall victim to the situation Emerson described, "Pep without purpose is piffle."

Perhaps an account of how some effective reformers succeeded in effecting basic changes in a particular system is appropriate. Through three great processes of change—study, planning and experimentation—the junior high school educators of Jefferson County, Colorado, developed team teaching as a way of organizing for instruction. They began by careful observation and study of team teaching experiments in the senior high schools of their county. From such observations and subsequent discussions it was concluded that future junior high school plants must incorporate more appropriate planning or space to accommodate the alteration in instruction. Although from plant to plant some variations in facilities were deliberately planned, generally, teaching areas were designed as two-room or three-room clusters. One of the authors visited Creighton Junior High School, the three-room cluster type, at the end of its first year of operation. At Creighton, classrooms within each cluster are separated by vision panels and in each unit classroom there are microphones and speakers to permit teacher-pupil communication when the triad is being used for large group instruction. Any one unit of the triad may be used equally well for a class of traditional size or for small group instruction. Although at the time of our visit, the principal was reluctant to admit complete success based on valid assessments, he did claim that flexibility in grouping, more effective use of teacher time, and upgrading of the quality of instruction had contributed to the achievement of some original goals.

TRADITIONAL FUNCTIONS

Since the teaching function gave rise to the administrative positions mentioned earlier, traditionally, and currently, for the most part, those holding status positions of educational leadership in American schools are expected to bring to the office classroom teaching experience and vitality for instruction. According to the Department of Classroom Teachers of the NEA,[12] to some extent these expectations plus the demands of school programs have placed three major functions upon administrative personnel: (1) to carry out assigned administrative and supervisory tasks; (2) to advise and coordinate many persons and processes so as to improve and facilitate instruction; and (3) to participate in and bring leadership resources to a variety of professional and public groups. That this multiple function of educational leadership offers an exceptional challenge is accepted by all those who have served in administrative positions. Among the uninitiated are, unfortunately, many laymen and professionals who neither understand nor support the endeavors of the educational leader. Obviously, here is one major problem of the profession.

Educational leadership of high quality provides both administrative and supervisory services. Only the challenge of the former aspect, administration, will be elaborated upon here, since the elements and characteristics of effective supervision will be treated in subsequent chapters. Administration consists of organization, coordination and operation, or more simply stated, design, arrangement and fulfillment. It is the first of these components, organization, says Griffiths,[13] that has been largely ignored in the literature and research of education. There can be little doubt that it is at the point of design, the actual first step in administration, that educational leaders experience confrontation with what is perhaps their greatest challenge. Griffiths and his co-authors selected at random 15 standard textbooks in school administration and found none which devoted as much as a chapter to the function of organization. Yet administration without the essential first stage of organization is utter chaos. Indeed, "the language of organization is the language of administration." [14]

For educational leaders as for business executives, sound architecture of the administrative machine is a requisite of the first order. To summarize, this definition of organization by Griffiths is offered:

> Organization is that function of administration which attempts to relate and ultimately fuse the purposes of an institution and the people who comprise its working parts.[15]

---

[12] *Conditions of Work for Quality Teaching* (Washington, D.C.: Department of Classroom Teachers, NEA, 1959).

[13] Daniel E. Griffiths and others, *Organizing Schools for Effective Education* (Danville, Ill.: Interstate Printers and Publishers, 1962), p. 3. Used by permission of the publisher.

[14] Griffiths, p. 3.

[15] Griffiths, p. 10.

While the structure-building component of administration is in itself, as we have stated, a critical test for the builder, it is only slightly more challenging than the major purpose of organization—coordination. Harmonious adjustment and functioning of portions of the master design are required if organization is to reach fruition through management or implementation. The challenge of educational leadership lies, then, in providing a structure, arranging the independent parts, and operating or managing the master plan in such a way as to insure the ultimate success of the educational enterprise. The whole process can then be called "education by design."

The fact that organization precedes the management phase does not negate the concept of interrelatedness as expressed by French, Hull and Austin: "The typical administrator constantly turns from the organizational phase of his work to its administrative phase, and though we call a person a school *administrator,* we are not implying that he is not also responsible for improved organization." [16] At this point prospective and incumbent educational leaders are reminded that the complexity of modern schools and the current emphasis on specialization suggest that the chief executive acts wisely when he delegates some of the functions of the total task of leadership.

Ways of looking at administration. A new era in the study and practice of school administration was born when the W.K. Kellogg Foundation of Battle Creek, Michigan, entered the field of public school administration in 1948. Supported by Kellogg funds and sponsored jointly by AASA, The Council of Chief State School Officers and the National Conference of County and Rural Area Superintendents, five regional conferences were held in 1948 and 1949 for the prime purpose of studying in depth pressing problems of school superintendents. Upon taking stock of the results of the five conferences, Kellogg officials and representatives of the sponsoring organizations decided to launch a program known as the Cooperative Program in Educational Administration. In essence, grants were made to selected universities to study the changing nature of public school administration in this county. Although in the planning stages only study of the superintendency was intended, ultimately the entire field of educational administration became the subject of research and exploration.

Kellogg-sponsored research projects and subsequent interest in research by the National Conference of Professors of Educational Administration and the University Council on Educational Administration have demonstrated the need for an acceptable administrative theory. Whether or not such a theoretical framework is a miracle or mirage remains to be seen.

Theory is not a personal attribute, a classification, a principle or a technique; rather, a theory is a set of assumptions guiding action with somewhat predictable results. The practice of administration then is the art and science of applying such a set of assumptions. School administrators through experience often develop a theory which works for them. Development of a description of reality in a set of rules for action—a theory—which can be taught in organized programs to the student of administration is another matter.

---

[16] W. French, J.D. Hull, and O. Austin, *American High School Administration: Policy and Practice* (New York: Rinehart and Co. Inc., 1962), p. 15.

In general the four primary sources of administrative theory have been: (1) comments and reports of practicing administrators, (2) survey research, (3) deductive reasoning of teachers of administration and (4) adaptation of models from other disciplines.[17] It is from deductive reasoning and adaptation of models that administrative theorists have sought to construct, for teaching purposes, a framework of assumptions to guide the administrative process.

Prior to the current emphasis on administrative research and theory development which began in earnest after 1950 there were three theories of educational administration. One was "balanced judgment," a system of concepts based on common sense principles; the second was based on the premise that the administrative function derives its nature from the nature of the services it directs; a third way of looking at administration was through study of "personality traits" of principals and superintendents. In the early days of the CPEA investigators discarded the "trait" approach in favor of the "situational" approach whereby the functions of school administrators were observed in actual situations and subsequently described in relation to specific situations.

It was in the early fifties that certain investigators, studying and analyzing administrator problems, began to view administration as "human relations." In general, it was practicing administrators, rather than teaching professors, who called attention to personnel problems as the most trying aspect of their job.

As a pre-service instructional method, case studies emerged in part from the theory of administration as "management." Advocates of this approach sought to dramatize, and capitalize upon, the similarities of educational administration to such other management professions as hospital administration, hotel management and business management. Although as early as 1925 authors of books on school administration called attention to the administrator's prime role of "instructional leadership," such a view of school administration was accepted by too few administrators. In the mid 1950's there was a renewal of interest in the "instructional leadership" theory where the principal or superintendent functions as an arranger and provider if not as a supervisor of instructional content and methods.

Still another view of school administration which grew out of studies conducted in the decade of the fifties is that of "communications." Skill in developing and maintaining multi-directional flow of information, interpretation and feedback among staff as well as among the many publics is regarded as a crucial element of the actual task.

Designed to clarify issues and stimulate research, a theoretical model has been provided by Getzels and Guba.[18] The basic notion of this view of administrative leadership emphasizes the social process wherein institutions are established to implement specific functions. In such a framework institutions are analyzed through study of expected behaviors of role incumbents. The principal, for example, is expected to perform particular functions and to act in specific ways in his relationships with teachers, su-

---

[17] Andrew W. Halpin, *Administrative Theory in Education* (Chicago: Midwest Administration Center, University of Chicago, 1958), p. 188.

[18] J.W. Getzels and E.G. Guba, "Social Behavior and the Administrative Process," *The School Review*, LXV, p. 423–41.

periors, other professionals, etc. It is this system of institution, role and role-expectation which comprises one dimension of another view of administration. The second dimension of this "social process" notion stems from an assumption that all institutions are made up of individuals who possess singular personalities and tendencies to act in certain ways, e.g., to be tolerant, to be persistent, to accomplish. Both dimensions constitute the basic idea that an individual's performance of functions in the social system depends on the expectations of others about him and on his own dispositions to act according to his personality needs. In essence the model outlined above expresses the concept that behavior results simultaneously from interactions among self needs and role-expectations.

Within the framework described here, Hills [19] identified three distinct leadership styles, that is, three modes of achieving the same goal. In the first style, the leader leans heavily on institutional roles and their expectations rather than on the needs of individual personalities in the social system. He is task-motivated, not person-oriented.

The second mode of leadership glorifies, in the case of a principal, the desires and wants of individual staff members and obviously diminishes the value of rigorous role definition. In this second style, goal achievement is just as paramount as in the first type of leadership, only the fulfillment of the objective is realized in a less direct manner; that is, through recognition and acceptance of relevant contributions of individuals involved in the enterprise.

Standing on middle ground between institutional demands and personal needs is the exponent of the third leadership style. Being intermediate between the first two styles, this pattern of leadership allows the leader to emphasize, as the situation demands, either role expectations or personal needs of individuals.

Griffiths [20] views the administrative process as one encompassing function-decision making. Here the key concept is that the distinguishing characteristic of administration is directing and controlling the decision-making process. It is not the function of the principal to make decisions; his task is to direct and control the process which is more than making decisions and choosing the alternatives. In Griffiths' theory the decision-making process includes also the acts of implementation; that is, action is implicit in a decision. That decision making is the heart of organization and the process of administration as well as the basis of all managerial action is revealed in one of four basic assumptions advanced by Griffiths, "The specific function of administration is to develop and regulate the decision making process most effectively."

Although Griffiths elaborates in *Administrative Theory* on four basic assumptions, six concepts and several propositions germaine to decision-making theory, the fact remains that principals commonly make their decisions without the aid of well developed decision theory. They may or may not depend on the scientific method to suggest appropriate steps in decision making. It is most likely, however, that the wisest decisions are made most frequently by principals who are guided by considerable insight into the intricacies of rendering sound judgments.

---

[19] R.J. Hills, "A New Concept of Staff Relations," *Administrators' Notebook,* University of Chicago, Vol. VIII (March, 1960).

[20] Griffiths, p. 57.

Miller [21] discussed common bases for decision and raised the question of the desirability of an emphasis on inner strength and personal control. According to this source, frequently the following bases for decision making are influential on the principal's action: orthodoxy and precedent, laws, the American way, and advisory committees. Whatever the principal's decision-making machinery may be, the authors heartily endorse Miller's suggestion that the inner strength-personal control factor is worthy of emphasis.

The idea of three-pronged leadership that has swept the business world may have significant implications for the school principal. This three-pronged approach to leadership, developed by Uris,[22] has been used by thousands of executives and supervisors throughout the United States and Canada. The essence of the concept is simply that there is no *one right way* to exercise leadership. Such factors as age, sex, training and experience, personality types and goals of followers determine the type of leadership to be applied.

For example various combinations of the above factors will cause the perceptive leader to choose any one of three leadership approaches: autocratic, democratic and free-rein. Obviously such a three-alternative approach is more flexible and more realistic in that each method works best with a singular situation. The demands of this style of leadership thinking on the principal are somewhat rigorous. Particularly it requires him to diagnose personalities, to arm himself with accurate descriptions of the people in the task force and to understand fully the goals of action. Although these demands are somewhat exacting, compliance with them is doubtless expected of all principals. Perhaps the beauty of this approach lies in its built-in feature of forcing the principal to assess more carefully each leadership situation in which he finds himself.

Figure 1-1 illustrates the essence of the three-pronged approach to leadership.

In presenting various ways of looking at administration the authors do not hope to make professional theorists out of practitioners who are surely enmeshed in the processes of action and implementation. However, some familiarity with models and efforts to construct theoretical bases for administrative leadership may provide them with fresh ideas for solving new and recurring problems.

THE ROLE OF THE SECONDARY SCHOOL PRINCIPAL

With few exceptions the secondary school has at least one designated officer with authority "in the line," usually the principal. Although this is a status position, it is desirable that the principal be able to shed the cloak of authority on occasion. For maximum goal achievement he must see his role as that of a team member. If teachers are to accept him in this role, he must succeed in shrinking himself as a threat symbol. Complicating the "team member" concept is the fact that his position of authority in the

---

[21] P.V. Miller, "Inner Direction and the Decision Maker," *School Executive,* 79 (Dec., 1959), pp. 27–29.
[22] A. Uris, *Mastery of People* (Englewood Cliffs, N.J.: Prentice-Hall, Inc., 1964), Ch. 17.

THE NATURE AND CHALLENGE OF EDUCATIONAL LEADERSHIP

The
   Leader
      deals with ———— People   of different *Personality* types for
                                                                                            specific *Purposes*

is AUTOCRATIC   Hostile
  with ————   Dependent
                           Youthful   and AUTHORITARIAN   to Achieve
                         Females   Personalities   COMPLIANCE
                         Inexperienced

                         Cooperative
                         Group-Minded
is DEMOCRATIC   Mature   and EQUALITARIAN   to Achieve
  with ————   Male   Personalities   COOPERATION
                         Experienced

                         Social-Isolationist
                         Individualist
is FREE-REIN   Male   and LIBERTARIAN   to Achieve
  with ————   Experienced   Personalities   CREATIVITY

Figure 1-1

Adopted from Auren Uris, *Mastery of People* (Englewood Cliffs, N.J.: Prentice-Hall, Inc.), Ch. 17. The model was prepared by the authors.

line and staff organization does require him to perform certain outside-the-team duties required by law.

The dream of every sincere principal is to release and guide the best efforts of the diverse personalities composing his staff into a smoothly-functioning team. Some elements in a "grand design" to jell the team through group identification were suggested by March and Simon.[23] Essentially their five factors for success are as follows:

1. Effective interaction among teachers is desirable.
2. Individual needs are satisfied in the group.
3. Individual perception of shared goals is important.
4. Perception of faculty prestige must be positive.
5. Competition between members of the faculty should be decreased.

Using the five factors as guides, the principal can inventory his own staff conditions.

---

[23] J.G. March and H.A. Simon, *Organization* (New York: John Wiley, 1958), pp. 65–70.

The results of the inventory should tell him how to proceed in making belongers out of isolationists.

Earlier in this chapter it was pointed out that every principal should have an overall concept of what his job should be. Day-to-day housekeeping duties, identified in numerous studies, of building principals which consume a disproportionate allotment of time need not blot this concept. The inner strength of the principal expressed through his concept of his total job must be sufficient to withstand pressure and allow him to use his time wisely.

One categorization of the content of the job of the junior high school principal is that suggested in a bulletin by the Council for Administrative Leadership in New York State.[24] The authors classify the junior high school principal's work into the following five areas:

1. Improving the educational program
2. Working with pupils
3. Selecting and developing personnel
4. Working with the community
5. Managing the school.

Each of these areas of responsibility will be treated in detail in following chapters; improving the educational program in Chapters Seven, Eight, and Nine; working with pupils in Chapters Eleven, Twelve, and Thirteen; selecting and developing personnel in Chapter Four; working with the community in Chapters Fourteen and Fifteen, and managing the school in Chapters Five, Six and Ten. It is generally, though not unanimously, agreed among scholars in the field of secondary school administration that the key role of the principal is the improvement of instruction. In the words of Conant,[25] "the difference between a good school and a poor school is often the difference between a good and a poor principal. A good school invariably means strong leadership by the principal . . . the question to be answered is: is the principal forced to spend a considerable fraction of his time doing routine tasks that could be done by either an assistant principal or secretary? If he is, he cannot perform his role as instructional leader; help should be provided." At least one study by Brown, Clark and Strong [26] has indicated that lay as well as professional opinions indicated improvement of the instructional programs as the primary responsibility of the principal.

SELECTED READINGS

Association for Supervision and Curriculum Development, *Perceiving, Behaving, Becoming.* ASCD Yearbook, 1962.

---

[24] Council for Administrative Leadership in N.Y. State, *The Administrative Organization of the Modern Junior High School* (Albany, N.Y., 1958), p. 26.

[25] J.B. Conant, *Education in the Junior High School Years* (Princeton, N.J.: Educational Testing Service, 1960), p. 37.

[26] Harry L. Brown, R.S. Clark, and H.R. Strong, *An Analysis of Lay and Professional Attitudes Toward the High School Principalship.* Published doctoral dissertation, Teachers College, Columbia University, New York, 1955.

Bennis, Warren G., *Changing Organizations*. (New York: McGraw-Hill, 1966), p. 233.

Brickell, H. M., *Organizing New York State for Educational Change*. The University of the State of New York, Albany, New York, 1961.

Brown, Harry L., Clark, R. S. and Strong, H. R., *An Analysis of Lay and Professional Attitudes Toward the High School Principalship*. Published doctoral dissertation, Teachers College, Columbia University, New York, 1955.

Campbell, M. V., "Teacher-Principal Agreement on the Teacher Role," *Administrator's Notebook,* February, 1959.

Caplow, Theodore, *Principles of Organization*. (New York: Harcourt, Brace and World, 1964), p. 383.

Conant, J. B., *Education in the Junior High School Years*. (Princeton, N.J.: Educational Testing Service, 1960)

Council for Administrative Leadership in New York State, *The Administrative Organization of the Modern Junior High School*. Albany, New York, 1958.

Doherty, Robert E., editor, *Employer-Employee Relations in the Public Schools*. (Cornell University, Ithaca, New York: New York State School of Industrial and Labor Relations, 1966)

Fiedler, Fred, *A Theory of Leadership Effectiveness*. (New York: McGraw-Hill Company, 1967)

French, W., Hull, J. D. and Austin, D., *American High School Administration: Policy and Practice*. (New York: Rinehart and Company, Inc., 1962)

Getzels, J. W. and Guba, E. G., "Social Behavior and the Administrative Process," *The School Review,* Vol. 65, pp. 423–41.

Getzels, Jacob W., Lipham, James M. and Campbell, Roald F., *Educational Administration as a Social Process*. (Evanston, Illinois: Harper and Row, Publishers, 1968)

Griffiths, Daniel E., Clark, D. L., Wynn, D. and Iannaccone, L., *Organizing Schools for Effective Education*. (Danville, Illinois: Interstate Printers and Publishers, 1962)

Halpin, Andrew W., *Administrative Theory in Education*. (University of Chicago, Illinois: Midwest Administration Center, 1958)

Likert, Rensis, *The Human Organization*. (New York: McGraw-Hill Company, 1967)

March, J. G. and Simon, H. A., *Organization*. (New York: John Wiley, 1958)

McKenzie, G. N., "Role of the Supervisor," *Educational Leadership,* Vol. 19, November, 1961.

Miller, P. V., "Inner Direction and the Decision Maker," *School Executive,* Vol. 79, December, 1959, pp. 27–29.

Moore, Hollis A. Jr., *Studies in School Administration*. Washington, D.C.: Committee for the Advancement of School Administration, American Association of School Administrators, 1957.

National Education Association, *Conditions of Work for Quality Teaching*. Washington, D.C.: Department of Classroom Teachers, NEA, 1959.

Ohmann, O. A., "The Leader and the Led," *Personnel Magazine,* November–December, 1958.

Saunders, Robert L., Phillips, Ray C. and Johnson, Harold T., *A Theory of Educational Leadership*. (Columbus, Ohio: Charles E. Merrill Books, Inc., 1966)

Scott, William G., *Organization Theory*. (Homewood, Illinois: R. D. Irwin, 1967), p. 442.

Smith, B. O., "The Anatomy of Change," *The Bulletin,* National Association of Secondary School Principals, Vol. 43, November, 1959, pp. 46–55.

Stinett, T. M., Leinman, J. H. and Ware, Martha L., *Professional Negotiation in Public Education*. (New York: The Macmillan Company, 1966)

The American Society for Public Administration, *Public Administration Review*. Washington, D.C., March–April, 1968.

Thompson, James D., *Organizations in Action*. (New York: McGraw-Hill Book Co., 1967)

Trump, J. L. and Bayham, D., *Focus of Change—Guide to Better Schools*. (Chicago: Rand McNally and Company, 1961)

Trump, J. L., "R/Ingredients of Change," *The Bulletin,* National Association of Secondary School Principals, Vol. 47, May, 1963, pp. 11–20.

Uris, A., *Mastery of People*. (Englewood Cliffs, N.J.: Prentice-Hall, Inc., 1964)

Willower, D. J., *Leadership Styles and Administrator Perceptions*. Albany, N.Y.: Council for Administrative Leadership, April, 1961.

Wynn, Dale Richard, *Organization of Public Schools*. Washington Center for Applied Research, 1964, p. 107.

TWO

Fundamental Principles of Administration and Supervision

In Chapter One we classified the principal's duties into five areas, one of which was improving the educational program. There is rather general agreement among authorities in the field of administrative leadership that the prime function of the building principal is that of improving the educational program. Early in the history of education both superintendents and principals conceived of the above function in a narrow sense; it simply meant inspecting and rating the teacher and his methods of instruction. Such a supervisory role for principals was not common until early in the present century, actually following assumption of that role by superintendents.

ADMINISTRATION AND SUPERVISION IN PERSPECTIVE

An early study states the belief that "administration and supervision are coordinate, correlative, complementary functions having as their common purpose the provision of means and conditions favorable to teaching and learning." [1] This investigation emphasized that democratic supervision is characterized by the absence of an inflexible, hierarchical system of relationships between the superior and inferior officers. The 1958 Yearbook of the American Association of School Administrators [2] divided the secondary school principal's duties into four areas: planning, organization, supervision, and evaluation. Obviously, planning and organization can best be described as administrative in

---

[1] Max R. Brunstetter, "Principles of Democratic Supervision," *Teachers College Record,* 44 February, 1943), pp. 374–75.

[2] American Association of School Administrators, 1958 Yearbook, *The High School in a Changing World,* pp. 302–304.

21

nature; although the Yearbook suggested that planning should assume first place, logically, in the principal's list of duties, it agrees with other sources that his major responsibility is to provide leadership in developing the program of instruction.

In smaller secondary schools enrolling less than 300 pupils, it is traditional, for the most part, that the principal initiate and carry on supervisory leadership. In schools of 300 to 900 pupils it is desirable that, in addition to his own efforts to help teachers, the principal should have the assistance of some specialistic supervisors who might fill the roles of assistant principal, department head or chairmen of purpose committees.

In larger schools enrolling more than 900 pupils there should be highly competent supervisory or resource personnel in the central office to strengthen the supervisory function. As a service from that office, they are employed to work in the separate schools of the system. Selected because of teaching skills, human relations skills and understanding of the teaching-learning situation, these assistants are responsible to the building principal.

Mackenzie [3] defined "supervisor" as a generic term to include all whose unique or primary concern is instructional leadership. Since it has been stated previously that the primary concern of the junior or senior high school principal is instructional leadership, it follows then, logically, that he is a supervisor. Later, the authors will describe some definitions from a recent source which will negate the possibility of the principal being a supervisor.

Throughout the 50 states, schools are adding additional staff members with the various titles of supervisors, consultants, directors, coordinators and administrative assistants. In the words of Burnham and King,[4] "Jointly, supervisors and administrators are responsible for furnishing the leadership required in studying, evaluating and implementing changes in the curriculum; interpreting the educational problems and programs to the public; developing in-service programs for staff members; providing orientation sessions for increasing numbers of new teachers; and developing and revising instructional materials to keep abreast of current developments."

In this source it is recognized that the supervisor's range of responsibilities is not as great as that of the principal. Working together to improve educational opportunities, the principal and supervisor occupy roles of equal status; one is neither the supervisor nor the director of the other. Such a team effort contributes to building a climate wherein the staff enjoys freedom and responsibility in initiating curriculum improvement projects.

Concerns about authority frequently hamper effective team efforts to improve the instructional program. In a properly organized junior or senior high school the source and nature of authority of administrative and supervisory personnel are precisely delineated in a carefully prepared set of policy statements. The authors do not mean to imply that it is either possible or desirable to compartmentalize neatly all functions into their respective and supervisory pigeonholes. Burnham and King [5] identify the following four concepts of authority:

---

[3] G.N. Mackenzie, "Role of the Supervisor," *Educational Leadership,* 19 (November, 1961), pp. 86–90.

[4] R.M. Burnham and M.L. King, *Supervision in Action* (A.S.C.D., 1961), p. 32.

[5] Burnham, pp. 44–45.

1. Legal authority which refers to a power to act resulting from the action of a legislative body.
2. Authority of position where the right to act is invested in a specific position.
3. Authority of competence in which a person, by virtue of superior skills, is granted the right to act.
4. Authority is viewed as the property of a goal-centered group related to group purposes and residing in a specific situation.

This fourth concept is most conducive to satisfying and enduring relationships between administrative and supervisory personnel as well as among various staff members. It is thought to be the most successful concept of authority because the power to act, potentially, may be granted to any member of the group.

In tracing supervision's administrative heritage, Gwynn[6] pointed out that supervision developed as an adjunct to school administration stemming from the superintendency and the principalship of the secondary school. For this reason, he said, conflicting ideas as to its relationships with other administrative functions have come along. From this kind of reasoning it may be inferred that Gwynn includes supervision as one of many functions of administration.

Stressing effective organization, Douglass, Bent and Boardman have no inclination to isolate supervision from administration, for both function together in all formal organizations. In their words,

> Administration has as its objective the establishment and maintenance of the best possible teaching and learning conditions. The objective of supervision is the same, but different methods are employed to attain it.[7]

Earlier in this chapter we implied that organization for supervision will vary with the size of the school and its program. In a large system, a medium to large secondary school frequently is served by a Director of Secondary Education or a Curriculum Coordinator and a number of subject specialists, any one of whom may be of advisory assistance to the principal or more directly to the teaching staff. It is fairly common in large secondary schools for the principal to have his own council for the improvement of instruction. In addition to certain supervisory personnel from the central office, this group might consist of assistant principals, the head librarian, the testing director and one or more department chairmen.

Although the principal may be fortunate enough to have one or more specialized helpers with specific supervisory duties, or even in some cases a supervisory staff, he nevertheless retains responsibility for the improvement of instruction. Linder and Gunn expressed the role of the principal as follows:

> However elaborate the administrative organization for improving instruction may be, this in no way absolves the principal from assuming the major responsibility

---

[6] J.M. Gwynn, *Theory and Practice of Supervision* (New York: Dodd, Mead and Company, 1961), p. 3.
[7] H. Douglass, R.K. Bent and C.W. Boardman, 2nd ed., *Democratic Supervision* (Boston: Houghton Mifflin Co., 1961), p. 17–18.

for the program in his school. All of these resources of assistance may be expected to stimulate the principal's initiative and give direction to his leadership but the responsibility remains largely his.[8]

In a recent pamphlet describing their new program of administrative internship in secondary school improvement, the National Association of Secondary School Principals had this to say about the principal's administrative and supervisory duties:

> Whether any principal works effectively for instructional improvement in his school depends largely upon the priorities he establishes for himself. A principal who places very high priority on educational exploration and experimentation searches continuously for ways to improve the program of instruction. A principal with no fixed priorities may find much of his time and energy slipping away in routine administration of the buildings and grounds or in an endless succession of talks with students and parents. The principal whose sights are set on instructional leadership in no sense abandons the community, but delegates his management functions, in large measure, to competent assistants. He becomes, in fact, *the educational leader* of his school.[9]

From the foregoing sources it is possible to sum up the viewpoints of authorities concerning the relationships of administration and supervision:

1. Supervision is an arm of administration.
2. Supervision is the joint responsibility of the principal and supervisor.
3. The principal and the supervisor function together in the formal organization.
4. The principal and the supervisor occupy roles of equal status.
5. Regardless of the nature and amount of supervisory assistance at his call, the principal is ultimately responsible for improving the program of instruction.

A sociological portrait of a supervisor by Lucio and McNeil [10] presents quite clearly their view of the changing supervisory functions of the principal. They suggest that the general supervisory functions of the principal have diminished in the wake of the trend toward enlarged school systems with many new specialists. Other factors detracting from the principal's key supervisory role according to Lucio and McNeil are the growth of professional organizations and the improved preparation of teachers. Especially in larger secondary schools of big systems where supervisory assistants may be plentiful, the principal-supervisor is now more of a personnel agent, skilled in handing personnel problems. Lucio and McNeil emphasize that the old supervisory functions of the principal are now performed by a team with the principal acting only after consultation with other authorities and specialists.

The authors cited above feel that it is not always desirable to sharply distinguish

---

[8] I.H. Linder and H.M. Gunn, *Secondary School Administration* (Columbus, Ohio: Charles E. Merrill Books, Inc., 1963), p. 222.
[9] National Association of Secondary School Principals, *Design for Leadership* (1963), p. 2.
[10] W.H. Lucio and J.D. McNeil, *Supervision* (New York: McGraw-Hill Book Co., 1962), p. 29.

the supervisor from teacher and administrator on the basis of status position and influence. They assume that within the line-and-staff system the principal is acting as an administrator when he exercises initiative in projects to improve instruction, makes decisions, coordinates the work of individuals, and issues directions. The principal's supervisory role is fulfilled when he exerts influence rather than authority in making decisions, taking action and controlling others. Within this kind of framework at times a supervisor may need to act administratively, and the principal frequently lays aside the mantle of authority in favor of consulting, advising and persuading.

According to Lucio and McNeil the present-day theory of supervision restricts the principal's supervisory role to the maintenance of curriculum balance and to the quality of classroom teaching. Although he is charged with overall responsibility, each principal assigns to a team of instructional experts within his building the specific task of improving teaching-learning processes.

Harris [11] has perhaps done more than anyone else to clarify terms and suggest a theory of supervision. The author treats supervisory behavior as a special form of leadership behavior. Emphasizing the need for a total view of school operation, Harris relies on a two-dimensional grid as a framework for viewing and analyzing various functions. Using the two dimensions of *instruction relatedness* and *pupil relatedness* he is able to distinguish five functional areas, none of which may be sharply delineated: supervision, teaching, management, special services, and general administration (Figure 2-1).

Obviously supervision may be described by behaviors which are highly related to instruction but little related to pupils. Included in this area are the duties of supervisors, coordinators, directors, consultants, administrators, and others which indirectly influence the teaching-learning processes. The general administration function is uniquely characterized by behaviors such as policy-making, communicating, and coordinating which tend to fall in center positions, thus giving it a role of centrality. Harris does not deny that principals, for example, sometimes become justifiably involved in both instruction-related and pupil-related activities. What he does apparently deny, however, is that a principal is both an administrator and a supervisor, for after carefully defining the terms of "supervisor" and "supervisory personnel," he concludes that the principal cannot be a supervisor. Rather, the principal more properly is classified under the heading, "supervisory personnel," and the term "supervisor" is reserved for those whose primary responsibilities are for providing leadership in supervisory activities.[12]

HUMAN SKILLS IN SUPERVISION

At the 1964 Chicago convention of the National Association of Secondary School Principals, Peter F. Drucker, widely known business consultant and professor of management, New York University, suggested in a speech that probably the most important contribution a secondary school principal could make is to have time available for

---

[11] Ben M. Harris, *Supervisory Behavior in Education* © 1963. Reprinted by permission of Prentice-Hall, Inc., Englewood Cliffs, New Jersey.

[12] Harris, p. 23.

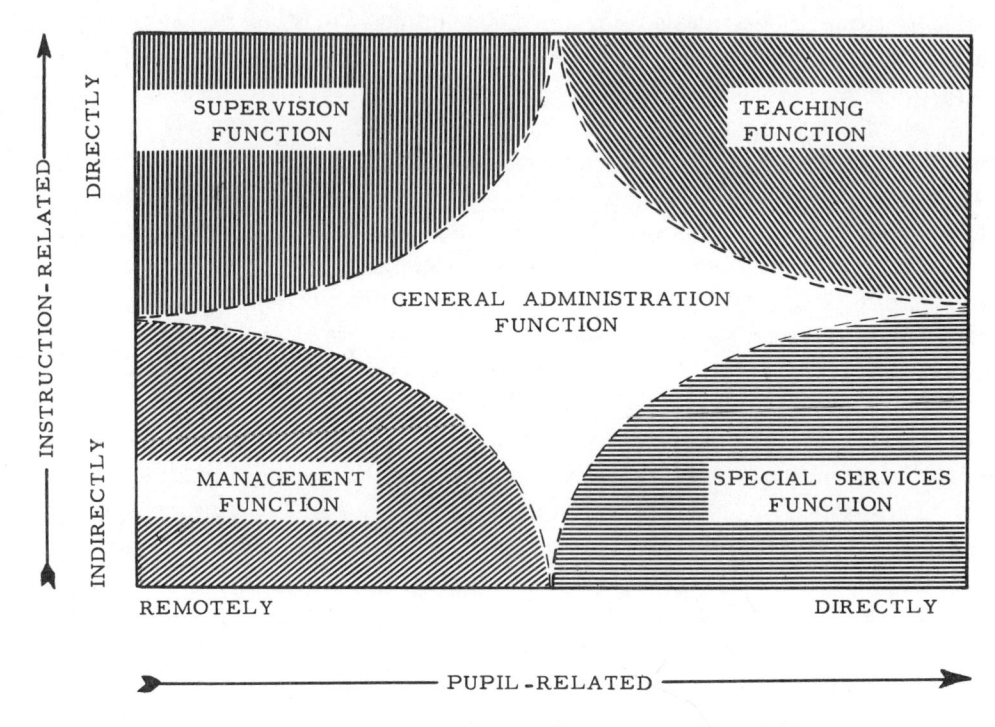

MAJOR FUNCTIONS OF THE SCHOOL OPERATION

FIGURE 2-1

individual youngsters and their parents. Drucker went on to say, "And nobody, if he does the job well, can have greater impact on a youngster in need of support. . . than the principal." This is the human side of the principal's job. Perhaps we can include staff personnel in Drucker's view of the principal's sphere of influence.

The above point of view by a management specialist is probably shaped by a concept of the great importance of the individual as an end in himself, which is certainly a reflection that supervisory thought and action are concerned rather strongly with relationships with individuals. Knowledge of self and others tested in practice helps the principal develop human skills for effective self-development and influence on others.

The quality and timing of reinforcement by the principal for mature teacher behavior is a major factor in the supervisory relationship. A reinforcing principal is likely to be one who recognizes the dignity of the teaching role and the necessity to get a clear view of how each teacher perceives reality. Such a principal makes decisions on the basis of what a teacher has rather than what he lacks; on what he does best rather than on what he does poorly or not at all.

One key concept in the human skills dimension is the objective acceptance of others. Once a principal-supervisor learns that he really can accept at face value the unique pattern of traits of each staff member, he is well on the way to becoming a person of influence and authority. Moreover, he likely will discover sooner or later that teachers will "catch" the spirit and accept their pupils with their diverse personalities.

It is a known fact that many school administrators pride themselves on the skillful manner in which they exercise procedural techniques in manipulating staff personnel. Such mechanical and sterotyped procedures as "How to be a sympathetic listener," or "Steps to use in cooling off an intense complainer," may in the long run fall short of their intended goals. Rather, the authors recommend that the secondary school principal in influencing others give serious thought to such indigenous group concerns as purposes, problem definition, hypothesis-forming, planning and evaluation.

Now and then a principal gets carried away with his prowess in the arena of interpersonal relations and attempts to offer therapy to teachers plagued with personal problems. The authors tend to agree with the position of Lucio and McNeil on this matter: [13]

> The personal and psychological problems of individuals are outside the purview of the supervisor's professional responsibility. Supervision, like teaching, is not therapy. The supervisor should clearly differentiate between giving professional counseling and giving personal therapy. Professional counseling about matters directly pertaining to teaching is one of his prime responsibilities; personal counseling or clinical therapy invades the private and personal life of an individual and has no place in the supervisory function.

It is doubtful that there are many valid "rules" of supervision. Industry reportedly is spending large sums of money to train supervisors in human-relations skills. Results are much less satisfactory than desired, for a myth persists that there are specifically "right" and "wrong" ways to supervise. Research findings, however, suggest that there are not specific rules of supervision which will work well in various situations. Since the supervisory process is quite complex, it is usually best to apply broad principles of human behavior which adapt to specific situations.

The fact that different subordinates react differently to a given supervisory act is partially accounted for in a number of research studies described by Likert.[14] Perceiving clearly that the supervisory act alone does not determine the subordinate's response, he concluded, "The subordinate's reaction to the supervisor's behavior always depends upon the relationship between the supervisory act as perceived by the subordinate and the expectations, values and interpersonal skill of the subordinate." [15]

From this proposition the junior or senior high school principal might well conclude that supervision is always a relative process. For effective action and communication, the supervisory leader adapts his modes of behavior for reckoning with the expectations, values, and human skills of those with whom he is communicating and interacting. Likert suggests that this principle applies in all person-to-person interactions.

Knowing that he cannot be all things to all persons, the wise supervisor recognizes and admits his limitations, a trait which in itself reduces guilt feelings of the teacher in difficulty. It is from such a strong humanistic foundation that the effective supervisor develops and applies his technical support to the instructional process and program.

---

[13] Lucio and McNeil, p. 156–157.
[14] R. Likert, *New Patterns of Management* (New York: McGraw-Hill Book Co.), Ch. 7.
[15] Likert, p. 94.

TECHNICAL SKILLS IN SUPERVISION

To say the least, it is quite difficult to differentiate sharply those supervisory skills which are either human or technical in nature. In reality there is a great deal of interrelatedness of the two dimensions. Having discussed some human skills, now is the time to define technical skills as those skills based on scientifically determined knowledge which are applied to effect change in behavior. Armed with human understandings plus valid theories and propositions, a secondary school principal is well equipped to cope with the supervisory demands of change and reality in the modern school setting.

Current literature abounds with descriptions of approaches to school improvement.[16] Although supervisory devices are many and varied, our purpose here is only to focus attention on three major aspects of supervisory responsibility, namely, the performance review, research methodology and curriculum development. Readers will find in Chapters Five and Six some elaboration on successful techniques, both human and technical, for upgrading the staff and their instructional methods.

Without question the assessment of teacher performance requires technical skills usage essentially on the part of the supervisor, who, in many junior and senior high schools, is the principal. One promising proposal for carrying out the performance review is offered by Lucio and McNeil.[17]

The success of this appraisal procedure, simple though effective, depends on careful planning, identification of and agreement on specific requirements to be met, and predicted outcomes. Planning starts with the supervisor's influence in committing teachers to explicit and measurable tasks followed by establishment of an environment wherein teacher success is highly probable. Evidence of the simplicity of the procedure is revealed in these phases: (1) reasonable teaching objectives are defined, (2) every effort and resource is brought to bear on goal achievement, and (3) the quality of performance is judged in terms of success in reaching previously established goals.

Contributing to the environment for teaching success are such factors as joint supervisor-teacher definition of objectives, procedures for purpose-achievement, and measuring devices. With such involvement in the review of performance the teacher is more likely to accept the results of the assessment.

RESEARCH METHODOLOGY

In the early 50's we began to talk and read about "action research." The present decade certainly has emphasized research in both the content and methods aspects of instruction. Nowadays, we are likely to hear such terms as "field testing," "curriculum research," and "cooperative research." The point is that the principal in his supervisory role is expected to utilize research and experimentation as one device for seeking evi-

---

[16] For a recent alphabetized list of supervisory devices, categorized on a group-individual basis and appropriately discussed, see J.M. Gwynn, *Theory and Practice of Supervision,* Ch. 16.

[17] Lucio and McNeil, pp. 212–218.

dence more dependable than mere "guesswork" in causing or evaluating change in the educational program. Today, there is great need for ongoing staff research projects, both individual and cooperative, to verify or disclaim the theories and proposals of several prime movers in modern-day curriculum improvement.

At the point of researching curriculum problems, the leader has some obligation to develop proposals cooperatively and assist in their implementation. Traditionally, with the exception of a few "lighthouse" junior and senior high schools and some laboratory schools, principals have neglected this dimension of supervisory services. In spite of the current ground swell of research emphasis and practice, today there are several controversies over school practices, ranging from team teaching to optimum grouping for instruction. Basic research has apparently not produced satisfactory evidence to convince practitioners of the relative values of these and other proposed changes. Secondary school principals are seldom ready to accept fully the concepts, unsupported by sufficient favorable evidence, of theoreticians far removed from the scene of action.

CREATIVE SUPERVISION

In the educational world as in the business world the leader has to combine creative thinking with judicial thinking in arriving at decisions. Relying on more than self, he uses his imagination to pool the experiences of others and to secure composite judgments through group processes. Essentially, the message is that the truly effective building principal is a paragon of creative action as well as an excavator of creative talent. Two statements by experts may assuage those principals who suffer anguish at such a notion of creativity on their part. Dr. J. P. Guilford concluded: "Like most behavior, creativity probably represents to some extent learned skills. There may be limitations set on these skills by heredity; but I am convinced that through learning, one can extend these skills within those limitations." In an address at M.I.T., Alex Osborn, noted authority on creativity, summed up as follows: "I submit that creativity will never be a science— in fact, much of it will always remain a mystery. . . . At the same time, I submit that creativity is an *art*—an applied art—a workable art—a teachable art—a learnable art —an art in which *all* of us can make ourselves more and more proficient, if we will." The writers point to the sessions on creativity at the 1963 and 1965 conventions of the National Association of Secondary School Principals as evidence of that professional organization's concern with and belief in creativity as a learnable attribute.

What are some of the research and experience factors making up an atmosphere for enhancing the art of creative supervision? Richards[18] believes that the creative supervisor must synthesize into effective action three areas: theories of learning, techniques of problem solving and group processes. He reminds us that although we learn in groups and by group action, it is the learner's personal involvement that constitutes meaningful learning. In the problem solving phase Richards sees the supervisory role as

---

[18] J.A. Richard, "The Art of Creative Supervision," *Educational Leadership,* 21 (Nov., 1963), pp. 80–83.

one of (1) active questioning to ascertain problems to be solved, (2) providing informational sources, (3) encouraging the group to discover other resources, and (4) stimulating construction of a hypothesis with subsequent steps for optional solutions. According to Richards,[19] "A sensitivity to the readiness of a group and of the individuals who may make up sub-groups is a prime requisite of the creative supervisor."

Another way of looking at creative supervision is that of recognizing the contributions of the allied concepts of human relations and interaction, guidance, curriculum reorganization and improvement, and the theory of instructional teams.[20] Modern supervision is creative supervision which is, in effect, a union of the values of both the democratic and scientific concepts of the function. Thus it is that cooperative effort and scientific research combine to free teachers for inquiry and advancement with an educational program keeping pace with a dynamic society.

BASIC TENETS FOR ADMINISTRATIVE AND SUPERVISORY LEADERSHIP

SELF-REALIZATION FOR THE PRINCIPAL

In an earlier portion of this chapter attention was given to "human skills" in supervision. Such skills may be improved through help one finds in books, courses, seminars, friends, or even therapists. More than likely, however, without occasional introspection and personal analysis the above aids fall short in helping the principal understand and improve himself.

There is some truth in the concept expressed by an unknown writer, "We love ourselves regardless of our faults; why not love our enemies likewise?" It has previously been established that a major task of the school principal is that of helping others to understand and accept themselves. Studies by Jersild[21] as well as Linscott and Stein[22] have shown that self-understanding and acceptance are the starting point in helping others do likewise. One of the authors of this book annually interviewed more than 200 experienced school administrators and candidates for administrative positions, and it is his observation that not all of them sufficiently understand and accept their own behavior patterns.

It is probably safe to say that there are several practicing and aspiring principals who are not fully self-accepting. How, then, are they to proceed in helping others to grow toward the adequate self? In all likelihood, these principals who question their own adequacy are aware of personal deficiencies even though they are unable to diagnose precisely just what those deficiencies are; of course, in life situations it is quite simple

---

[19] Richard, p. 83.
[20] For a thorough discussion of instructional teams, see Gwynn, J.M., Chapters 2, 13, and 20.
[21] A.T. Jersild, *In Search of Self* (Teachers College, Columbia University: Bureau of Publications, 1952).
[22] N.N. Linscott and J. Stein, editors, *Why You Do What You Do* (New York: Random House, 1956), p. 305.

for others to do that for them. An old cliché states, "One tends to see himself as others see him." When a principal, in performing his administrative and supervisory duties, discovers that his view of self is less than fully satisfying, then it is time to search out his values and concerns, as well as any possible anxieties, prejudices and intolerances which may exist. Then appropriate steps should be taken to build the self-image into one of adequacy, for in the setting of administrative and supervisory leadership, an inadequate self-image is crippling to the individual.

By the very nature of his responsibilities it is important that the principal, in relation to other members of the staff, demonstrate more clearly such qualities as maturity, optimism, self-understanding, tolerance and empathy. This view serves to underline the unfortunate situation in which the leader sometimes finds himself, one in which his own problems stall the forward march. With regard to at least one limitation, the following analogy is pertinent, "The tight skirts of prejudice always shorten the steps of progress."

It is the authors' premise that superior school leaders and leaders of high potential in the educational enterprise are individuals who believe firmly that change in self can and should occur. For suggestions to the principal on this matter we have adapted the views of Kelley on the fully functioning self: [23]

1. The fully functioning personality thinks well of himself.
2. He therefore sees his stake in others.
3. He sees himself as a part of the world in movement—in process of becoming.
4. The fully functioning self develops and holds human values.
5. He knows no other way to live except in keeping with his values.
6. The fully functioning person is cast in a creative role.

Although, as Combs suggests, adequate people may have negative views of self, their total behavior is fundamentally positive. He states these characteristics of the behavior of adequate persons: (*a*) a positive view of self, (*b*) identification with others, (*c*) openness to experience and acceptance, and (*d*) a rich and available perceptual field.[24] Perhaps the last of these characteristics deserves explanation.

The term "perceptual field" as used here refers basically to both the amounts and kind of information and understanding one has of the world around him, especially as he relates to that world. It is admitted that the junior high school principal rarely is expected to possess all the technical know-how that exists in education; yet it is imperative that he does have depth and breadth of knowledge to the extent that he is able to make wise judgments and decisions. In so doing he finds self-satisfaction and at the same time exerts positive influence on his fellow workers.

Discerning readers will note that at this point a principle will be ignored, "Always finish on a positive note." Rather, the authors have chosen to point out some of the very best thinking habits that a principal can use to insure his inadequacy:

---

[23] E. Kelley, *Perceiving, Behaving, Becoming,* Association for Supervision and Curriculum Development, 1962 Yearbook, Chapter 3.

[24] A.W. Combs, *Perceiving, Behaving, Becoming,* Association for Supervision and Curriculum Development, 1962 Yearbook, Chapter 5.

1. Forget the many blessings of his job and overemphasize the burdens.
2. Think that he is indispensable.
3. Think that the position of principal automatically insures him dignity and respect.
4. Forget others.
5. Nourish a pessimistic outlook.

Guiding Principles. Already we have argued that it is folly to think of separating administrative theory from administrative practices, for it is theory that provides principles as guides to action. The staff leader who lacks basic guides to action is constantly spinning his wheels in solving anew recurring problems. A great number of persistent educational problems can be boiled down to basic principles. Armed with a sound framework of theoretical assumptions, the principal can more frequently make wiser decisions in less time.

To be of maximum value principles should be applied flexibly and should be adjusted through reality testing. Unique situations are likely to call for modification or even abandonment, at times, of firmly entrenched principles. Careful evaluation of the application of principles to practical problems is one way to improve administrative and supervisory behavior.

The writers strongly recommend that every principal put into writing his principles for administrative and supervisory behavior. Nothing clarifies thought processes as well as written expression. In the first two chapters it has been pointed out that administration of the instructional program is a prime function of the secondary school principal. In terms of this function the following principles are indicative of the kind the principal should consider in formulating his own platform:

1. In order to be maximally effective, component activities of the instructional program must be selected and distributed in proportion to their educational priority and relative need for them.
2. In order to be maximally effective, the school must provide all students with common educational experiences leading to the development of the personal and social competencies required to live effectively in our society.
3. In order to be maximally effective, the mechanical organization must provide all students the opportunity to select and pursue unique personal and vocational interests.
4. In order to be maximally effective, the instructional program must be designed sufficiently to enhance the placement of primary emphasis on the educational development of the individual and the utilization of subject matter only insofar as it contributes to the attainment of this end.

Moving to the supervisory process itself, it is reiterated that supervision involves human relations, the complexity of which has thus far prevented development of adequate theory. However, one possible framework is that of Harris [25] who proposes the following:

---

[25] Harris, pp. 32–36. Used by permission.

1. Practically, we can think of supervision as a set of interrelated tasks which are carried on to facilitate maintenance of, or change in, the teaching function.
2. Supervision involves activities which can be identified as having differential impact on the people or the situation and which hence promote the maintenance of, or changes in, instruction.
3. Supervision is carried on in relation to the influences of a dynamic society characterized by an accelerating rate of change.
4. "The supervision function is carried on in the midst of an enormously expanding fund of human knowledge."
5. Supervision is concerned primarily with changing rather than maintaining the teaching-learning processes. . . .
6. Supervision, in facilitating change in instruction, is concerned with the rate, direction, and quality of change.
7. Direction, rate, and quality of change may or may not be desirable, depending upon the values applied in judging them.
8. Supervisory activities influence direction, rate, and quality of change.
9. Effective supervision involves skillful application of basic skills and processes to the tasks of supervision.

Competencies Needed by Junior High School Principals. A famous actor was asked what a stage performer should know. His answer: "All about acting and as much about everything as possible." In terms of his own role, this admonishment applies to the junior high school principal. He should know all about administration and supervision—and as much about everything else as possible. But, knowledge is only one of many requisites. In perusing the literature of educational administration one would have little difficulty in listing 50 or more qualifications.

In 1960 Vrentas sought help from 65 Illinois junior high school principals of three-year schools in identifying competencies recommended for this level of administration. The condensed data revealed that moral character and an understanding attitude toward discipline are competencies of the highest order. Other attributes deemed essential by more than 90 per cent of the respondents were patience and interest in pupil problems. The data further revealed that a majority of the principals were of the opinion that a prospective junior high school principal should have undergraduate preparation in a specific curriculum for junior high school teachers as well as previous administrative experience as an elementary principal. The majority of the principals were of the opinion that the ideal junior high school principal might be thought of as a person 30 to 35 years of age, with a Master's degree and five to ten years of teaching experience in the elementary and junior high schools.

To the aforementioned characteristics the authors add a leaping mind, boundless energy, purposeful enthusiasm, the knack for practical action in emergencies, and some intangible element of life and leadership style which inspires in others self-improvement and loyalty to the cause.

In the debatable area is the issue of the nature of the principalship at different levels. In New York City the bylaws of the board of education prescribe the general duties of *all* principals. No differentiation is made in assignments for the three divisions

—elementary, junior high and senior high school. New York City schools have since reorganized using the Middle School concept. Yet, at least to one junior high school principal in that city, it is obvious that the nature and scope of administrative duties do differ from level to level. Saunders [26] analyzed the job of the junior high school principals. The investigator noted essential differences in the job of the junior high school principal, which she classified into (1) known and accepted differences and (2) factors evident to the practicing junior high school principal. Under the first of these categories she calls attention to the need for expert handling of the constellation of behavior patterns found in early adolescence; to the task of providing both exploration and provisions for strengthing the basic skills; and to the vastly different cultural and socio-economic backgrounds of the pupils. According to Saunders the factors obvious to the practitioner include the pressure of policies from below and from above, the burden of training and supervising inadequately prepared assistants, lack of stability of the staff, and the presence of inexperienced and unskilled teachers on the staff.

In an attempt to determine if there are specific and unique competencies particularly important for junior high school principals, Rose [27] sought opinions from selected superintendents and principals in the states of the North Central Association. The problem became important to him when an examination of professional literature pertaining to the junior high school established two important facts. First, functions and purposes of this school are somewhat different from either the elementary or the senior high school. Secondly, the junior high school organization has recently undergone a great growth spurt. Examination of current practices of preparing, certifying and selecting junior high school principals showed them to be usually identical to that of senior high school principals. In fact, Rose concluded that identical competencies are desirable in junior and senior high school principals, an apparently incongruous situation. If the functions and purposes of the junior high school are different, he reasoned, why are there not unique qualities of leadership at each level? Having secured for administrators their evaluations of the importance of competencies for junior and senior high school principals, Rose analyzed the data and found that there are discrete factors considered important by superintendents in the selection of junior high school principals. These factors include:

1. Superintendents prefer junior high school principals to be 25 to 35 years of age upon entrance to the profession as compared to 36 to 45 years of age for senior high school principals.
2. Superintendents suggested that the following factors are particularly desirable for junior high school principals.
    a. A thorough knowledge and understanding of adolescents.
    b. A desire to work with this age group.
    c. Teaching experience in the elementary school and junior high school.
    d. An interest in junior high school curriculum problems.

---

[26] Juliet Saunders, "Job Analysis—Junior High School Principals," *The Bulletin,* National Association of Secondary School Principals, 43 (Nov., 1959), pp. 46–55.

[27] H.C. Rose, *A Study of the Competencies Needed for Junior High Principals.* Unpublished doctoral dissertation, University of North Dakota, 1961.

In this study respondents rated sixteen competencies more important for junior high school principals than for senior high school principals. Ten of the sixteen competencies represented differences of opinions by the sample of administrators which were statistically significant well beyond the .01 level. The ten competencies rated *much* more important for junior high school principals follow:

a. Knowledge of child growth and development.
b. Background of successful experience as an elementary teacher.
c. Background of successful experience as a junior high school teacher.
d. Background of successful experience as an elementary school administrator.
e. Background of successful experience as a junior high school administrator.
f. Knowledge of development and function of elementary schools.
g. Knowledge of development and function of junior high schools.
h. Understanding current issues, problems, and practices of core curriculum.
i. Knowledge and understanding of sound elementary school curriculum practices.
j. Knowledge and understanding of effective block time teaching techniques.

Few men and women possess genius for educational leadership, which means that most junior high school principals will need to take advantage of all professional growth opportunities. Chapter Three will present some of the ways in which principals can participate in self-development experiences. It is most unlikely, however, that techniques and knowledge can substitute for personal patterns of behavior. That is to say, professionalism is second to character in running a school.

It is not enough to push a pet project or funnel too much energy into one aspect of the administrative task. Within his building, the prime sphere of the junior high school principal is that of the whole rather than any one part. It's his job to survey, plan and decide where the school will be tomorrow, next year, the next decade—then organize and motivate his staff toward that goal. It is not his job to finish the task; neither is he permitted to lay it down.

The above guidelines to administrative and supervisory action are only suggestive and by no means exhaustive of the concepts that the modern principal needs to understand and apply. If leadership is to be superior, the principal should perceive and apply appropriately many more principles of much greater comprehensiveness than have been expressed here.

SELECTED READINGS

American Association of School Administrators, *The High School In A Changing World.* AASA Yearbook, 1958.

Brunsetter, Max R., "Principles of Democratic Supervision," *Teachers College Record,* Vol. 44, February, 1963, pp. 374–375.

Burnham, R. M. and King, M. L., *Supervision in Action,* Association for Supervision and Curriculum Development, 1961.

Combs, A. W., *Perceiving, Behaving, Becoming,* Association for Supervision and Curriculum Development, ASCD Yearbook, 1962.

Council for Administrative Leadership in New York State, *How Teachers View School Administration,* January, 1959.

Douglass, H., Bent, T. K. and Boardman, C. W., *Democratic Supervision.* (Boston: Houghton Mifflin Co., Second Edition, 1961)

Engleman, Finis, "Theory vs. Practice," *The School Administrator,* March, 1962.

Gwynn, J. M., *Theory and Practice of Supervision.* (New York: Dodd, Mead and Co., 1961)

Harris, B., *Supervisory Behavior in Education.* (Englewood Cliffs, N.J.: Prentice-Hall, Inc., 1963)

Hills, R. J., "A New Concept of Staff Relations," *Administrator's Notebook,* University of Chicago, Vol. VIII, March, 1952.

Jersild, A. T., *In Search of Self.* (Teachers College, Columbia University; Bureau of Publications, 1952)

Kelly, E., *Perceiving, Behaving, Becoming.* Association for Supervision and Curriculum Development, ASCD Yearbook, 1962.

Likert, R., *New Patterns of Management.* (New York: McGraw-Hill Book Co., 1961)

Linder, I. H. and Gunn, H. M., *Secondary School Administration.* (Columbus, Ohio: Charles E. Merrill Books Inc., 1963)

Linscott, N. N. and Stein, J., *Why You Do What You Do.* (New York: Random House, 1956)

Natioinal Association of Secondary School Principals, *Design for Leadership,* Washington, D.C., 1963.

Richard, J. A., "The Art of Creative Supervision," *Educational Leadership,* Vol. 21, November, 1963, pp. 80–83.

Rose, H. C., *A Study of the Competencies Needed For Junior High School Principals.* Unpublished doctoral dissertation, University of North Dakota, 1961.

Saunders, Juliet, "Job Analysis-Junior High School Principals," *The Bulletin,* National Association of Secondary School Principals, Volume 43, Nov., 1959, pp. 46–55.

THREE

The Principal's Program of Self-Improvement

There has not been a time in recent years when the secondary school principal has not needed to work hard to keep abreast of the contemplated and actual changes in the administration of schools. The tempo is quickening. In the months ahead the principal will be called upon to make many decisions about new ideas for administering the curriculum, the students, the staff, building programs, materials, and equipment. He must have access to information of sufficient depth to make the decisions required. He must be able to distinguish between change and improvement.

He will be called upon to make new kinds of decisions related to areas unknown to his counterpart of two decades ago. Today the world is truly moving into the school —and with the world, its problems; and with these problems, new unsettled questions are generated in the school.

The continual development of knowledge, understanding, and skill by the principal in order to furnish the leadership which will be required of him in the years ahead is a necessity. How can he provide for his own professional growth within an already tight schedule?

PROFESSIONAL GROWTH

There are many avenues to professional improvement. Some are quite formal. One immediately thinks of graduate course work, credit hours, advanced degrees, and all that this entails. Other routes are less formal though they do represent an organized effort at improving the principal in his job. Among the examples of this type are conventions, workshops, institutes and conferences.

GRADUATE WORK

The pursuit of knowledge through graduate work is a popular way of improving one's professional capabilities. Graduate schools have recognized the administrator's difficulty in arranging long periods of time on campus. The result has been evening or Saturday courses, extension classes within the buildings of a school system remote from the university campus, and short post sessions following the regular summer session on campus. In this way a principal can take a course such as business administration or school finance to help fill gaps in his professional background.

Often these courses, however, are geared to the teacher who hopes to become an administrator and are designed to meet basic state requirements for certification as an administrator. In some instances universities have designed, and made available through the aforementioned avenues, courses for the practicing, certificated administrator who already possesses the master's degree, and who may or may not be interested in a sixth year or doctor's degree. These courses are generally in areas like personnel administration or school law.

There are few courses open to the practicing administrator through evening, Saturday or extension work in those areas which have become increasingly important to the principal in recent years. These are courses in related fields, such as economics, political science, data processing, business administration, race relations, and labor management. These are courses which may not be designed specifically for the school administrator but which contain knowledge he needs in order to cope with some of the problems reaching his desk with increasing frequency.

Some colleges of education have risen to current challenges and have made room in their advanced graduate degree programs to include these needs. It is hoped others will follow suit rapidly.

The question of whether to take courses as a part of a program leading to an advanced degree or just to take courses one desires or for which one feels the need, must be faced as one continues to pursue graduate work beyond the master's degree. Of course, the first rule is the obvious one—take courses which will help to improve one's ability as an administrator. It would be hoped, however, that this can be accomplished within a degree program. There are many reasons why there are advantages to such a program. The person gains the attention of a faculty member who may take a personal interest because he becomes partly responsible for that person's success in the program. A good program, tailored to an individual's needs, as is true on many campuses today, meets the requirement of providing relevant courses plus a master plan. Furthermore, the discipline of a planned program has a built in prod—or motivator.

Lastly, there is always the time when that advanced degree will mean the difference between being considered for a position or not even being allowed to apply. There are certain doors which only the advanced degree unlocks, regardless of experience, ability, and intelligence. One never knows when he will come to such a door. The wise policy is to be ready just in case.

PROFESSIONAL LITERATURE

Regardless of the several avenues one chooses to aid his professional growth, among them must be a certain amount of reading in professional literature. There is just no way to keep up with the latest advances in the field unless one does a reasonable amount of reading in professional periodicals and books. It is the easiest part of a professional program of growth to procrastinate, but nonetheless, it should be pursued with determination.

In the area of educational administration, one should seek good books. Much of a principal's reading must be devoted to specific specialties or weaknesses in his background, or those new areas such as programmed instruction and computer-assisted learning. Periodically, however, a good general treatise on the administrative art should be read—to remind one of some of the things he should be doing, but has pushed aside in the press of daily problems. There are a number of these around, but a good place to start is Ray E. Brown's *Judgment in Administration.* (New York: McGraw-Hill, 1966.) This is an excellent, readable treatment of some of the most basic elements of administration and its associated decision-making process.

From time to time books about various facets of education will appear, written by well-known people. Principals should read these if for no other reason than that they will be discussed by the professional and layman with whom he will be working. It is worthwhile to be well enough informed to react. James B. Conant's *The Comprehensive High School* (New York: McGraw-Hill, 1967) is such a book.

With research playing an increasingly important role in the school, the principal should include several references in his professional library related to this subject. Some should be devoted to how to do both simple and in depth research in the school setting. Others should deal with reports on research important to improving learning in the school. Examples of volumes which fit in these categories are: *The Handbook of Research on Teaching,* by N. L. Gage (Chicago: Rand, McNally and Co., 1963), and *The Encyclopedia of Educational Research,* edited by Chester W. Harris and Marie R. Liba (New York: The Macmillan Co., 1960). Individual research studies such as that of James S. Coleman, reported in *Equality of Educational Opportunity* (Washington, D. C.: Government Printing Office, 1966), which raise some important questions about basic premises in education, should also be a part of a principal's program of professional reading.

One of the areas of reading which should be included is the learning process and implications for the school. Certainly among the "musts" in this field are: Jerome Bruner, *The Process of Education* (Cambridge: Harvard University Press, 1963); Philip H. Phenix, *Realms of Meaning* (New York: McGraw-Hill Book Co., 1964); and Harry S. Broudy, B. Othanel Smith, and Joe R. Burnett, *Democracy and Excellence in American Secondary Education* (Chicago: Rand-McNally and Co., 1964). These are works to which one should return from time to time. There are other works, of course, which fit into this category, for this group is by no means exhaustive.

The principal's reading program should spread to as many areas which border administration as possible. Examples of books of recent origin which might be included in such a list are: Harmon Zeigler, *The Political World of the High School Teacher* (Eugene, Oregon: Center for the Advanced Study of Educational Administration, University of Oregon, 1966); Gilbert Burck and the Editors of *Fortune, The Computer Age* (New York: Harper and Row, 1965); American Association of School Administrators, *Imperatives In Education* (Washington, D. C.: AASA, 1966); Gertrude Noar, *The Teacher and Integration* (Washington, D. C.: NCTEPS—NEA, 1966); Calvin W. Taylor and Frank E. Williams, editors, *Instructional Media and Creativity* (New York: John Wiley and Sons, Inc., 1966); and Edgar L. Morphet and Charles Ryan, editors, *Implications for Education of Prospective Changes in Society* (Denver, Colorado: Designing Education for the Future, an eight state project, 1967).

Professional periodicals are an important part of the principal's reading. Among the best for keeping up to date on items pertinent to the schools are: *Phi Delta Kappan, NASSP Bulletin, Nation's Schools,* and *Education USA*. Geared to the layman, but including material of importance for educators, are *Saturday Review, Time, Newsweek,* and the educational supplement of *The New York Times.*

To keep up with each of these periodicals and to read each of the books cited would not be possible for most principals during the current year. By the same token, not to do a reasonable amount of this type of reading is wilfully short-circuiting oneself. New and renewed ideas are being thrown about in educational circles and the press continuously. The U. S. Office of Education is looking with great favor upon "innovative" practices. Industry is entering the educational technology field with an eye on a multi-billion dollar market. The only answer for the wise principal is to set up a regular reading program which includes both books and periodicals. A definite program with a relatively small amount of time each day, strictly adhered to, will bring surprises as to the amount of such reading which can be accomplished. It is indeed worth the effort.

INSTITUTES, WORKSHOPS, CONVENTIONS, AND CONFERENCES

Institutes and workshops are opportunities for professional growth. Whether offered by the school system, professional associations, or educational institutions, these are excellent ways of improving oneself. They not only provide the chance to do some work on one's own in preparation for a contribution to the group, but they also allow the sharing of ideas and common problems with fellow administrators. The mere knowledge that other principals have encountered similar problems is valuable therapy. To get their reactions and attempts at solutions is enlightening. Furthermore, the camaraderie and enjoyment associated with the industry which are a part of well run workshops are worthy by-products to the central purpose of professional growth. For these reasons the workshop is a highly recommended device for improving one's professional ability.

Conventions also contain an element of fellowship which principals find valuable. To get away from the school for a few days may prove a worthy catharsis. Beyond this it gives one the opportunity to hear how others are approaching common problems.

Group sessions also provide the opportunity for interacting with the experts through questions from the floor. A seasoned convention goer stated that he always attempted to come home from each convention with one good idea he was going to devote some effort to trying-out in his own situation. Over the years some important changes have taken place in his school as a result.

The principal is automatically involved in a number of professional conferences. These can be approached from two points of view. The first is to do no preparation if it can be avoided and as little as possible if some is required. This approach may "get one through" most conferences. This is tempting to the busy administrator. The other tack is to take a little extra time and not only arrive at the conference better prepared, but professionally stronger in the process. The extra reading, consulting with knowledgeable people, or other resource activity pursued, contributes to a more highly qualified administrator, and a more worthy participant in the conference.

PROFESSIONAL ORGANIZATIONS

Professional organizations offer an opportunity for self-improvement. Getting involved in the work of such groups will provide numerous avenues for broadening one's perspective and concurrently for being of service to one's colleagues. Of course, some organizations are more active in improving the profession than others. There are ample opportunities for these groups to provide a responsible voice for the principals of an area or state, however, and it is a rewarding experience to be a part of such an activity. With the recent activities of the federal government and business in education, an authoritative voice for principals, regionally and nationally, is becoming more important.

WRITING—SPEAKING

While it may not be universally true that "writing maketh the exact man," certainly one of the best ways to organize one's ideas is to put them on paper. By so doing, a person cannot only organize and clarify his own thoughts, but it enables him to take stock of what is, what is presumed, what is hoped, and what cannot be validated. It is a good way of helping one face some of his job's realities. Often a person does not really encounter some of the fantasies in his repertoire until he sees them in writing.

Principals have an obligation to the profession to write about their successes and failures. Not only is it valuable to the writer to organize and test his ideas in this way, but it helps the professional growth of his colleagues. With all of the new ideas being tried, much more writing should be done about them. This writing should then be submitted to professional journals for consideration.

If the manuscript is not accepted, it should still be preserved for principals interested in similar problems. In the past, locating such information has been almost impossible. A service which offers promise for helping with this herculean task is the file of such studies being assembled by Phi Delta Kappa. The plan is to collect studies from school systems across the country and put them into a computerized system. A person may ask for studies on a particular subject and receive print-outs of those available at a nominal cost. This will provide access to a heretofore closed source of information in the field.

One last word, as one writes about studies, he should try to present the picture as near the actual fact as possible. The tendency to paint a nominal success in glowing hues is a natural one, but the profession is best served by something nearer the truth. Failures deserve to be reported too. A lot of blind alleys would not be repeatedly traversed if those who first found them let the rest of their friends know. After all, to make a mistake and recognize it is not a disgrace. This, too, is professional growth.

Speaking has many of the same values as writing for professional growth, especially if one prepares by first roughing it out in writing. Another advantage which may come to one who speaks is related to the audience. In writing, the principal usually addresses his thoughts to other professional people. In his speaking, however, he frequently is working with groups of lay people. This requires a different approach, a different language, and provides another benefit in growth for the principal. It often requires more work to put one's remarks into the layman's language so he may be understood. This is not always easy, but in the end, by finding ways of expressing oneself so his audience may understand, he better clarifies the topic in his own mind and thus makes it more valuable to him.

GROWTH AS A PERSON

It is said that one of the really hard jobs of life is looking at oneself. It is important, however, that this be done occasionally in order to direct one's growth as a person. It is a rewarding process, for from it one cannot only assess what one is doing, but further, what he should be doing toward improving himself as a person.

READING

Just as reading is an important aspect of professional growth, it is equally important for one's personal growth. It is easy to become so involved in one's job that reading becomes devoted to professional writings and the daily newspaper. Such a program of reading is well calculated to produce a principal very narrow of outlook and unaware of the real world around him and his pupils. Such a principal can never be truly effective in providing leadership for a continually developing curriculum to fit the world in which our young people live. Reading on a broad scale is a necessity.

Such a reading program should probably include three general areas:

1. To expand one's general knowledge
2. To enhance one's understanding and appreciation of himself, his fellow man, his physical environment, and his spiritual world
3. For fun

It is possible to find books which will fulfill elements in each category from the best seller lists. In fact, lists and reviews in Sunday supplements such as the *New York Times Book Review* are excellent sources of sufficient information for making reading choices. It is well to remember that busy administrators often have the largest gap in "reading for fun."

As with professional reading, it is appropriate to reiterate that over the course of a year a surprising number of books can be read if a person makes use of 15–30 minute pieces of time sandwiched between other activities. It is a good habit to acquire.

COMMUNITY ACTIVITIES

Engaging in activities in the community provides three outlets for the principal. It enables him to associate with non-educators in an activity for community betterment. This affords him the opportunity of getting to know members of the community and to be known by them apart from activities related to the school. This association can be of value personally as well as to the benefit of the school. In time of school crises it is well to be able to count among one's friends a reasonable supply of non-educators. This reason is important enough to cause some school districts to have an unwritten policy of distributing its principals among service clubs and other civic organizations in the community.

A second factor is that the principal brings skills to these groups which are of value in carrying out their activities. This affords the principal the opportunity to be a contributing member of the community and offers a change of pace from educational matters.

In addition to what one contributes, these activities provide avenues for personal growth which are of importance to a well-rounded person. What one can gain from association with people of various backgrounds and stature is of value to development as a real person. Such activities are, therefore, highly recommended.

Two cautions are offered. The tendency of chairmen of such activities is to automatically steer educators to youth activities. There is merit in this, both to the organization and to the individual. However, the senior high principal whose community activities consist entirely of teaching the senior high class in Sunday School, serving as chairman of the youth talent program of the service club, managing a local team of little leaguers, and working with a boy scout troop, is enjoying a change of pace from his school work, but he is not getting much opportunity for strictly adult activities. At least some of these projects should be strictly adult.

The other recommendation is to beware of becoming so enmeshed in community activities that the personal growth value is inundated by the loss of time for job, self, and family. This is a difficult problem because the very nature of the principal's position places him in a logical spot to be sought out for certain community activities. Once he has demonstrated an ability and willingness to serve, his "fame" will spread and requests for help will multiply rapidly. These people know that busy people are those who get jobs done. At this point one of the hardest personal qualities to develop must be acquired —the ability to say "no."

RELAXATION

Finally, the principal must develop the ability to relax. He owes it to himself and to his family—indeed to his school and his profession. This is the perspective-gaining element. The pace at which most principals move makes it hard for them to relax; the tendency is to "keep on the move." There is so much to do, so much to read, that when one finds a few "unscheduled" minutes, he is likely to use every one to read, outline the solution to a problem, or get involved in some activity. The principal must, therefore, discipline himself to put all this aside and relax.

Of course, relaxation takes many forms for different people. For some golf is an escape to an afternoon of complete relaxation. For others—the ones who break or throw their clubs—this is not an activity which rightly falls within the category of relaxation. Whatever the activities that fit one's needs—walking, driving, photography, chess, or whatever—leave some time in your days and weekends to allow for these activities.

Lastly, schedule some thinking time. As Romine states, "Time to think is one of the conditions most needed to maintain sanity in modern living. Caught up in a cyclone of activity, we seldom question our direction, assess the real significance of our endeavor, or evaluate results." [1]

Romine has succinctly stated several important elements related to the need for thinking and given some suggestions as to how one might encourage it in himself.[2]

> Some of us are no longer good company for ourselves, and we fear to be alone. We have weakened or lost the ability to let our minds range the rough terrain of truth seeking an adventure in ideas. Often, too, we have reduced our sensitivity to life around us by a lack of sufficient feeling and solicitude for others. . . .
>
> Determination to set aside a few minutes regularly each day or week is crucial. Most people fear a schedule as a prison, but it can help one to find time and use it wisely, even for doing nothing. It is encouraging, too, if promising ideas can be reserved for reflection, to be tasted as one savors good food, slowly and thoroughly.
>
> Getting away from people occasionally is restful in itself. It enables one to rediscover the pleasure of being and thinking alone. Group decision is important in many matters, but it is no substitute for independent thinking. A walk in the hills or the woods alone, where the soul can breathe as well as the body, will do much to put one in a contemplative mood. Listening to appreciate music in a quiet place serves in a similar fashion.
>
> Some of us have been so busy keeping up with the Joneses that we haven't caught on to ourselves. The reassessment of goals and activities might surprise us. Success in enjoying occasional thoughtful solitude may not come easily. The more difficult it is the more we probably need it. . . .
>
> Unhurried reflection may also save time and energy that are often wasted under

---

[1] Stephen Romine, "Take Time to Think," *News and Views,* College of Education, University of Colorado (March, 1964), p. 1.

[2] Romine.

conditions of stress. Many people race their motors without having their minds in gear. They are constantly busy but the results are discouraging.

One of the most important parts of growing in the principalship is developing the ability to look at oneself, to map out a program of self-improvement, and to discipline oneself to continually devoting some time to accomplishing it. All elements are important and none should be emphasized at the expense of the others. Professional improvement is essential to fill the gaps in original preparation and to keep abreast of the rapid changes occurring and proposed for our schools.

But the most able professional will not be as successful as he will need to be in the coming years, unless he devotes some time to improving himself as a person. This requires working on one's personality and his philosophy of life—and it means taking time to relax. All are important elements in the continual development of the principal. This part of a principal's life cannot be ignored without reducing his proficiency as the leader in the school. This assigns it a pretty high priority.

SELECTED READINGS

American Association of School Administrators, *Imperatives in Education.* (Washington, D. C.: AASA, 1966)

Brown, Ray E., *Judgment In Administration.* (New York: McGraw-Hill Book Company, 1966)

Broudy, Harry S., Smith, B. Othanel and Burnett, Joe R., *Democracy and Excellence in American Secondary Education.* (Chicago: Rand-McNally, and Co., 1964)

Bruner, Jerome, *The Process of Education.* (Cambridge: Harvard University Press, 1963)

Noar, Gertrude, *The Teacher and Integration.* (Washington, D. C.: NCTEPS-NEA, 1966)

Part 2

THE PROFESSIONAL STAFF

FOUR

Personnel Requirements and Selection

Secondary school administrators are feeling the full force of the shortage of competent teachers and are faced with the task of making the best choices of those who will teach the students.

REQUIREMENTS

The determination of staff needs for a given school unit requires exhaustive study, careful planning, and meticulous specification. These requirements will continue as the members of boards of education and administrators compete with other taxing groups for public funds and as they strive for prudent management.

A two-fold consideration of requirements must be made. First, the qualitative aspect requires a meaningful description of each professional position that is established in the staffing of a school unit. Second, the quantitative aspect must be described, proposed, and defended for each school year.

QUALITATIVE

The qualitative aspects of staffing are determined as answers are sought for the several questions which follow:

"What educational goals are to be achieved through the program of instruction?"

The determination of these goals is to involve representatives of the community as well as the members of the professional staff. It would be a gross error to specify goals without community involvement as such action would jeopardize positive school and community relationships that are necessary for understanding, acceptance, and financial support. "What the schools do" is rightfully determined by the community. "How the instructional program is conducted" is to be determined by the professional staff. Hamlin [1] discusses the delegation of responsibilities and has set forth a structure for community involvement that may establish a true school-community.

"What are the professional competencies needed to carry out the instructional program?"

The education controversy of the mid-century, the "Focus on Change," the staff utilization studies, private corporation grants, and federal aid require every administrator to examine the program of the school and the manner in which the professional staff *is* utilized. His awareness of the teaching process and the nature of learning must be evident in his pronouncements and in his professional behavior. These will be the determinants of the professional competencies needed for the members of the staff and will be discussed in Chapter Five.

"How should the members of the professional staff be organized to permit them to function at an optimum level?"

This question is raised here to establish the third element of qualitative requirements to guide the job interviewer. The answers to this question will be discussed in Chapter Five.

QUANTITATIVE

The quantitative aspects of staffing are challenged most frequently as they affect or are affected by the annual budget. When the staffing recommendations of administrators are challenged, they should be ready to submit the bases for their requests. Justification should find its basis in the answers to the first and second questions under the qualitative aspects of staffing. These answers may prove to be insufficient as the dollar value of the requests for funds rises above the financial resources of the school district. At this point, the administrator seeks to rank order all the requests.

With the establishment of realistic educational goals and the specification of professional competencies, the administrator and his staff evaluate staffing requests with respect to the rank order. Administrators must bring about a confrontation of issue with issue, achieving final decisions that have been focused on merit and not on personal dynamics or rank.

A standard for pupil-teacher ratios has less and less justification as programs of large and small group instruction, independent study, and the use of para-professionals and clerical aids become realities in the schools.

More significant is the standard of 50 professionals for every 1,000 junior and/or senior high school students. This standard includes all those assigned to a school, but the

---

[1] Herbert M. Hamlin, *Citizen Participation in Local Policy Making for Public Education* (Urbana, Illinois: College of Education, University of Illinois, 1960), pp. 19–23.

central or headquarters staff are not counted. They should be counted separately, and a standard of one administrator or supervisor for every 1,000 students is a working ratio. The goal of a professional staff should be to achieve an optimum ratio. This ratio will vary, as pointed out by studies in New York State:

> The size of the optimum administrative staff in a local school system is a function of the size of the school system, the wealth of the community, the expressed purposes of the school system, the administrative functions that are felt to be necessary for the achievement of the purposes, the pattern of organization of the administrative staff, and the capacity and ability of individual staff members.[2]

SELECTION

Several well-defined administrative tasks, when properly performed, will lead to decisions for effective practice in personnel selection. Responsibility for selection must reside in the secondary school principal for the same reason that Lapchick[3] supports autonomous teacher selection in the elementary school. When principals make the effort to assume such an active role, teaching in the schools may be improved. The position of principal is described as an example.

POSITION: Principal, secondary school—a line officer directly responsible to the superintendent of schools.

RESPONSIBILITY: Serve as the administrative head of the secondary school through providing educational leadership in administration and supervision.

    Be solely responsible for the conduct of the program in its entirety.

    Meet all certification requirements of the state.

    Strive to maintain personal and professional fitness through community service and involvement in activities that promote continuous development of leadership capabilities.

    Negotiate with the staff on all items that pertain to the professional assignments within the building and the administration, organization and supervision of the staff and program.

ASSIGNMENT: Procure, develop and retain competent members of the staff.

    Maintain effective communication with and between staff members.

    Institute the means for continuous study, assessment and development of the program of the school.

    Organize for optimum utilization of the competencies of the professional staff.

    Achieve full use of the instructional materials and physical plant to realize the objectives of the program.

---

[2] New York State, Council for Administrative Leadership, *Handbook for the Study of Administrative Staff Organization* (Albany, New York: State Department of Education, 1957), p. 5. Used by permission of the publisher.

[3] Joseph D. Lapchick, "Who Should Hire Elementary Teachers," *School Management*, 9 (February, 1965), pp. 81–82.

Provide pupil personnel services and government organization to serve the individual and group needs of the boys and girls.
Develop fiscal policies that will foster development of the program.
Insure continuous evaluation of the learning and teaching processes.

PROFESSIONAL POSITIONS

Written descriptions of the established professional positions should be a part of the policies, rules, and regulations of the board of education. In the absence of such descriptions or policies the administrator responsible for selection should initiate the writing of such descriptions. Further guidance in developing descriptions may be found in the studies from New York State.[4]

THE SEARCH

Searching for promising and competent personnel is not a seasonal task. It is a year around opportunity to identify individuals who possess qualities that match the requirements of professional positions in the school. The principal may obtain valuable leads from his teachers to seek out the outstanding performers in other schools. Some acquaintances—that have been made by teachers and principals at institutes, in college and university classes, at conferences, and in former positions—will be worthy of follow-up.

College, university and private placement offices will continue to be a primary source of candidates for school administrators to consider. Vacancy notices to placement agencies must contain clear and concise descriptions of the position and qualifications desired. Such notices and brochures will permit the placement officers to review the candidates registered with them and to make intelligent referrals.

Recruitment activity of secondary school principals is generally limited to the placement agencies. This is insufficient in light of the extensive activity that characterizes recruitment by industries. A staff needs to select those students who have potentialities for teaching. These students should have opportunities to experience what teaching really is as tutors or teacher aides. Some chapters of the Future Teachers of America provide classroom experiences for their members as they assume duties as teacher aides for a period of six to ten weeks. These experiences have assisted many high school students to select education as their vocation with assurance that their selection is a knowledgeable one drawn from their experience.

Junior and senior high school students who possess the personal and intellectual qualities needed by teachers should be invited to confer with their teachers, counselors and principals about the teaching profession. One study of teacher supply and demand concludes with a list of five overriding facts that should be known by undergraduates as they select their field of major study. These are as follows:

---
[4] New York State, pp. 17–19. Used by permission of the publisher.

1. The total number of college graduates in teacher education is increasing faster than the finances of schools will permit their employment.

2. The greatest shortage will continue to be at the elementary school level.

3. The supply of secondary school teachers is out of balance. Surpluses exist in some areas while there are shortages in other subject areas.

4. Choices are being made by undergraduates without knowledge of the needs in the schools.

5. Teachers are needed whose "personal qualities and specific preparation fit them for a career of service" to students whose family backgrounds have not prepared them for the public school programs.[5]

The number of unfilled positions at the time of fall school openings leaves the first statement open to question. The second statement should be examined in light of current data.

The Research Division of the National Education Association—through the work begun by Ray D. Maul and continued by William S. Graybeal—has provided much information with respect to teacher supply and demand. Martin H. Bartels utilized their basic data and developed an *index of teacher demand*.[6] The index is a simple ratio of new teachers employed to new teachers prepared. In a recent paper [7] Dr. Bartels has ranked the teaching fields by index of demand. These rankings appear in Figure 4-1 and should be made known to students in teacher education programs as they plan their major and minor areas of study.

The guest speaker at the 1965 Spring Conference of the Junior High School Association of Illinois was Gordon F. Vars. Dr. Vars urged the formation of a "Jun-Hi Teach Corps" to make a better world for the adolescent. He cited the major problems in obtaining enough qualified teachers:

(1) getting enough young people to want to go into education, (2) selecting those who want to teach and who possess the personal qualities, (3) finding those who have academic preparation and certification with competency in the teaching fields, (4) possessing preparation in the teaching of reading and study skills, and (5) having had a meaningful and successful student teaching experience.[8]

The principal should seek nominations from teachers, fellow principals and professors of persons who have demonstrated the competencies needed for a position. This requires an administrator who will accept and encourage the professional advancement of members of his staff.

---

[5] National Education Association, Research Division, "The Problem: Teacher Supply Demand," *NEA Research Bulletin* 42 (December, 1964), p. 119.

[6] Martin H. Bartels, "Index of Teacher Demand Through 1964," *The Educational Forum*, XXX, No. 2 (January, 1966), pp. 217–220.

[7] Martin H. Bartels, "A Sharp Upturn in Teacher Demand," unpublished, 1968, p. 6.

[8] Gordon F. Vars, "Preparing Junior High Teachers: A Prof's Eye View," *Junior High School Staff Personnel* (Danville, Illinois: The Interstate Printers and Publishers, Inc., 1966), pp. 9–16. Used by permission of the publisher.

TEACHING FIELDS RANKED BY INDEX OF DEMAND *

(1) Rank	(2) Teaching Field	(3) Demand	(4) Supply	(5) Index of Demand (3)/(4)
1.	Junior High School (General)	1376	54	25.48
2.	Elem. Phys. & Health Education	690	154	4.48
3.	Trade, Industrial, Vocational, Technical	697	160	4.36
4.	Elementary Music	707	205	3.45
5.	Distributive Education	201	63	3.19
6.	Librarian	1142	405	2.82
7.	Special Education	2372	1149	2.06
8.	Ungraded (Total)	4126	2381	1.73
9.	Art, Elementary	335	212	1.58
10.	Mathematics	4667	3112	1.50
11.	Elementary Total	41453	27925	1.48
12.	Elementary, Regular Classroom	39655	27268	1.45
13.	English, Language Arts (Total)	8244	7242	1.14
14.	Natural and Physical Sciences	4228	3764	1.12
15.	Secondary Total	37259	41126	.90
16.	Foreign Languages (Total)	1829	2124	.86
17.	Physical and Health Education, Women	1596	1904	.84
18.	Industrial Arts	1164	1454	.80
19.	Foreign Languages, Elementary	65	86	.76
20.	Guidance Counselor	612	827	.74
21.	Agriculture	476	648	.74
22.	Business Education	2262	3217	.70
23.	Social Sciences	4735	7010	.68
24.	Music	1587	2424	.65
25.	Art, High School	967	1528	.63
26.	Home Economics	1731	2750	.63
27.	Physical and Health Education, Men	1496	3672	.41

FIGURE 4-1

* Includes data from 24 states.

The screening process by the school administrator begins with the first contacts in-person or on-paper that he has with candidates. He may improve his efficiency in the entire selection process as he organizes the file for each candidate—correspondence, application, credentials, transcripts, recommendations and notations of telephone conferences and interviews. The interviewer must examine college transcripts and letters of recommendation to establish their authenticity. The author's experience suggests that falsification of records or letters is quite rare; nevertheless, placement of one applicant under such conditions is a risk that should not be taken. It is advisable for interviewing officers to make their own requests for transcripts and recommendations directly to the college or individual referent.

All applicants should complete the application form that is used by the school district. If there is no standard form, the staff should consider adopting a form that will accumulate the information they desire. An example of such a form is illustrated in Figure 4-2. The use of such a form will enable interviewing officials to have in writing the essential information sought on every candidate, to pinpoint specific items readily, and to make omissions apparent.

In those instances when numerous applications have been received for a given position, the administrator must glean from his file on each candidate the pertinent information that will enable him to select those who he will interview. Failure to locate the pertinent information, or an incomplete file on the candidate may exclude a superior person from consideration. Functional clerical procedures are a necessity. Administrators who are keenly perceptive of the clues locate the qualities and the competencies that are sought for a given position will be efficient in their screening. In the screening, the following qualities and categories must be assessed: (1) educational preparation, (2) teaching, (3) scholarship, (4) ability to meet state certification requirements, (5) previous experience, (6) personal qualities, (7) recommendations and (8) identification with the school-community. Administrators will need to add to this list the other items that are pertinent in their setting.

Upon completion of this initial screening, the candidates are to be scheduled for interviews as soon as possible.

INTERVIEWING

The interview will be most fruitful if the interviewing officer and the candidates have clearly perceived the purposes for each of them. The interviewer desires to obtain the person who is best qualified with respect to professional capacity and personal, social, physical and emotional attributes. What the dossier and correspondence with the candidates have not revealed, the interviewer must assess in the interview. Failure to make adequate preparation will not produce a fruitful interview. It is also the case with the candidate who does not prepare for the interview by having purposes well in mind and by having his dossier complete with application, references, transcripts and personal data. Candidates must be aware that administrators do make judgments about them.

Application for Teaching Position in
Hometown Community Unit School District
Hometown, U.S.A. 10010

Name in Full _____ Date of Application _____

Home   Area ____
Address _____   Tel. No. _____
         (Street)   (City)   (State)   (Zip)

Present   Area ____
Address _____   Tel. No. _____
         (Street)   (City)   (State)   (Zip)

Date of Birth _____ Citizenship _____

General Health _____ Physical Handicaps _____ Height ____ Weight ____

Marital
Status _____ If married, state age of each child _____

Full Name of Spouse _____

                                                           Year
EDUCATIONAL PREPARATION   High School _____ Grad. _____
                                      (City)   (State)

Dates of Attendance	Name and Location of College or University	Major Subject	Sem. Hrs.	Minor Subject	Sem. Hrs.	Degrees and Dates Awarded

Semester Hours of Professional Education _____ Semester Hours Student Teaching _____

Student Teaching (subject, grade, school): _____

Kind of Certificate held or eligible for: _____

Where are Credentials or Dossier on File? _____

PROFESSIONAL EXPERIENCE

Dates of Prof. Exp.	Number School Years	Name and Location of School, Col., or Univ.	Subjects Taught and Grade Level	Salary

FIGURE 4-2

PERSONNEL REQUIREMENTS AND SELECTION 57

Applicant's   Hometown Com. U. S. D.
Name _____ Application Page 2.

Are you under contract for the coming year? _____

Have you ever failed for reappointment? _____

If so, where and state reasons _____

_____

_____

Why do you wish to leave your present position? _____

_____

Why do you wish to teach in our schools? _____

_____

What professional associations do you belong to? _____

_____

_____

List the extra-class activities you have sponsored or feel competent as sponsor _____

_____

OTHER EMPLOYMENT EXPERIENCE (include military, business, trade and industrial)

Dates	Number Years	Name and Location of Employer	Duties and Responsibilities

REFERENCES

Name	Address	Vocation & Title	Relation to Your Work

FIGURE 4-2 (*Continued*)

Letters of application that are poor in grammar and composition, contain misspelled words, are written on torn or untidy paper and are poor in penmanship give the administrator an impression that is not a credit to the applicant.

For several years, the author has used a tape recording to open the interview. In this twenty-five minute presentation the candidate is urged to take those notes he might wish to have and to write questions that occur to him. This permits the candidate to relax and focus all his attention on the presentation. The administrator is free to devote himself to other matters while the candidate is listening to the tape. Secondary school principals who reflect on variances between interviews are well aware of omissions and the brevity of some interviews. These variances are not uniformly conditions of disinterest in the applicant; rather, the pressures of a particular day may have caused him to cut short some interviews. Such a condition may plague the principal later in reviewing the applicants he has seen in an endeavor to make a choice. He recalls items he omitted; consequently, he lacked the applicant's reaction to them! The use of a tape recording to present the general items of interest and value to all candidates permits the administrator to conduct complete interviews in spite of a very busy day or week. Instead of relating the "school story" numerous times, the interviewer is free to assess personality and competence. He is permitted to focus on the educational program and to determine how the applicant's education and experience background may contribute to the program of education.

Upon the conclusion of the tape, the face-to-face interview begins. First, the questions the applicant wrote down are discussed. Second, the specific information concerning the position applied for is presented and discussed. Third, the administrator checks the dossier to be sure it is complete, or he requests that certain items be furnished. It is good procedure to name for the applicant the references that are in hand. This gives the applicant the opportunity to be sure the references he requested were sent.

When a desired letter of recommendation has not been included in the dossier, a form could be mailed to the person from whom a statement is desired. The use of a form will enable the interviewing officer to receive those ratings and statements on the qualities of the candidate that are of primary importance. A letter of recommendation will not always be complete with responses regarding all the qualities sought by the interviewing officer. Fourth, the principal should have the candidate elaborate upon his professional experiences with statements of the assignment, methods of instruction he used and descriptions of progress achieved by the students. The candidate should be asked to indicate how his educational preparation will enable him to perform the duties of the position under consideration. Fifth, the salary schedule should be presented and the candidate's salary estimated for the ensuing year and a projection made for potential earnings. Sixth, when the applicants have not been communicative (generally a result of nervousness), the author has drawn them out with questions and simply let them talk. Questions that are effective are as follows: "What are your long-range professional goals?" "What is your philosophy of education?" "What is your conception of discipline?" "Select a unit you have taught. Describe how you planned it and the materials you selected. How were the students involved in the learning activity?" This will achieve

PERSONNEL REQUIREMENTS AND SELECTION 59

the "dynamics of interaction" sought by Kahn and Connell [9] as a technique of interviewing. Seventh, the tour of the building, classroom visits and conferences with department heads and teachers are conducted. First hand observation may enhance the prospective teacher's interest, and subsequent conversation will be enriched and more meaningful for the teacher and the principal. And finally, it is made clear to the candidate what the next steps are. Will additional interviews be needed? When will a decision be reached? It is an ethical procedure for administrators to notify all applicants when a position has been filled and for applicants to notify administrators (to whom they have applied) when they have accepted a position elsewhere.

It is advisable for those who conduct interviews to keep a record of each interview. Such records will provide material assistance in the succeeding steps leading to the procurement of competent personnel.

The review of applications is conducted upon the conclusion of the first round of interviews. With such a review, the administrator determines whether he has all the information for a given applicant to determine his fitness to assume the duties of a specific position. He checks the chronology of education, experience, military service, and other employment. Omissions may have been an intentional omission of a major illness or an unsuccessful professional appointment. The assessment of personal and professional qualities must be made between candidates. The review should cover the same qualities and categories presented for the screening earlier in this chapter.

Interviewing may be productive when these guidelines are followed:

1. Prepare a dossier on each candidate
2. Study each dossier carefully
3. Select candidates for interview
4. Structure the interview

   a. Introduction by tape
   b. Personal interview
   c. Conference with department chairman or representative
   d. Tour of instructional area
   e. Outline next steps

5. Review each dossier of candidates interviewed
6. Obtain additional data or recommendations if needed
7. Rank the candidates
8. Decide on one to nominate

---

[9] Robert L. Kahn and Charles F. Connell, *The Dynamics of Interviewing—Theory, Techniques, and Cases* (New York: John Wiley & Sons, Inc., 1958), p. 103.

THE NOMINATION

A properly conducted search culminates in a nomination which should result in the beginning of a successful professional relationship. Teachers need to demonstrate that the signing of a contract has meaning. There are too many instances in which some teachers consider the contract to teach as a unilateral agreement that is binding only upon the board of education. To safeguard contractual obligations for all members of the profession, it must be established that the contract is bilateral—binding both parties to the agreement. Teachers must demonstrate their willingness to meet their obligation by teaching for the full term of the contract. Requests for release to accept another position before completion of the school year should not be granted. Should the teacher fail to report, the board of education should institute proceedings to revoke the license to teach. In the spring of each school year, it would be appropriate for the principal to review with his staff the procedures for appointment, retention, dismissal, tenure and contractual obligations.

The signing of a contract by a certificated person should signal the end of his search and indicate he will present himself ready to assume his duties upon the opening of school. He should notify all others to whom he has applied to withdraw his application as he has accepted another position. This procedure is followed by very few candidates; nevertheless, it is the most courteous and appropriate action. When this has been done, the administrator will not expend time and effort needlessly in processing applications for candidates who are no longer available for employment.

The administrator assembles the credentials, interview sheets, contract, transcripts and recommendations for presentation to the board of education at its next regular meeting. These papers comprise the original entries in the formation of the personnel file for each member of the staff. The principal is to be prepared with verbal explanation of his choice in matching the requirements of the position with the professional and personal qualities of the candidate. The administration of the school is to assume full responsibility for the selection and recommendation of qualified personnel. This is not a function of the school board; consequently, the principal's task is to conduct the search, screening, interview, review and nomination with such thoroughness as to preclude any question or doubt in the mind of any school board member regarding the recommendation.

As soon as possible after confirmation of the contract, the principal or the director of personnel should notify all the persons who applied that the position has been filled. This is a courtesy that should be observed by the candidates and the administrators when positions have been accepted and when contracts have been signed and approved.

SELECTED READINGS

Argyris, Chris and Harrison, Roger, *Interpersonal Competence and Organizational Effectiveness*. (Homewood, Illinois: Dorsey Press, Inc., 1962)

Chruden, Herbert J. and Sherman, Arthur W. Jr., *Personnel Management,* 2nd ed. (Cincinnati, Ohio: South-Western Publishing Company, 1963)

Davis, Keith, *Human Relations in Business.* (New York: McGraw-Hill, 1957)

Fawcett, Claude W., *School Personnel Administration.* (New York: The Macmillan Co., 1964)

French, Wendell, *The Personnel Management Process: Human Resources Administration.* (New York: Houghton Mifflin Co., 1964)

Ginzberg, Eli, *The Development of Human Resources.* (Niles, Illinois: McGraw-Hill, 1967)

Marting, Elizabeth and MacDonald, Dorothy, eds., *Management and Its People: The Evaluation of a Relationship.* (New York: American Management Association, Inc., 1965)

Megginson, Leon C., *Personnel: A Behavioral Approach to Administration.* (Homewood, Illinois: Richard D. Irwin, Inc., 1967)

Pigors, Paul, Myers, Charles A. and Malm, F. T., *Readings in Personnel Administration,* 2nd ed. (New York: McGraw-Hill, 1959)

Van Zwoll, James, *School Personnel Administration.* (New York: Appleton-Century-Crofts, 1964)

FIVE

Staff Utilization and Supervision

During the last 40 years, many forces have had an impact on public education. The behavior of public school educators in the period from the Depression of 1929 to the involvement of the United States in the Second World War deluded many adults into a belief that the public schools could serve all the needs of the youth—even in the face of failures by numerous agencies to adequately meet these needs. These beliefs were shattered in the post-war period by such well known critics as Bestor, Fuller, Lynd and Rickover. Educators became defensive. In time, however, these attacks forced educators to examine the goals, programs and use of human resources.

Many educators came to realize that failure of home, church or community agencies did not constitute a mandate to the public schools to fill all the voids. This realization was followed by a commitment of many educators to strengthen these groups. Such a commitment was evidenced through the active participation of educators in the groups serving youth. Their activity was (1) to refer youth who had specific needs that could be met by the agency, (2) to participate in policy making, fund raising and management of these agencies and (3) to serve as workers in the programs of an agency. Such community participation of educators served to strengthen and improve services to youth in many communities.

The most significant opportunities for educators to achieve a "breakthrough" have come in the studies on staff utilization and the related experimental programs.

STAFF UTILIZATION

In May, 1956, the Executive Committee of the National Association of Secondary School Principals appointed a Commission on the Experimental Study of the Utilization of the Staff in the Secondary School. Dr. J. Lloyd Trump was appointed Director of the Commission. Finances for the work of the Commission were provided by the Fund for the Advancement of Education and the Ford Foundation. Under the direction of Dr. Trump a large number of experimental programs were initiated in secondary schools across the nation. Under his authorship several publications described a new focus on change in organization and methods for instruction. He set forth for secondary school principals new patterns for utilizing the competencies of individual teachers and developing new relationships in the organization of the entire professional staff.[1]

REORGANIZATION OF INSTRUCTION

The impact of the staff utilization studies and the related experimental programs has been extensive. The Institute for the Development of Educational Ideas sponsored an extensive study of innovations in accredited secondary schools.

In a summary prepared by Richard J. Mueller,[2] tabulations are reported in three areas for responses representing 7,237 schools—eight in curriculum, seven in technology and twelve in organization-miscellaneous. Dr. Mueller reports that many school programs have undergone change. As the administration and teachers have learned of successful practices in staff utilization, they have adopted selected portions or adapted the practice in their own programs.

> The typical accredited high school has adopted an average of six innovative practices in curriculum, technology, or organization within recent years. The tendency is for the larger more affluent schools to have instituted innovations, with schools in some areas of the nation indicating greater change than others.
>
> School administrators were asked to check the status of 27 selected innovations in their own schools. Although the quantitative data of this investigation indicate rather limited adoption of the 27 listed innovations, administrators' comments on the questionnaire strongly suggest that current innovative trends are having a broad impact on textbooks, use of teaching aids, and basic organizational changes.
>
> Many of the administrators stated that although their schools were not using a particular curriculum "package," their teaching staffs were utilizing parts of new programs and were currently investigating new concepts and ideas in curriculum.[3]

Descriptions of specific programs in the schools may be found in the bulletins [4] of the National Association of Secondary School Principals. Broad, sweeping revisions

---

[1] J. Lloyd Trump, *New Directions to Quality Education: The Secondary School Tomorrow* (Washington, D.C.: National Education Association, 1960), p. 3.

[2] Richard J. Mueller, *National Inventory of Secondary School Innovations 1967* (DeKalb, Illinois: Northern Illinois University, 1967), following p. 20. Used by permission of the publisher.

[3] Mueller, p. 4.

[4] National Association of Secondary School Principals, *The Bulletin*. Vol. 42 (January, 1958), "New Horizons in Staff Utilization." Vol. 43 (January, 1959), "Exploring Improved Teaching Patterns: Second Report on Staff Utilization Studies." Vol. 44 (January, 1960), "Progressing Toward Better Schools: Third Report on Staff Utilization Studies." Vol. 45 (January, 1961), "Seeking Improved Learning Opportunities: Fourth Report on Staff Utilization Studies." Vol. 46 (January, 1962), "Locus of Change: Fifth Report on Staff Utilization Studies."

affecting the entire program of a school have been described for Lakeview Junior-Senior High School,[5] Decatur, Illinois; Melbourne High School,[6] Melbourne, Florida; and Barrington Middle School,[7] Barrington, Illinois. Others are known to educators as a result of presentations at conventions and observations in school visits. The group of staff utilization studies is having a continuing impact in numerous schools as curriculum improvements are attempted and improved. Some of these improvements are in a given subject area, in the classrooms of a given teacher and on a school-wide basis. These innovations will enable other teachers to observe firsthand the benefits that are to be derived from such changes.

The federal funds which have been made available through the National Defense Education Acts, the Vocational Act of 1963, the Economic Opportunities Act and the Elementary and Secondary Education Act are having profound effects on programs for education. These effects have only been initiated and will not be fully realized for several years. The apparent positive effects generate much hope and optimism.

How may superior educational programs be developed? They may be developed to the extent that each of the following characteristics is strongly evident: (1) the quality of the human relationships developed between the teacher and the learner; (2) the reality of the learning skills assimilated by the learner; (3) identity of the self apparent to the learner and (4) the vitality of a desire for self-education leading to self-renewal.

CHANGES IN STAFFING PATTERNS

The new curricular programs, the changing concepts for organizing the learning experiences and the continuing competition with business and industry for qualified personnel are each forcing administrators to conceive new staffing patterns. This has been termed "The Instructional Revolution."

> . . . the number of inexperienced teachers is so staggering that American schools must still meet a challenge to educational quality: to discover ways of having the best and more experienced teachers exert an influence beyond the walls of their classrooms—an influence on other teachers and on the course of study.
>
> Many schools have taken the first step in this direction by recognizing and using the fact that some teachers, while equal to others in college degrees and years on the school payroll, are "more equal" than others in ability. It is a waste of talent, it is felt, to assign such superior teachers equal kinds of responsibilities, in equal-sized classrooms, before an equal number of students. This kind of waste drives better teachers from the profession. And as many bright young people who might otherwise

---

[5] David W. Beggs III, *Decatur-Lakeview High School: A Practical Application of the Trump Plan* (Englewood Cliffs, N.J.: Prentice-Hall, 1964).

[6] Bartley Frank Brown, *The Nongraded High School* (Englewood Cliffs, N.J.: Prentice-Hall, 1963).

[7] Ford Foundation, Educational Facilities Laboratories, *Barrington Middle School: A Report 1966 / Barrington, Illinois* (New York: Ford Foundation, 1966).

become teachers observe that superiority and mediocrity get equal treatment in the schools, they never enter the field.[8]

Staffing decisions which have basis in function, daily time allotment, and professional competence of the individual staff member will lead to higher levels of utilization of professional competencies. Dr. Trump has made such a determination. He illustrates that local financing is not a deterrent but adequate and within the means of many school districts to reorganize instruction.[9]

INSTRUCTIONAL METHOD AND TEACHING AIDS

The textbook will continue to be a basic source for instructional programs until teachers have reached an optimum level of growth and development needed for their professional assignments. It is imperative that administrators organize within the educational unit a procedure for the examination, selection and evaluation of materials and equipment to supplement the basic text. This procedural development is best initiated and carried on through an Instructional Materials Center.

Instructional Materials Center. High priority is attached to the organization of an Instructional Materials Center as a true center of the educational resources within the educational unit. The center must be staffed with professional people who are competent in providing services required for extensive use of all forms of printed materials and the equipment necessary for their maximum use. The professionals must have regular clerical assistants assigned to them for use in the center. When the Instructional Materials Center has been properly staffed and provided with space in which to function, the professionals may then strive for harmonious blending of student capabilities, teaching talent, learning materials and instructional aids. When the required professional staff, necessary clerical assistants, sound financing and adequate facilities have been functionally organized, the Instructional Materials Center may provide the classroom teacher with shopping center conveniences of "one-stop shopping."

This functional organization must have well-defined procedures that are clearly understood by all professional staff members with respect to examination, procurement, dispensing, scheduling and inventory. These materials and items of equipment are maintained to provide maximum availability to all the classroom teachers. Educators must make more extensive use of technological aids. A listing of the materials and equipment available in the center is made to be sure that the description of the center is clear:

> All supplementary printed and graphic materials (books, pamphlets, pictures, maps, graphs). Two-dimensional items (opaque and transparent) and the equip-

---

[8] Ford Foundation, *Time, Talent, and Teachers* (New York: Ford Foundation, 1960), p. 7. Used by permission of the author.

[9] J. Lloyd Trump, *Images of the Future: A New Approach to the Secondary School* (Washington, D.C.: National Education Association, 1959), p. 25.

ment necessary for projection. Three-dimensional objects (models, torsos, skeletons, mock-ups, sculpture). Films (slides, strips, motion, sound). Disc recordings and tape recordings (including those that are available commercially as well as produced by the school staff).

This discussion has focused on the Instructional Materials Center as a service to teachers. The center must also be viewed as a work and study area for the student. Individual study areas should be provided that have a sufficient amount of work surface screening or partitioning that permit him to concentrate on the task before him. The student should have listening and viewing stations available for his use.

Teaching Method. The author has attempted to focus on the fact that textbook oriented classroom activities and fixed class sizes are not absolute determiners of quality education. It is apparent, however, that professional staff members should make use of all of the resources that are available with regard to materials and community resources in achieving their educational goals. The classroom experiences must promote the total growth and development of each individual student. Teachers are demonstrating that large group instruction, small group instruction, individual study, team-teaching and lay assistants enable teachers to achieve a degree of educational progress that has not been possible heretofore in the self-contained classroom. These innovations do not have to be instituted in all classrooms of a given attendance unit. Interested teachers must be given support, facilities and materials. One or more of these forms of classroom experiences may be organized in isolated situations in a particular building. Such innovations should be observed and studied by other teachers in the attendance unit who may grow in acceptance of these new forms and become secure in trying them out in their classrooms. These innovations have proven to be a real challenge to the teacher and have produced a marked improvement in the teacher's perception of self and a much higher level of satisfaction with his professional tasks. There has been an observable increase in student interest and a noticeable decrease in student misconduct when these programs have been successfully organized and executed.

FACILITIES

Facilities have a direct bearing upon staff utilization. Many significant developments have been made in remodeling existing school plants, permitting the staffs in schools to implement successful staff utilization studies or to modify the studies to local needs and conditions.

School planning entered a new era late in the 1950's with much dialogue and cooperative planning between educators and architects. Evidence of this effort may be found in the literature [10] and the facilities designed by the avant-garde. Cooperative efforts between educators, the manufacturers and the suppliers is evidenced in the design and construction phases of the Barrington Middle School.[11]

---

[10] Educational Facilities Laboratories, Inc., *New Schools for New Education* (New York: Ford Foundation, 1960).

[11] Educational Facilities Laboratories, Inc., pp. 17, 19.

SUPERVISORY FUNCTION OF THE PRINCIPAL

A position was taken earlier by the author that the building principal is solely responsible for the administration of the school. The principal is responsible for the supervisory functions of the school. In fulfilling such a function he may share some aspects of supervision with departmental chairmen, team leaders or teachers who have responsibilities and authority beyond the classroom assignment. The principal is the instructional leader serving as a chairman of the faculty in curriculum development. His awareness and continuing study of the numerous elements that comprise the educational program will enable him to hold a position of leadership at the leading edge.

This chapter will focus on the principal's supervisory function as it relates to the classroom. A larger concept of supervision will be developed in Chapter Six.

Program of Instruction. Well-developed supervisory activities will provide (1) assessment of the appropriateness of the curriculum revealing strengths and weaknesses and the qualities of articulation and integration; (2) observations of uses of instructional materials, supplies, equipment, and facilities providing a basis for budgeting and purchasing and (3) possibilities for improving the utilization of the professional competencies of the staff.

Personnel. Principals are called upon to make recommendations concerning tenure, retention, dismissal and promotion of members of their staffs. When the principal has met his supervisory responsibilities, he will be able to make firm recommendations drawn from first-hand contacts. The new curricula incorporated into the schools require new talents and changing roles of the classroom teachers. Despite the increasing complexities in making personnel assignments, a supervisory principal will have much to guide him in making well-founded decisions.

In the supervisory role, the principal has many opportunities to develop meaningful communication with teachers. Having achieved such communication, it could very well be the most valuable effort he has made. He may be in a position to have his hand on the pulse of the program, to sense the level of student responsiveness and to perceive the needs for personnel and material.

Interpret the Program and Needs. The design to be presented in this chapter envisions first-hand contacts that will enable the principal to promote an understanding of the program and garner active support of the community. It is of inestimable value for a principal to be able to respond to an irate parent, "When I was in that classroom last week, this is what I saw. . . ."

In presentations to the central administrative staff and the board of education, the principal may interpret a program and describe needs at the classroom level. He is able to defend requests from a meaningful participatory experience in preference to an "on-paper" request.

Students. The principal can achieve a more realistic perception of the students as they engage in their study than if he were dealing only with those students who are referred to the administrative staff. This perception enables him to place in proper perspective the matters which are brought to his attention regarding student behavior.

The students develop an image of the principal as one who is interested in the educational program and a participator in it. The mere presence of the principal in the classroom presents opportunities for contacts and exchanges that would not occur otherwise. This accessibility will prove to be of value to students and the principal.

Shared Responsibility. In the larger attendance units the principal will need to share some of his supervisory responsibilities with supervisors, directors, coordinators and/or department chairmen. These persons are not to operate independently of him, but rather in a unified effort for adequate supervision. The authors emphasize *sharing* as the principal must be active in supervision for the reasons stated above. Adequate staffing with administrative assistants and competent office services personnel are prerequisites to the principal's attaining the instructional leadership of his school.

A DESIGN FOR EFFECTIVE SUPERVISION OF INSTRUCTION

The author will describe a design that is operational in many settings. At the outset, the principal needs to define a design, a plan, or a structure that is workable in his situation. His design is to be clearly understood by each member of the professional staff with respect to purpose, role and follow-up. When understanding has been achieved, acceptance will be forthcoming. The design should be somewhat compelling; so the principal will get out from behind his desk and into the classroom. A quantitative goal should be set to compete with the many demands that reach the principal's desk. For example, he could plan to visit all the classrooms of probationary teachers by the end of the first semester and visit one-third of the tenure teachers by the end of the year. Having set such a goal for himself, he has also the expectation of the staff that he will visit.

Purpose. To maintain the school as a viable institution serving the youth and the community, several purposes determine the nature of effective supervision of instruction: (1) increase the effectiveness of the professional staff, (2) improve instruction and method, (3) continue curriculum development and (4) evaluate the program. These purposes will reveal the nature of professional activities for the staff and the nature of administrative activity in classroom visits and in-service programs.

Supervisory Visits. It is imperative that the principal establish a climate that is not threatening to a teacher. This is done as he interacts with the whole staff, with committees and with individuals. He stresses the staff relationships by developing a concept of a unified team effort. In the orientation to the supervisory program, stress is placed upon the *planned* visits. The surprise, brief visit is not a part of this design. The administrator must develop a perceptible interest in the assignment of each individual member of the staff. A pervasive element in establishing the climate is communication. Such communication is characterized by a resolve within each group—faculty and administration—to speak for itself, to rely on the other to do so, and for each to listen and thus comprehend and understand the other. Having achieved this level of communication, all aspects of a given situation are focused on the professional considerations to the exclusion of the personal elements that breed anxiety, uncertainty and insecurity.

The principal's design for supervisory visits is presented to the faculty at the opening of each school year. In this presentation, an invitation is extended for each teacher (to be visited) to confer with him on a mutual selection of time and class that will be scheduled for his visit. The teacher is urged to suggest a time that will provide the maximum opportunity to observe a variety of classroom experiences that are indicative of the classes assigned to the teacher. The teacher may select a given class with the express purpose of gaining the principal's perception of the teacher's handling of a particular problem or of seeking his counsel in improving a situation that is not what the teacher would like it to be. He discusses this design in each interview with prospective members of the staff to develop supervisory visits as an integral part of the professional activity for the school.

In the *pre-visit conference,* the teacher describes the work in which students are presently engaged for the class to be visited. The teacher relates the outline of the subject taught, the extent of student participation and the plan for the sessions the principal will observe. The principal emphasizes that the teacher is not to change the overall lesson plan or to stage anything for his benefit. The principal desires to see the instruction as it normally progresses. He should assure the teacher that he does not expect to find all the students in one class to be as well oriented and as dedicated as in another. Groupings occur either by chance or choice. These variances between classes should not place a teacher's professional standing in jeopardy. What is done to improve a student's concept of himself is of prime importance. The teacher supplies a seating chart or roster and copies of instructional materials and guides that will be used.

The *visitation* is made to three consecutive sessions of the same class. Over this three-day period, the principal has the opportunity to observe a progression of learning experiences from one day to the next, to become better acquainted with individual students and to participate in the learning experience. This participation for the author has taken the form of contributing to the discussion in social studies, completing a project in an art class, writing a test with the students in an algebra section and acting as a teacher's aide in an English class during time set aside for individual study. Active participation as a member of the group lends greater meaning to the classroom experiences and permits close observation of the work of individual students. It will aid in breaking down the stilted atmosphere that may be present at the entrance of the principal.

The principal should be on time and remain for the *entire* session. A ten- or twenty-minute visit does not enable a visitor to perceive the complete context of a learning situation. This requires that the office staff handle matters during a classroom visit that need the attention of the principal. Given the opportunity, many matters can be resolved by a secretary or an assistant principal in the absence of the principal.

The principal should do *no* writing. The teacher needs support; writing during a visitation is distracting to a teacher who wonders what is being written. This was made very evident to the author when, during one visit, he noted that a down spout was separated from the gutter. He wanted to be sure to call this to the attention of the maintenance staff, so he wrote a brief reminder. The author felt that he had established good rapport with the teacher and they communicated well; nevertheless, the teacher remarked in the lounge, "I wonder what he wrote down."

In this design, no checklists are used. Checklists are not really objective instruments. A preoccupation with completing a checklist in many instances hinders total involvement of the observer and fails to assess the human relationships in a learning experience. After a visit, the principal should note on a blank piece of theme paper (1) the nature of the instruction, (2) teacher activity, (3) student involvement and (4) observations of student reaction to the learning experience. In reflection on the visit, he makes notations of significant practices, use of instructional materials and multi-media aids, assessment of rapport and teaching method. He writes statements of strength for support and reassurance, as well as suggestions for improvement in method or use of materials.

A *post-visit conference* should be held as soon as possible after the conclusion of the third observation. Every effort should be made to confer within 24 hours. Even with the most ideal teacher-administrator relations, a teacher will have some anxieties until the conference is held, and the principal should allay these feelings to avoid any adverse effects on the teaching.

During this conference, the principal discusses the points on the written report just enumerated above. This is the time for the teacher to clarify the use of one method or procedure in preference to others. The principal should encourage the teacher to relate negative as well as positive aspects of the whole teaching situation. The elements that prohibit the teacher from improving or enlarging the instructional opportunities should be declared and examined. As he concludes the conference, the principal indicates to the teacher his desire to return later in the year should the teacher have a particular activity for him to observe.

A carefully conducted conference will enable the teacher to gain considerably in his perception of himself and to be reinforced in significant educational method. The teacher should be strengthened in the performance of his professional duties.

Administrators who are apprehensive about staff reactions to supervisory visits should be reassured that classroom teachers will come to welcome such participation. Teachers can gain much support through a team effort of teachers and administrators in conducting and improving the program of education. A teacher should not have to be a solitary performer. He values the time, interest and professional assistance of the principal.

SELECTED READINGS

American Association of School Administrators, *School Administrators View Professional Negotiation.* (Washington, D. C.: The Association, 1966)

Association for Supervision and Curriculum Development, *The Way Teaching Is.* (Washington: National Education Association, 1966)

Beggs, David W. and Buffie, Edward G., *Nongraded Schools in Action.* (Bloomington, Indiana: Indiana University Press, 1967)

Brown, Frank B., *The Appropriate Placement School: A Sophisticated Nongraded Curriculum.* (West Nyack, New York: Parker Publishing Co., 1965)

Bruner, Jerome S., *The Process of Education.* (New York: Vintage Books, 1960)

Conner, Forrest E. and Ellena, William J., eds., *Curriculum Handbook for School Administrators.* (Washington, D. C.: American Association of School Administrators, 1967)

Frymier, Jack R., *The Nature of Educational Method.* (Columbus, Ohio: Charles E. Merrill Books, Inc., 1965)

Klahn, Richard P., ed., *Evaluation of Teacher Competency.* (Milwaukee, Wisconsin: Franklin Pub., Inc., 1965)

Leeper, Robert R., ed., *Humanizing Education: The Person in the Process.* (Washington, D. C.: The Association for Supervision and Curriculum Development, 1967)

National Education Association, Project on the Instructional Program of the Public Schools, *Current Curriculum Studies in Academic Subjects,* by Dorothy M. Fraser. (Washington: The Association, 1962)

National Education Association, Project on the Instructional Program of the Public Schools, *Deciding What to Teach,* by Dorothy M. Fraser. (Washington: The Association, 1963)

National Education Association, Project on the Instructional Program of the Public Schools, *Education in a Changing Society,* by Richard I. Miller. (Washington: The Association, 1963)

National Education Association, Project on the Instructional Program of the Public Schools, *Planning and Organizing for Teaching,* by John I. Goodlad. (Washington: The Association, 1963)

National Education Association, Project on the Instructional Program of the Public Schools, *The Principals Look at the Schools: A Status Study of Selected Instructional Practices.* (Washington: The Association, 1962)

National Education Association, Project on the Instructional Program of the Public Schools, *The Scholars Look at the Schools: A Status Study of Selected Instructional Practices.* (Washington: The Association, 1962)

National Education Association, Project on the Instructional Program of the Public Schools, *Schools for the Sixties: A Report of the Project on Instruction.* (Washington: The Association, 1963)

National Education Association, *Evaluation of Classroom Teachers,* Research Report 1964-R14. (Washington, D. C.: The Association, 1964)

National Society for the Study of Education, Committee on In-service Education of Teachers, Supervisors, and Administrators, *In-service Education for Teachers, Supervisors, and Administrators.* (Chicago: The University of Chicago Press, 1957)

Stinnett, Timothy M., Kleinmann, Jack H. and Ware, Martha L., *Professional Negotiation in Public Education.* (New York: The Macmillan Co., 1966)

SIX

Morale and Professional Growth of the Staff

Morale is a realistic and vital element of staff relations that may have a deleterious or salutary affect on instruction. It has a quality of elusiveness. Some conditions cause morale to degenerate. Other conditions—though not remedying an unhappy condition—will improve morale and instill positive attitudes. How, then, does an administrator develop and promote desirable morale?

MORALE

Morale is a quality that is not developed in isolation. It is developed in the normal functioning of an organization when the individuals perform their duties at satisfactory levels of achievement. This examination of morale will be made with respect to three aspects of its development: (1) the mental and emotional attitudes of an individual toward the responsibilities assigned to him, (2) a sense of common purpose with respect to teachers in the attendance unit and to adults in the greater school-community and (3) the state of individual psychological well-being based on a sense of purpose and confidence in the future.

HUMAN RELATIONSHIPS

Each person who attains a degree of extroversive character is able to perceive talent and competence in his colleagues. In this context, respect for individuals will enjoy sustained growth. The principal is the one who must develop extroversive qualities in his personality. With consistent behavior in the routine operations, the principal may enable the members of his staff to develop expectations in administrative behavior that will approximate actual responses. And, conversely, the principal develops expectations of staff behavior that will approximate actual responses of individual members of the staff. This is not to say that "second-guessing" is a foundation for staff behavior. Rather, the principal's performance and response in the routines are predictable by the staff; so, they may make decisions (regarding their behavior in the day-to-day operations) that are void of apprehensions. When these conditions characterize staff relationships, teachers perform their duties with assurance. Respect for individuals and attainment of personal integrity within each member of the staff are prologue to the development of these qualities in the students as they participate in the educational program.

Professional Interest. The literature which describes the classroom as the setting for learning focuses upon the relationship between the teacher and the learner. So it is that the principal of the educational unit should examine his behavior and test his decisions to determine how he establishes the setting for education.

Every action of the administrator must be permeated with professional awareness and interest. It is more than an alert or purposeful action at a staff meeting or in a classroom visit. It must become a quality of behavior that is evidenced in every contact. This would range from the formal contacts in the professional staff meeting to informal and brief encounters. The demonstration of such behavioral qualities will arise from procedures that keep lines of communication functioning and the door open revealing the principal as an intent listener. These principles roll off the tongue easily. They must be evidenced in leader behavior.

Personal Interest. The element of personal interest may be questioned, but an administrator lacking this quality is ignoring the fact that each member of his staff is a person as unique as each of the students. The personal needs for acceptance and achievement are just as real for teachers as for students. In his discussion of objectives, principles, and functions of personnel administration, van Zwoll takes the position that

> Personnel administration is regarded as a special facet of human relations. It is directed toward getting the most efficient service possible for the attainment of the objectives of the organization within which employer-employee relations exits. Subordinate to securing efficient service but corollary to it is a concern for the employee as an individual with aspirations and problems which have implications for his effectiveness as an employee and which for that reason deserve consideration.[1]

Objections to this position will be made on two fronts: (1) The principal lacks the qualifications for adult counseling, (2) the principal is to concern himself exclusively with the professional aspects of his duties.

First, the principal should be a student of personnel practices and theory. His effectiveness as an educational leader in improving an educational program is through the individual members of the staff. He may serve students only as effectively as he partici-

---

[1] James A. Van Zwoll, *School Personnel Administration* (New York: Appleton-Century-Crofts, 1964), p. 16. Used by permission of the publisher.

pates in meaningful ways with the classroom teachers. He is in a position to examine his role, in conference with the certificated counselors on the staff. Although he does not engage in therapy, he does make referrals to individuals and agencies qualified to give continued assistance.

Second, the administrator who concerns himself only with the professional relationships of his staff, while excluding the personal relationships, is not fostering the interpersonal relationships that should be developed in the educational process. He must demonstrate for his staff the nature of the personal relationships he would have the teachers establish with the pupils. Failing in this area he cannot expect the educational program in the school to change behavior and to prepare the students for adult roles. Dr. Melby stresses the primacy of the personality of teachers when he states,

> . . . if you study our schools carefully you find that knowledge is not the teacher's most important equipment for his work. The teacher succeeds in terms of what he is, not in terms of what he knows. Many very erudite teachers have a bad effect on the children they teach. Studies with disadvantaged children show us that the child's self concept is the biggest single factor in learning, yet our educational procedures with their preoccupation with subject matter, our grading systems and report cards, our middle class teachers with their lack of understanding of the disadvantaged child—all these—literally doom the slum child to failure.[2]

The prospect of being doomed to failure is not limited to the slum children! Later in this chapter, under professional growth, the authors will focus on the teacher's perception of adolescents.

Conflict Situations. Occasions will arise when the principal will be called upon to resolve conflicts and assist in solving problems which arise. He should not rely on his own independent judgment. He must have guides for his action.

With respect to those day-to-day situations that require decision making, there are several frames of reference. First, he recalls those policies, rules, and regulations which apply. Applications are not always clear-cut, but require some interpretation to reach reasonable decisions. Second, he will need to apply administrative theory to real life situations in decision making. Third, he must test the decision with standards of morality and the expectations of the school-community. Fourth, the secondary school administrator must assess his decisions in light of outcomes that are best for the children in the school and that will aid in the achievement of the objectives of the program. These are all instances in which the principal is the primary agent.

Those situations which may not be solved readily or which require a broader effort are to involve other personnel in the professional effort that leads to a decision. First, the literature and research are to be examined for pertinent applications to problems at hand. Second, consultants, who have demonstrated competence in the area under study, may be retained. Third, the staff should be organized for continued study of the problem.

These administrative procedures should promote the best use of an individual's

---

[2] Ernest O. Melby, "Needed: A New Concept of Educational Administration," *The Community School and Its Administration,* III (July, 1965), p. 2. Used by permission of the publisher.

time and talent and achieve the desired results as efficiently as possible. The desired outcome and competencies, interests and desires of the staff members should be factors in determining how a staff is organized for study. The attack can be launched on one or more of the following fronts: individual tasks, small groups, instructional areas, and the complete staff. The emphasis is not on structure, but rather on optimum and purposeful involvement of the staff. The study should be structured to progress through these phases: (1) identification of the problem, (2) gathering of data, (3) description of alternatives and objectives, (4) trials, (5) selection of a course of action and nature of subsequent evaluation, (6) implementation of the decisions and (7) evaluation of the actions. This is closely related to John W. Gardner's prescription for social action.

> If social action is to occur, certain functions must be performed. The problems facing the group or organization must be clarified, and ideas necessary to their solution formulated. Objectives must be defined. There must be widespread awareness of those objectives, and the will to achieve them. Often those on whom action depends must develop new attitudes and habits. Social machinery must be set in motion. The consequences of social effort must be evaluated and criticized, and new goals set.[3]

Follow-up. The quality of human relationships is readily perceived by an individual staff member in the audience he is granted and in the actions he perceives. In all face-to-face relationships sincere individuals will be assessing the degree of communication. The spoken word and empathy of the listener are the indicators of the level of communication achieved in any contact. A principal cannot ignore these facets of communication if he is to achieve and maintain educational leadership. As a listener and through follow-up he must demonstrate that he is a partner in communication.

Leadership is exercised with other human beings, and leadership is developed out of purposeful and meaningful human relationships.

INSTITUTIONAL ELEMENTS

All too often there is too much reliance on the institutional elements of organizational patterns in line and staff relationships. Priority has been given in this chapter to the human relationships.

Foundation. Organizational structure serves as the foundation. The structure should be well defined, operational, and understood by the individuals who have tasks to perform. The authors purport that effective organization (Chapter One), personnel requirements and selection (Chapter Four), and staff utilization and supervision (Chapter Five) each have potential for developing morale.

Communication. Effective communication should be consciously developed and maintained. The principal should be one who is available to the staff for consultation

---

[3] John W. Gardner, "The Antileadership Vaccine," *1965 Annual Report,* Carnegie Corporation of New York (New York: the Corporation, 1965), p. 5. Used by permission of the author.

as they feel the need for it. He must demonstrate the ability to listen and to follow up the verbal and written communications which he has received. He needs to be enthusiastic in his support of teachers as they try new techniques that are worthy of the effort. Teachers need the principal's support and reassurance in their failures as well as in their successes with innovations. Effective communication within a school district is of primary importance. Administrators and teachers should be called upon to develop and maintain the procedures and the processes that will make effective communications a reality. All parties will need to develop the ability to listen and to speak frankly in language that is both clear and concise. Complete communication is necessary with no holding back of information. It is inefficient for professional staff members to be compelled to interpret what one means. When clarity and conciseness characterize communication, members of a staff will be assured that in all forms of communication they may act upon what has been said and not dissipate their energies trying to determine what is "between the lines."

Educators who teach and use the skills of speaking, writing and reading have erroneously assumed that in the employment of these skills as means, communication is achieved. Communication is possible when individuals will listen and will read. Even with such a willingness, communication is achieved only with understanding. R. L. Jenkins cited from industry four failures in communication: (1) failure to see the other person's point of view, (2) failure to size up others correctly, (3) failure to show appreciation or give credit and (4) failure to listen correctly.[4] Teachers and administrators who use the common acts of communication must consciously strive to achieve understanding. It is through effective communication that a sense of common purpose may be developed, building morale.

Appreciation. Mental and emotional attitudes may be positively influenced as the individual feels that his efforts are appreciated by his colleagues and administrators. A principal has opportunities to express appreciation to individuals in his supervisory activities. His observations in the classroom provide him with a factual basis for such expressions. Individual states of psychological well-being are enhanced by sincere approval, support and commendation.

When the principal can relate the school program and the efforts of teachers (as individuals and as a group) to the greater school-community, a sense of purpose may be reinforced and confidence in the future will result. With the extensive personal involvement teachers experience with the students in their classes, teachers need to be supported and reassured. As the teacher grows in command of his personal life, his potential to be a better teacher enlarges.

PARTICIPATION

As institutions grow in size and complexity, the need increases for individuals to be actively involved as participants in the daily conduct and future development of the

---

[4] Russell L. Jenkins, "How to Avoid Four Failures When You Talk to Workers," *Business Management,* 21 (February, 1962), p. 52–3.

institution. Feelings of desperation may appear as persons consider themselves lost in the machinery and the quality of being human vanishes in a corporate structure.

Individual conferences that are scheduled on a formal basis during a school year with a live administrator will insure that each staff member will have a face-to-face contact. Informal conferences are valuable and will be held on timely matters, but the principal must not rely solely on these. Individual conferences cannot always be held with the chief school officer as the size of the educational unit may require delegation of responsibility to another administrator or professional with responsibility. Department chairmen can be very effective in this role.

Face-to-face contacts will need to be used continually; however, the complexities of local, intermediate, and state units require the utilization of diverse modes of communication. An administrator must employ many media to achieve a quality of communication that will foster maximum utilization of professional competencies. Failure to achieve such a quality will result in frustrations and tensions developed out of uncertain behavior in the attempts of individuals to achieve meaningful communication with their colleagues. Attitudes will be developed as an individual has a clear understanding of the responsibilities assigned to him. When he is able to view these responsibilities as positively related to his own goals and to the group endeavor, he may be more confident that his efforts will contribute to the total effort of the group.

Participation in group conferences and activities will be discussed under the larger topic of in-service programs for the professional staff.

PROFESSIONAL GROWTH OF THE STAFF

The justification and a commission for in-service activities is improvement of the program of education through continuing growth in professional competence and in personal satisfaction for each member of the staff. Successful activities will promote morale. In-service activities are not solely for new staff members; they are to be planned for the entire staff. The need and scope of such activities will be developed more fully in the discussion to follow. Orientation programs for new teachers are well-meaning but overwhelming at the outset. In-service activities that are an integral part of the professional staff meetings during a school year will prove to be of greatest benefit to each member of the staff. The administrator who recognizes that motivation and involvement are prerequisites to a successful in-service program will be rewarded with evidence of professional growth and improved attitudes.

PROFESSIONAL STAFF MEETINGS

Group conferences that are regularly scheduled enable each staff member to plan for regular participation in meetings which are called for specific purposes. When such a structure is provided, individuals may select the appropriate times for their participation in administrative and professional matters. Plans for these meetings should involve representative staff members in the determination of the emphases and the topics which will be the focal points for professional activity during a school year. All professional staff members should participate in selecting the theme for a given school year. An agenda should be prepared and distributed prior to each meeting. The principal could call on a representative group to assist him with the preparation of an agenda. The group might include department chairmen, principal's cabinet, chairmen of standing committees, or representative teachers.

The theme should be given a large portion of the time allocated in the agenda. Many administrative matters can be dispensed with in memoranda to the staff. Those that require discussion should be held, conscientiously, to a small portion of a professional staff meeting. Each meeting focuses on a sub-topic of the larger theme. This permits long-range planning to involve presentations by consultants or study groups at opportune times during the year. To promote careful planning and to involve all staff members, provision can be made for both large and small group sessions. The following monthly cycle has proven to be effective in some schools:

First Week	Professional Staff Meeting
Second Week	Instructional Leaders Meeting
Third Week	Instructional Area Meeting
Fourth Week	Intramural Instructional Area Meeting

The Professional Staff Meeting, for the entire staff, provides for large group presentations and discussion. It is the means for orientation to new topics, developing a structure for attacking a problem, reporting the findings of study groups, reaching decisions, and achieving consensus on next courses of action.

The Instructional Leaders Meeting is for department chairmen, instructional area chairmen, grade level chairmen, or that group in the organizational structure of the school that is representative of the classroom teachers with respect to instruction. These leaders and the principal make agenda and detailed plans for study of the theme. They determine the sub-topics, describe activities, form study groups, engage consultants, and schedule presentations to the large and small groups. Consideration should be given to permit individual quests by faculty members who have the desire to pursue study of a topic within the larger theme.

Instructional Area Meetings are scheduled for teachers in a department, a core program, or a team in keeping with the organization of the instructional program. In the larger schools where there are a number of teachers in a department, a more formal departmental organization may be needed to involve all members of a department. Krebs [5] outlines a structure for departmental advisory councils.

Intramural Instructional Area Meetings give opportunities for involvement of teachers in small groups for study and discussion outside their instructional area. These meetings are scheduled in response to needs and provide opportunities for diversity in groupings.

---

[5] Alfred H. Krebs, *Organizing and Working with Departmental Advisory Councils in the Public Schools* (Danville, Ill.: The Interstate Printers and Publishers, Inc., 1965), p. 24.

Principals should develop the elements that will feed vitality into the professional activities under discussion. The administrator should make this a creative effort. His failure to do so results in continued time loss and dissipated professional energies at impotent assemblies of the staff. Creative efforts should be reflected in the ways he brings together the staff, material, and the resource and consultant personnel of the region. In the fusion of these three elements, a truly creative approach will have the potential to capture the interest of the professional staff and move the staff enthusiastically into group activity. Such an approach is to be made in a manner likened to the master teacher who views himself as the one professionally competent and responsible for the progress of the individual student. The principal as the "master teacher" is responsive to the learner and maintains a readiness to learn. He establishes a basis in the psychology of learning with motivation his charge and close observation of individual responses his responsibility. The principal's task is to adapt and revise procedures as the group progresses much as a master teacher would lead his students. Creative approaches, which possess qualities for effective combinations of staff, material, and other professionals, will produce dynamics in human relationships that interest and challenge the individual members of a staff.

A number of approaches may be examined to provide a focus for in-service activities that will achieve professional growth in a staff.

AREAS FOR STUDY

The authors will not attempt an exhaustive listing of areas for study which might be undertaken by a staff. They will acknowledge those which have universal need. They will develop those areas which have not been adequately studied and merit consideration by many professional staffs.

Curriculum. The primary concern of a staff is the development of appropriate curricula and the selection and preparation of units of instruction, materials, textbooks, and multi-media aids. An infinite number of studies may be made of this area.

Policies. The study of policies, rules, and regulations or their development—where none exist—will increase understanding of individual roles and may promote efficient use of the time and talent of each member of a professional staff. Written policies will enable the members of a staff to act with knowledge and assurance in professional matters. This will develop good staff morale in that individuals may read the policies and, therefore, carefully plan for themselves and predict the principal's action and decision rather accurately. This is one basis for achieving a productive and efficient level of professional behavior which draws upon assessments that produce knowledgeable actions. The author proposes involvement of teachers in the determination of policies to contravene the status as described by one writer.

> In the educational hierarchy, he is low man on the totem pole. In the power structure, he is the one without power. In the line of order, he is the one who takes orders from everyone else. He has little chance to exercise creativity, to show in-

telligence, or to use democratic procedures. He has no say in the important decisions affecting the schools. The educational system in America today is a vertical hierarchy and the teacher is at the bottom.[6]

Improvement of Instruction. Many teachers and administrators have participated in graduate study and earned advanced degrees as salary schedules have provided rewards for those efforts. In recent years other inducements have been offered as stipends for participation in workshops and summer programs sponsored by the National Science Foundation and others under the National Defense Education Act. Some salary schedules award credit for approved professional activities—independent study, writing, research and travel—which relate to the individual's assignment.

Individual staff members may contribute to their professional growth as they use audio and video tapes to look at themselves. They will grow as they permit others to listen and to look at their teaching and relate what they heard and saw. Many teachers are able to make inter-school visits. Much can be achieved as administrators schedule intra-school visits for specific purposes. Resources within the building may be tapped with little or no expense. Opportunities for experimentation within the teacher's own classroom are overlooked and need to be developed as a valid contribution to professional growth.

Demonstration of significant teaching practices and successful new programs within a school and between schools permits teachers to observe increased opportunities for professional growth. In recent years this practice is in wider use and needs to be developed further to reach many teachers. Brickell [7] reported that (in the opinion of most of the teachers and administrators interviewed) the most persuasive experience for educators is an observation of a successful new program in the actual instructional setting followed by demonstrations in their own schools.

Local school units should take the initiative in sponsoring workshops, short courses and extension courses to serve specific needs of their staff. When the need has been defined, the professors in the colleges and universities will cooperate with local units in offering the opportunities needed for study. In a similar manner, field service personnel could be a significant resource to a local unit in conducting a school survey, in curriculum development, and in organizing experimentation and research.

Consultants may be retained to provide competent direction and to bring resources to a staff that are not available within the local unit.

IN-SERVICE APPRAISAL

Administrators should plan with individual members of their staffs the nature of graduate study which they undertake. License for such cooperative planning derives from the salary increment provisions in salary schedules for graduate study. When such

---

[6] Anne Mitchell, "The Crux of the Matter," *Saturday Review,* 49 (January 15, 1966), p. 66. Used by permission of the publisher and the author.

[7] Henry M. Brickell, *Organizing New York State for Educational Change* (Albany, New York: New York State University, 1961), pp. 27–29.

is the case, a teacher may be expected to engage in study that will increase his proficiency in his present assignment or future assignment needed in the school district.

A long-range plan should be initiated with a review of transcripts of a teacher's professional record with respect to subject matter preparation and professional education study. The review should determine areas of strength and deficiency in undergraduate and graduate study with respect to the teacher's present assignment. A teacher is called upon to determine his immediate and long-range goals which will be considered with the needs of the school district.

The greatest degree of flexibility in cooperative planning may be achieved after the staff member has earned the master's degree. Graduate study programs are clearly defined to that point. After five years of study, consideration should be given for acceptance of specified study in undergraduate level courses. With respect to a current assignment, such courses would serve to meet deficiencies, to enlarge upon a major or minor area of study, to refresh and to retrain teachers for new curricula. A teacher might receive equivalent credit for several planned professional activities—independent study, major papers, research, and travel.

This planning may be formalized with statements in triplicate for copies to be retained by the teacher, the building principal, and the director of personnel. Review of the plan will be necessary as study progresses and as goals are changed or achieved.

SELECTED READINGS

American Association of School Administrators, *A Climate for Individuality,* statement of the Joint Project on the Individual and the School. (Washington: National Education Association, 1965)

Arnspiger, V. Clyde, *Personality in Social Process,* Values and Strategies of Individuals in a Free Society. (Chicago: Follett Publishing Company, 1961)

Broudy, Harry S., *Building a Philosophy of Education,* 2nd ed. (Englewood Cliffs, New Jersey: Prentice-Hall, Inc., 1965)

Broudy, Harry S., Smith, B. Othanel and Barnett, Joe R., *Democracy and Excellence in American Secondary Education.* (Chicago: Rand McNally, 1964)

Full, Harold, *Controversy in American Education.* (New York: Macmillan Co., 1967)

Gardner, John W., *Self-Renewal,* The Individual and the Innovative Society. (New York: Harper and Row, Pub., 1963)

Goodlad, John I., *School Curriculum Reform in the United States.* (New York: The Fund for the Advancement of Education, 1964)

Jersild, Arthur T., *When Teachers Face Themselves.* (New York: Teachers College, Columbia University, 1955)

Kuethe, James L., *The Teaching-Learning Process.* (Glenview, Illinois: Scott, Foresman and Co., 1968)

National Society for the Study of Education, Committee on Personnel Services in Education, *Personnel Services in Education,* edited by Nelson B. Henry, 58th yearbook, part II of the N.S.S.E. (Chicago: The University of Chicago Press, 1959)

Rossi, Peter H. and Biddle, Bruce J., *The New Media and Education.* (Chicago, Illinois: Aldine Publishing Company, 1966)

Sergiovanni, Thomas J., "New Evidence on Teacher Morale: A Proposal for Staff Differentiation," *North Central Association Quarterly,* 42 (Winter, 1968).

Siegel, Laurence, *Instruction: Some Contemporary Viewpoints*. (San Francisco: Chandler Publishing Company, 1967)

Watson, Bernard C., "The Role of the Principal in Collective Negotiations," *North Central Association Quarterly,* 42, (Winter 1968).

Part 3

THE PROGRAM OF STUDIES

SEVEN

Requirements and Optional Subject Offerings

This chapter centers the reader's attention on curriculum content as organized in required courses, elective courses, and special programs. In a discussion of requirements and optional offerings one must start by indicating the grades to be considered in the school unit. While the junior high school normally includes grades 7-8-9, there are also other groupings. Some schools, for instance, include only grades 7 and 8, others 6-7-8, and a few 6-7-8-9. Since most junior highs which include grade 6 follow a curriculum quite similar to that found in the sixth grade in elementary school, we will confine our discussion here to grades 7-8-9.

Senior high schools also are organized in several grade patterns. The most common patterns include grades 10-11-12, 9-10-11-12, and junior-senior high schools of grades 7-8-9-10-11-12. This discussion will consider grades 10-11-12 as senior high school grades.

REQUIRED SUBJECTS—JUNIOR HIGH SCHOOL

Three sources are recommended in considering requirements for junior high schools. They are: Grace S. Wright and Edith S. Greer, *The Junior High School* (Washington, D. C.: U. S. Department Health, Education and Welfare, 1963), pp. 54–59; Junior High School Committee, CASSA, *The Junior High Schools of California* (Burlingame, California: CASSA, 1961), pp. 4–5; Junior High School Project, Cornell University, *The Intellectual Responsibility of the Junior High School* (Ithaca, New York: School of Education, Cornell University, 1962), p. 14.

Note: This chapter was prepared in part by Dr. Karl Plath, Superintendent, Highland Park High Schools, Highland Park, Illinois.

These three references have been cited to show that while much variation exists, there is also much similarity between recommended requirements and current practice. The last reference is probably the one which would include the greatest number of requirements. A comparison between this recommendation and general existing practice will show a difference only in ninth grade social studies and science. These subjects, which the staff at Cornell would require, are required by fewer than three-fourths of the schools, but still by a healthy majority.

The authors would agree that recommendations and practices cited are valid for schools as they are generally conducted today. Rather than set up their recommendation of the number of required and elective courses, they feel that good schools in the immediate future are going to take a slightly different approach to this matter. This will be explained after the senior high school requirements are discussed.

REQUIRED SUBJECTS—SENIOR HIGH SCHOOL

Required subjects for senior high schools show a broad pattern. Continuing after the ninth grade, English is normally required in two of the three final years. Mathematics, science, and social studies are most often required for one of the last three years. Foreign languages are elective.

Several variations from the traditional pattern have been recommended. Conant [1] spoke strongly for a heavier required academic program for academically talented and highly gifted students. Bush and Allen have spoken in favor of more flexibility while advocating "continuous, rigorous study in breadth and depth in all basic subject matter fields throughout the six secondary school grades." [2]

The authors' preference is to favor a minimum of required courses. They favor stress on course selection based on a strong counseling program supported by a maximum individualization of program within each subject.

CONSTANTS, VARIABLES, AND ELECTIVES

Experienced administrators are aware of the difficulty of providing a curriculum to meet the needs of all students when a state or local board requirement suddenly thwarts what common sense dictates. Thus, instead of having a series of required and elective courses, a combination of constants, variables, and electives is recommended.

Certain courses, called "constants," are a part of the curriculum for all students, not only through junior high grades, but through at least part of the senior high grades as well. Language arts or English is a good example of this type of course. Physical education is also a constant for the junior high school.

---

[1] James B. Conant, *The American High School Today* (New York: McGraw-Hill Book Company, Inc.), pp. 57–64. Used by permission of the author.

[2] Robert N. Bush and Dwight W. Allen, *A New Design for High School Education* (New York: McGraw-Hill Book Company, Inc., 1964), p. 9. Used by permission of McGraw-Hill Book Company.

Another category of subjects may be classified as "variables." These subjects are characterized by the fact that while certain proficiencies and understandings should be required of all students by the time they have completed their secondary school education, varying abilities and proficiencies determine whether other subjects should be a requirement at a particular grade for a particular student.

One student might, because of high proficiency in a subject, be allowed to bypass a particular level of that subject and proceed to an advanced one. Another student, after two years of sequential courses in a subject such as mathematics, might have attained about as high a level of achievement as may be expected, considering his ability. It might be wise to let him have a "breather" from this subject for a year and then continue it again in senior high school. These subjects are thus called "variables" because, although ultimately certain requirements will be met, how and when will vary with the circumstances.

The third group of subjects will be called "electives." These may be chosen freely to allow greater specialization or additional exploration. Instrumental music, advanced art and drama are illustrative of the elective group.

Constants, variables, and electives will exist in curricula of both junior and senior high schools. As the student advances in his secondary school experience, the variable and elective part of his program becomes greater.

GUIDANCE AND SUBJECT AREAS

Although a later chapter will discuss guidance and the pupil personnel services, it is pertinent here to mention the importance of proper guidance in course selection to the secondary school student. Whether formally through the school structure or informally through parent-pupil discussion, the pupil must be assisted in choosing the elective and variable courses that best meet his needs. Maximum educational benefit, a correct profile for college admissions, and optimum preparation for post-high school living all generate from a well-planned sequence of courses.

SUBJECT AREAS

Over the past few years the schools have enjoyed the greatest interest in curriculum study and revision in several decades. In a book of this type it would be impossible to pursue in detail the many aspects under consideration in each curriculum area. It will be the intent here, rather, to point out a few of the interesting investigations currently being undertaken.

English. Getting off to a later start than science and mathematics, English is currently receiving a great deal of attention. Structural linguistics and functional grammar have a prominent place in professional literature at this time. Certainly some fresh approaches to the study of the language will be common practice in secondary schools in the years immediately ahead. At the present time the scholars have not settled for themselves just which is the most productive approach to the study of grammar. In view of this fact, it seems reasonable that some of the more enthusiastic supporters of one approach or another are currently making claims which cannot be endorsed by the majority of the scholars in the field.

The other language arts skills are also a part of a good secondary school English program—listening, speaking, writing, reading, correct usage, and the development of an appreciation for an understanding of good literature.

Project English is a concentrated effort at improving the teaching of English in our schools. The approach is made through four areas: Basic research, applied research, curriculum study centers and demonstration centers. This project began formal work early in 1962 and offers promise for a number of changes in the English curriculum of the secondary school.[3]

While reading is too rarely taught as a separate subject in the secondary school, educators are concerned about the need for attention to this area of the curriculum. Most good secondary schools have a remedial reading program, but too few include any kind of developmental reading program. While this is considered to be a part of the regular English program in many schools, it probably exists more "on paper" than in fact. It is an aspect of the curriculum which should receive attention.

Senior high school English departments build upon the pupil's junior high curricula in both the required courses and in the electives offered. One major emphasis is logical written expression; this emphasis is based on a structural content sequence. Competent literary analysis, an appreciation of our literary heritage, and competent public speaking are other major goals.

In addition to the required English courses, many senior high schools appeal to students' diverse interests through courses such as journalism, creative writing, drama, stagecraft and great books. More recently the English departments have combined with art, music, and social studies departments to offer courses in the humanities.

A good summary of trends in the teaching of English is found in The *Curriculum Handbook for School Administrators* edited by Conner and Ellena.[4] They cite the following trends:

1. The learning of English is now seen largely as a process of inquiry and discovery.
2. New approaches to learning English concentrate on concepts related to the "structure of subject" and avoid attempting to cover the entire field.
3. New methods of teaching English require a variety of learning and teaching materials.
4. The time devoted to English studies varies with individual need.
5. The interrelated content and skills of English must be taught in a continuous, unified program.

---

[3] J.N. Hook, "Project English: A Concentrated Attack on Old Problems," *Illinois Education,* LIII (March, 1965), pp. 286–289. Used by permission of the publisher.

[4] Forrest E. Conner and William J. Ellena, editors, *Curriculum Handbook for School Administrators* (Washington, D.C.: American Association of School Administrators, 1967), pp. 64–68. Used by permission of the publisher.

Physical Education. The physical education program of today is generally far removed from the "toss them a ball and let them play" curriculum prevalent a number of years ago. The organized physical education curriculum stresses sound physical development, teaches skills in sports and games, and develops special classes for the physically handicapped and unskilled.

Two activities in the physical education area that are receiving increasing emphasis are swimming instruction and health education. The swimming pool in junior or senior high schools is no longer a rarity. These schools often require students to learn to swim as one of their graduation requirements.

Health educators recommend individual subject status for health education rather than having it as part of physical education. An already overcrowded curriculum has hindered their making much headway toward achieving this aim, however.

Growing out of a sound physical education program are extra-curricular activities in intramural sports, extra-mural sports, and interscholastic sports. These activities offer competition for all skill levels. While girls' extra-curricular activities generally offer many fewer opportunities for inter-school competition than do the boys', the physically skilled girl does have some opportunities for competition.

Social Studies. Like English, social studies started late but is currently receiving much attention. The ultimate outcome is not clear at this time. The big problem is getting the proponents of the separate disciplines within this broad field to agree on what should be included and how it should be approached. The historian wants history taught as a separate subject; so does the geographer, the political scientist, the economist, the sociologist, the anthropologist, and the social psychologist. There is much conflict yet to be resolved before a real overhaul of the junior high school social studies curriculum can be accomplished.

The following trends may be noted in the social studies: [5]

1. Joint efforts have been made by social science scholars and public school educators. (Examples are cited such as: The Report of the State Central Committee on Social Studies to the California State Curriculum Commission, the USOE's Project Social Studies, and the NEA's Project on Instruction.)
2. The content has been changing. There has been a reassessment of the scope and sequence. (Political science, anthropology, and economics, for example, are having a more prominent part in the content along with history and geography which have dominated the content in the past.)
3. Methods of teaching the social studies have been undergoing changes. (Critical thinking, and independent study, for example, are becoming more popular.)
4. The American heritage is being emphasized. (Rights and dignity of the individual, and the judiciary and parliamentary systems, for example.)

Consistent with the above trends, the following course titles may appear in the senior high school's social studies curricula: History of Western Civilization, History of

---

[5] William W. Crowder, "Some Trends in Elementary School Social Studies," *Social Education* (November, 1964), pp. 388–390. Used by permission of the publisher and the author.

Non-Western Civilization, Modern European History, Political Science, Sociology, Economics, and Afro-Middle Eastern Studies.

Mathematics. One of the first areas to receive the attention of the academicians, the mathematics picture is now beginning to come into sharper focus. With several major approaches to the subject evolving simultaneously, some confusion existed at first. The various textbook publishers have begun to release new volumes which show quite a synthesis between the so-called new mathematics and the proven parts of the old. Since these are so well known, they require no further comment.

Another recent practice which is being replaced in many schools, but deserves mention, is that of the more capable pupils starting algebra in the eighth grade, to be followed by geometry in the ninth grade. Some students, easily capable of handling such a sequence, have found that in high school they have abilities and interests in areas other than mathematics. They then reason that with two years of "high school" mathematics behind them, they will pursue the subject no further but rather devote their time to another area.

If they plan to attend a university which requires that two years of mathematics shall have been taken beyond the ninth grade, they find they must continue into advanced algebra to meet this requirement. It has become apparent that those schools which allow the eighth grade algebra-ninth grade geometry sequence need to provide a careful guidance program in conjunction with it.

For the interested and able mathematics student, however, the algebra-geometry sequence above offers the opportunity to study calculus before the traditional freshman college year. Similarly, algebra as an eighth grade course allows a place on the schedule for a course in digital computation as a senior.

Mathematics, as well as other secondary school curricula, is being increasingly affected by computer developments. It is not uncommon now for school mathematics classes to have access to a high-speed computer through a telephone wire arrangement. This enables students to explore more problems faster and in greater depth than under the traditional classroom arrangement.

Science. The revamping of science courses has followed a similar pattern to that of mathematics. While some of the programs such as PSSC Physics haven't had a direct effect on the junior high school, others such as BSCS Biology and introductory physical science have made their way into the curriculum.

Another recent consideration by junior high schools is the development of earth science or earth and space science as a part of the curriculum. At the moment, curriculum specialists, teachers, and administrators are weighing carefully the many factors involved to determine whether this should become a standard part of the junior high science offerings. A good discussion of the issues is included in the *NASSP Curriculum Report* of May, 1965.

The impact of the National Science Foundation continues to be felt in secondary science curricula. A revision of PSSC Physics, known as the Harvard Physics Program, is under trial in a number of secondary schools. It is hoped that this curriculum will attract more boys and girls to physics.

Industrial Arts. Like other areas of the curriculum, industrial arts is undergoing change. Two elements seem to be included most often where changes occur. In some schools a part of each industrial arts course is related to the technology of that subject as it is affected by the economy and industrial world today. As an example, in metal shop the place of metals in our society is studied along with working with metals in the shop. Also studied are production methods of modern industry, quality and strength of materials, structural design, technology, and similar areas.

The second change is to a general shop rather than several specific area shops. The idea is to have one large shop area containing spaces for wood working, metal craft, metal casting, plastics, and so forth. The student begins a project by drawing working plans. He then goes to the appropriate area of the shop to work. Some projects may involve the use of four or five areas of the shop before a project is completed. The rationale is that this procedure is more realistic for the future adult as he will use these skills in his leisure time. Since the profitable use of leisure time is one of our concerns for the years ahead, this organization would seem to make educational sense.

Senior high school industrial education builds on the pupil's general shop experience or personal experiences. Courses are designed for the student who wishes immediate job placement after high school, for the student who wishes advanced training in a technical area after high school, and for the college-bound pupil.

Recent developments in this field include substantially increased federal funding under the Vocational Education Act of 1963, the growth of work-study programs in secondary school, and the development of area vocational schools. In the latter, pupils spend part of their day in their home school and are transported to an area school for specialized training during the remainder of the day.

Home Economics. The status of homemaking in the curriculum has undergone much change in the past fifteen years. Until the launching of the first satellite this course was often required in the seventh and eighth grades and frequently in the ninth, for all girls. It was also usual to find a year required in the senior high school as well.

As the big push for academics developed, this requirement has gradually been reduced until no more than one or two semesters of home economics are required in the junior high school (usually at seventh grade), and there is no requirement in the senior high school. This has been due not only to the "academic excellence" binge but also to a lack of understanding by the public of what the home economics educators were trying to do. Many felt that the mother could teach her daughter all she needed to know in this area. Actually, there is much more to a good home economics course than is usually realized.

For some time prior to Sputnik, these courses were undergoing revision. The familiar clothing and cooking classes had been brought up to date and supplemented with the study of family living. The latter included many areas. An understanding of teenage girls pointed to the need for helping them appreciate good grooming. The high cost of installment buying created a need for including a study of budgets and the wise use of family finances. The high divorce rate in our country indicated a need for much better understanding of the "give and take" of marriage, as well as understanding one's self, mate, and family. These are but a few examples within the broad areas of child care, human relationships, consumer economics, mental health, physical fitness, and applied science, which were added to the home economics curriculum.

Unfortunately, the critics of home economics seized upon minor aspects to point up the need for eliminating this "frill" to make room for "respectable" subjects. They said that "girls spent 'most' of the time in these classes manicuring their nails and talking about dating." The voices trying to put the argument in perspective were drowned out by the critics.

Today, cooler heads have begun to highlight the important problems facing our nation in the years ahead. With more leisure time, with the greater need for strengthening the family unit, with the requirement of being a good homemaker, even for the career girl, this area of the curriculum is getting a second look. It will undoubtedly receive greater emphasis for all girls, including the college bound, as goals are reassessed for the secondary school.

Foreign Languages. Perhaps no facet of the curriculum has received more talk or created as much confusion in the secondary school as the recent changes in the foreign language programs. Nothing which has taken place in education in the past ten years has illustrated shoddy articulation as visibly as the foreign language movement. The true impact of this statement can be appreciated only by those people who between 1957 and 1963 were serving in communities which decided to get started immediately with the sudden pressure for foreign language in the elementary school. The creation of this problem need not be elaborated upon here since it will be developed more fully in the section on articulation.

Suffice it to say that a problem exists and the best efforts of teachers and administrators are going to be required, lest more states follow the misguided lead of the California legislature. In that state it was first decided to require foreign language of all junior high students, then changed to *most* students. It is hoped that, rather than maintaining an aloof attitude, the foreign language specialists will join in bringing order out of the chaotic state which currently exists in too many communities. Only in this way will the modern foreign languages become a contributing member of the junior high curriculum.

The approach to foreign languages is generally some combination of speaking, listening, reading, and writing. In fact, many foreign language educators view this as a continuum, in the order named. The older approaches to teaching foreign language tended to emphasize the right end of this continuum. The newer approaches place their emphasis at the left end, especially during the early years of study.

Now that the early novelty of foreign language laboratories has worn off and teachers are learning to use them effectively, they have found a useful place in the school. These will be discussed further in Chapter Ten.

Art—Music. These subjects are being considered simultaneously because they are so often found this way in the junior high curriculum. Various administrative arrangements are found, such as one semester of art and one semester of general music required in seventh or eighth grade. Probably the biggest problem in this area is securing teachers. The teacher of an advanced art course may not be interested in the "nonartist" in these general art classes. The "band man" or choral director who "ends up with" the general music course may hate it as much as his students will, because of his reaction to it.

The problem perhaps is one which should rest with the preparing institutions. The logical answer is to employ teachers of general music. Unfortunately, too many music departments in higher institutions are interested in performing artists and merely tolerate the teaching of general music. The same is somewhat, though not as severely, true of art departments. It is hoped this picture will change and that more general music teachers will emerge from the teacher training institutions.

Among the more interested and ingenious teachers in art and music departments exciting and challenging things are happening. The many media available to the artist are being utilized in good exploratory art courses. It is hoped that more of these ideas will spread. Certainly pupils in the cybernated age will need all the help they can get from these two areas if they are to have useful and satisfying outlets for the increased free time which will be available.

The importance of music in the curriculum is expressed by Leonhard.[6]

> Music merits an important place in the educational system because it represents one of the most significant human achievements, because it is a unique symbolic system which appeals to the life of feeling and of the mind, and because musical competence contributes unique esthetic richness to the quality of living. Furthermore, the right kind of experience with music can make a powerful contribution to the development of rational powers, and such development is almost universally accepted as the central purpose of education.

Art and music courses in the senior high school generally are elective subjects. Enrollment varies with the pressures of graduation requirements, college admissions standards, and the prestige of these subjects in the school and the community. Recent movements to join these areas with English and social studies in a humanities course should help to provide more senior high school students with an art and music experience prior to graduation.

Performing Arts. A new department, called the performing arts, is emerging in some junior and senior high schools. It usually includes drama, stagecraft, vocal and instrumental music, dance, and speech. It may also involve art, home economics and industrial arts. As in all things which contain elements for good, extremes can overshadow this good. The secondary school which has a performing arts group which "runs the school" has no place in a system which is endeavoring to meet the goals of secondary education as developed here. In the opinion of the authors it is equally as bad to ignore this important aspect of the curriculum.

To have constant interruptions to the regular routine to provide extra rehearsals for a play or a band concert is not educationally sound. The value which can accrue to the participating students and to the climate of the entire school, as a result of these activities, is sufficient to demand our best efforts at providing these experiences while keeping the entire curricular picture in focus.

---

[6] Charles Leonhard, "The Place of Music in Our Elementary and Secondary Schools," *NEA Journal,* 54 (April, 1963), pp. 40–42. Used by permission of the publisher.

One administrator tells his staff at the first faculty meeting in September, "You may anticipate losing one week during the year, a period at a time, for rehearsals for drama, band, chorus, synchronized swim, and similar shows. Plan accordingly now." He then sets a schedule of these activities so that no rehearsal comes on consecutive days during the same period, nor does any class have more than two interruptions for the same activity.

Administrators who have had close association with properly coordinated performing arts groups are convinced that the value which comes from such an activity greatly outweighs what is lost in one or two class periods of algebra, English, or foreign language.

Business Education. The business subjects usually included in the junior high school are general business and typing. The former may be anything from economics to consumer mathematics, but usually it is a course geared at aiding the prospective consumer. As such, it includes a basic study of economics and business as they apply to the consumer.

More recently, because of the need to provide a better understanding of economic systems for future citizens and voters, this aspect has been included in business courses at the junior high level. Other schools have included it in social studies. In each case, it is an elective. The importance of this subject suggests that it be included among the constants of the curriculum. This would mean that it should probably be included in the social studies area.

Typing, as offered in the junior high school, is usually non-secretarial in nature. In fact, the course is quite often called personal typing. For those students wishing to pursue a secretarial curriculum, beginning typing is usually deferred until senior high school. The concentration on writing in the English curriculum has popularized personal typing courses. It has even been suggested that typing might be added to the "variables" group of curricular offerings.

Several courses have been appearing in senior high school business curricula in recent years to supplement the traditional offerings. College typing and notehand, data processing, distributive education, and office occupations have joined the usual non-vocational and vocational offerings. As in industrial education, the Vocational Education Act of 1963 gave a boost to business education.

SPECIAL PROGRAMS

One of the major functions of the school is to design the curriculum, to tailor the methods of instruction, and to select the materials and media in order to meet the needs of all students. While pre- and early adolescents have many traits in common, they also have many differences, because like human beings of all ages, they are individuals. One way of providing for the individual differences among students is by appropriately placing the variables in the student's program according to his need. For one pupil this may mean fulfilling the requirement of a variable as soon as possible in order to free his schedule later for advanced courses. For another student it may, in contrast, postpone a variable in order to provide room in his program for an elective he particularly needs or desires. The selection of electives also provides a means of meeting these individual needs.

In Chapter Eight, various curriculum designs are discussed which, among other things, provide means of meeting the special needs of students, be they among the majority with good, normal, average abilities, or those of various degrees of deviation from the norm. In these ways, in the hands of a good teacher with adequate materials and media, the needs of the majority of the students will hopefully be met. For the remainder of this chapter, possible ways of meeting the educational needs of the atypical students will be discussed.

Handicapped Children. Pupils with physical or mental handicaps are in the one group of atypical pupils whose needs have been recognized for the longest period of time. This is not to say that having been recognized longest, their needs are now satisfactorily met in the school curriculum. It is true, however, that the problem has been recognized long enough and pressure has been brought to bear successfully so that many states have set up special programs with partial state aid.

It is important to note that there appear to be two approaches to meeting the needs of handicapped pupils of which the administrator should be aware. While the problem will differ with the handicap, one idea is that these pupils require such special help that they should be handled in a self-contained classroom with a specialist. The class should be quite small (five or six if the student has a severe physical handicap, or ten to twelve if mentally retarded).

A second approach is to have these pupils in a special class for part of their work and in the regular classroom for the remainder. If the latter policy is employed, there are definite problems which need to be resolved. If the specialists in this field suggest that a special class should be limited to five or six, or ten to twelve, then it is unrealistic to say that no adjustment in class size is required when one of these students is added to a regular class. If a blind student is considered to be one-sixth of a class size in a special class for the blind, it would seem reasonable to say that he is *at least* one-sixth of a class size in a regular class normally housing 30 students. In this case perhaps the class size with one blind student should be only 25. This example is meant to illustrate that class load must be considered if the handicapped student is added to the regular classroom. It is also well to point out that the validity of this practice is still controversial and suggests that specialists in this area need to work closely with those outside the area to help resolve the issue. It is an area of much needed research.

The Gifted. The education of the gifted is a topic of much interest. As a special group, the gifted or academically talented did not receive much attention until the past ten years when the swing to academic excellence began. While some schools have had special programs for these students for a number of years, the majority tried rather to handle their needs within the regular classroom.

Following World War II individual schools began to look to other ways of providing for these youngsters. While a variety of ideas were tried, most administrators said little about it for the climate was not sympathetic to these practices. To provide any type of special curriculum for the superior student was "undemocratic." In the few instances where publicity did accompany the program it was often tied in with other aspects of giftedness or talent. An example is the program at Portland, Oregon.[7]

With the push for academic excellence, the special programs for gifted students became respectable. It was pointed out that this practice was not undemocratic, that equal educational opportunity and identical educational experiences were two entirely different things. Homogeneous grouping became popular and with it, separate classes for the gifted students.

A look at homogeneous grouping over a span of several years reminds one that if you stand in one spot long enough you can quite often meet your educational colleagues coming back. The process of grouping was criticized so severely prior to World War II that few administrators had the nerve to try it. Then it became respectable, and by 1960, 74 percent of those junior high schools which utilized class sections practiced some form of grouping.[8] If one is to judge from the tone of professional writings and sessions at professional conferences, grouping is now being seriously questioned.

The authors strongly suspect that grouping is one of those processes in education which is likely to be debated for a number of years to come, simply because too many people have been highly successful with it, and too many others have been highly unsuccessful with it. The result is that it is one of those things about which the educator feels strongly according to his own experience.

There is ample coverage of grouping in the professional literature. A good summary of the research is given in the *Handbook of Research on Teaching*.[9] Many of the arguments given by either side are refuted by practice employed by the same people. As an example, the opponents of grouping often say that the members of the "low" group realize their plight because of being so grouped and thus attach a stigma to themselves and decide they cannot expect to succeed. These same people often recommend heterogeneous grouping in all classes but regrouping within the class as a way of handling the wide range of abilities. Surely even the pupil of the lowest ability is going to realize which group he is in within the class. In fact, being in such close contact with what the "faster" groups are doing will drive the point home even more emphatically. Thus, if the first argument holds, then the cure has to be judged on the same basis and we are no better off than before.

The authors feel that the value of grouping depends upon several practices. First, the basis for selection must be a number of factors rather than a single criterion such as I.Q. Most often, achievement scores, previous grades, and teacher recommendations are used. Second, something truly different should happen within the classroom after grouping is accomplished. If the groups are different, then the methods, materials, and degree of abstractness must also be different. Third, while the students will figure out the grouping, labels for the groups should be avoided. Fourth, opportunity must be pro-

---

[7] Clifford W. Williams, *The Gifted Child in Portland* (Portland, Oregon: Portland Public Schools, 1959).

[8] Grace S. Wright and Edith S. Greer, *The Junior High School* (Washington, D.C.: Office of Education, 1963), pp. 17–18. Used by permission of the publisher.

[9] N.L. Gage, ed., *Handbook of Research on Teaching* (Chicago: Rand, McNally and Company, 1963), pp. 1143–1144.

vided within the school day for interaction with students of varying abilities, i.e., do not keep the group together or with similar students throughout the day. Fifth, provide opportunity for success for everyone.

One of the problems with grouping is that most teachers want the gifted group. This is because many teachers feel that it is easy to teach them or that there are no problems in this group. A teacher with this approach should not be with gifted students. To teach a class of these students, offering the proper challenge to them will be one of the hardest jobs a teacher will encounter—the most rewarding perhaps, but certainly the hardest.

A look at some of the hoped-for outcomes of such a class should indicate why this is true. The goal is for these students to emerge as self-propelled, questioning, creative students with the ability to think abstractly, logically and constructively. It is hoped that they would increase their knowledge about many areas and inquire at great depth into certain areas of interest.

What does this say about teaching? It says the teacher must be a scholar in his field and generate an appreciation for scholarship in his students. He must, at the same time, recognize that he does not have all of the facts or understanding about some aspects of learning which his students may have, even though they are teenagers. He must, if he is to develop a questioning attitude, expect his own statements and ideas to be questioned. When this happens, the answer is not, "Because I told you so!" A teacher who is threatened by questions is not the teacher for a group of gifted students.

Another problem in teaching the gifted is the loss of perspective. As one works with this group, he has the tendency to forget what the other students are like. A number of hazards creep in at this point. Grading is illustrative of the problem. It is a natural tendency to devise more and more difficult tests in order to "spread them out." There is not a lot wrong with this as long as the teacher recognizes that he has distinguished between an outstanding "A," an excellent "A," a good "A," a fair "A," a weak "A," an outstanding "B" and a superior "B." It becomes a problem when the teacher deludes himself into thinking he has separated the group into A's, B's, C's, D's, and F's.

In using grouping as a device for handling the gifted student, the pupils should be regrouped for each subject. Experienced educators know that a large majority of those grouped for English will remain in the same group for mathematics and science. However, there are some in one group who do not belong in the other, and this should be handled by regrouping.

Another problem to watch for is the load imposed by these courses. For this reason some schools limit the number of special gifted groups a student may be in. To provide outstanding classes in English, mathematics, science, the arts, etc., and then to burden the student to the extent that he makes poor grades, impairs his health, or does not have time for anything beyond his school work is an indication of poor overall planning. Perhaps the best approach is to consider each student's case separately. Some students may be able to handle several of these classes with little trouble. Others may not. Again, it's the process of working with individuals.

We also need to remember that these students need some time to think—to sit quietly and supposedly do nothing, if you will. To not provide that opportunity is obstructing the path toward reaching the goals set for these students.

Grouping of gifted students has often taken some interesting and exciting turns by creative teachers and administrators. In some schools a group has been formed, not for a subject, but rather for special interests which cut across the whole field of the humanities, or the sciences, or the fine arts. Another school has coordinated leadership and a study of U. S. History and civics. The selection of the group includes the gifted with leadership potential. The ultimate aim—to get more of these students involved in leadership positions in the school.

As was indicated previously, marking can be a serious problem in special classes. Probably more gifted classes have been abandoned because of grading practices than for all other reasons combined. You may build a strong case for how much better prepared the students will be for college, etc., because of this class, but if you couple this argument with few A's, a large number of B's, a large number of C's, and an unusual number of D's and F's, you might as well face it, the product is not going to sell. Unfortunately, this is a problem which too few faculties face up to before going into a program of special classes. Certainly it is of paramount importance.

The ungraded secondary school offers some interesting possibilities in the area of the gifted as well as for students of all abilities. This will be mentioned in Chapter Eight.

The underachieving gifted student is worthy of special attention. The wasted talent here is worth our best effort. Various studies have indicated that the usual programs for the gifted are no more stimulating to him than programs where no particular attention is given to the gifted.

The greatest promise offered so far for this type of student seems to be to elevate his self-concept. These students have a tendency to look down upon themselves, to not see any value in finishing a task, and to not care how well they do a job. The problem is to help him to recognize the importance of carrying a job through to completion, to do a task well for the sake of being able to look back upon it with pride. He must come to understand that success breeds success, and that being successful is important to his satisfaction in all of life to come. This was the approach of one of the early projects at the junior high level [10] which has since been utilized in a number of studies. Since even this process has not proven completely successful with all of those students with whom it has been used, and there are some students which this approach did not reach at all, other novel approaches to the problem must be tried.

Reluctant Learners. The reluctant learner is a member of another group which has received special attention of late. The ideas offered for dealing with the underachieving gifted student offer some promise with this student. The main problem, however, seems to be tied in closely with disinterest. This then leads back to one of the most basic elements of teaching—proper motivation.

New devices and techniques offer some possibilities for help. Special groups have also been tried in some schools. It is doubtful, however, that anything will come nearer a solution than a sympathetic, understanding teacher who really cares about boys and girls. It seems then that while special programs offer some promise for the student,

---

[10] Mark Smith, "Motivating the Under-achieving Gifted Pupil in Junior High School," *Journal of Secondary Education, XXVI* (February, 1961), pp. 79–82. Used by permission of the publisher.

perhaps the greatest assist will come from teachers truly oriented to this type of secondary school youngster and from good counseling programs.

The Troublesome Ten Percent. Dr. Charlotte Elmott and her associates conducted a study of this group of students in Santa Barbara, California. She describes them as those "whose behaviors give concern to their teachers and interfere with their successful use of the opportunities that the school provides."[11] While this study was concerned primarily with early identification and handling of these pupils' problems in the elementary school, the study pinpointed aspects which are applicable to dealing with the situation in the secondary school.

This group is generally described as (1) often having some form of health problem, (2) at least a fourth were dull or mentally retarded, (3) they frequently change geographic location, (4) almost half come from a home culture which is different from the dominant community culture, and (5) they are likely to be among the economically disadvantaged.[12]

The Santa Barbara study approached the problem from the point of utilization of school social workers. This study is indicative of the feeling among many that the students require concerted effort on the part of specialists outside the classroom. The teacher may aid in early identification and in working closely with specialists who are dealing with these youngsters beyond the classroom, but unless such professional help is available, the job within the classroom is extremely difficult and the rewards are few.

One suggested approach is something akin to the programs of job experience or diversified education which have become popular at the senior high school level. There are some problems involved in some states because of legal age limits for working children. If this can be worked out, however, it seems to offer promise. Such programs in Flint, Michigan, Kansas City, Missouri, and New York City have recently attracted interest.

One of the major problems in working with these pupils in the classroom is the lack of understanding by teachers and pupils of the other's living environment and accompanying set of standards. The teacher speaks of honor, the importance of doing a job well, of self-sufficiency, and meets smiles and a shake of the head, but neither understands the other's attitude because he has not experienced the other's world. It then becomes a question of teacher education institutions providing opportunities for contact and better understanding throughout communities and then programs such as "Higher Horizons" to raise the sights of this group. One doesn't have to ponder this statement long to realize the mammoth undertaking suggested here. The road ahead is not an easy one.

SELECTED READINGS

Bush, Robert N. and Allen, Dwight W., *A New Design For High School Education*. (New York: McGraw-Hill Book Company, Inc., 1964)

---

[11] Charlotte Elmott, Jane Criner, and Ralph Wagner, *The Troublesome Ten Percent* (Santa Barbara, California: Santa Barbara City Schools, 1961), p. i. Used by permission of the publisher.

[12] Elmott, p. 1.

Conant, James B., *The American High School Today*. (New York: McGraw-Hill Book Company, Inc., 1959)

Gage, N. L., editor, *Handbook of Research on Teaching*. (Chicago: Rand, McNally and Company, 1963)

Junior High School Committee, California Association of Secondary School Administrators, *The Junior High Schools of California*. (Burlingame, California: CASSA, 1961)

Junior High School Project, Cornell University, *The Intellectual Responsibility of the Junior High School*. (Ithaca, New York: School of Education, Cornell University, 1962)

EIGHT

Types of Curriculum Design

PRINCIPLES UNDERLYING CURRICULUM DESIGN

In this chapter various types of curriculum design will be explored. The purposes of any curriculum design or organizational plan are to facilitate achieving the goals or objectives of the school and to provide a structure which allows the effective and efficient utilization of staff and facilities.

Morphet, Johns, and Reller [1] state that the "only significant test of the worthwhileness of any organizational plan is its effect upon the educational program or the opportunity it affords the children to learn."

They further enumerate these principles of curriculum design or organizational plans: [2]

1. The value of any organizational plan must be determined fundamentally in terms of the opportunity it provides for the development of the desired educational program.

2. The organizational units need to be understood as instruments through which more adequate provisions can be made for caring for individual differences.

3. The plan of organization involving the various schools must provide for continuous educational development of children and youth.

---

[1] Edgar L. Morphet, Roe L. Johns, and Theodore L. Reller, *Educational Administration* (Englewood Cliffs, N.J.: Prentice-Hall, Inc., © 1959), p. 260. By permission of Prentice-Hall, Inc., Englewood Cliffs, N.J.

[2] Morphet, pp. 266–268.

4. The organizational plan must be continuously and periodically re-examined in a constructive manner with a view to assisting schools to meet educational purposes in a more effective manner or to provide a basis for modifying the plan.

5. The school should be large enough to make available necessary specialized competencies and services at reasonable cost; it should be small enough to be comprehensible to the student and to facilitate the recognition of and the provisions for individual differences.

6. In large schools some of the advantages of the smaller unit can be attained through the organization of "schools-within-the-school."

7. The school should be characterized by both homogeneity and heterogeneity.

CURRICULUM DESIGNS AND RELATED ELEMENTS

Various curriculum designs may be utilized in an effort to meet these ends. Some of them will be examined in the sections to follow.

CORE AND BLOCK OF TIME PROGRAMS

The core, fused subject areas, integrated learnings, and block of time programs are four approaches which, though not identical, have some elements in common. The core has been advocated by a sizeable group of junior high educators for a number of years. The core may be defined as that part of the total curriculum which is required of all students at any level. The term is used to designate all or part of the program of general education. It has not gained wide acceptance in senior high schools. Among the advantages offered are:[3]

1. It is in harmony with the best learning theory.

2. It unifies the learning experiences of pupils around real problems.

3. Using the problem-centered approach through experience learning, it offers a superior opportunity for pupils to learn to plan cooperatively and to work together.

4. It affords the opportunity for greater attention to individual differences among pupils.

5. It provides an excellent opportunity for the teacher to serve the guidance function with his pupils.

6. Because of the atmosphere in the core class and the higher motivation of pupils, discipline problems are reduced.

While these advantages are claimed for the core program, its advocates believe it meets some of the objectives for the junior high school in a unique way. Some of these are:

---
[3] Roland C. Faunce and Nelson L. Bossing, *Developing the Core Curriculum* (Englewood Cliffs, N.J.: Prentice-Hall, Inc., 1958), pp. 61–64. By permission of Prentice-Hall, Inc., Englewood Cliffs, N.J.

1. It provides an extended time for the student to be with one teacher, thus helping to bridge the gap between the elementary school with its self-contained classroom and the senior high with several teachers in several rooms.

2. It offers the opportunity for fusing or integrating subject matter, saving time, and reinforcing learning.

3. It provides the opportunity for the teacher to facilitate the guidance function.

Perhaps the biggest disadvantage of the core and block of time programs is the difficulty of finding teachers who are professionally prepared and dedicated to the idea of handling this type of teaching. It has been a problem for years and is becoming a greater one for three basic reasons:

1. Few colleges are interested in preparing teachers for such an assignment.

2. Some states have recently passed legislation increasing the number of semester hours of course work required to teach a subject in the secondary school. This makes it difficult to prepare for teaching in two subject areas.

3. The guidance function is becoming increasingly specialized especially in the senior high schools.

It is possible therefore that these practices may diminish in popularity in the years ahead. Nevertheless, through interdepartmental team teaching a number of the advantages may be salvaged.

A LONGER SCHOOL YEAR

In order to provide more time to accomplish the many objectives of the school, to utilize fully the school buildings, and to make full use of teachers' expertise, a longer school year has frequently been recommended. A summary of the most often recommended plans is given in *The Year-Round School* as follows: [4]

(*a*) A Full 48-Week School Year: Under this plan, students and teachers attend a 48-week, 4 quarter school year, with 4 weeks of vacation. This plan was first tried in 1912. Most school systems have abandoned it after trial, primarily because of the increased cost to the taxpayers and the acceleration of pupils through school to the labor market at an unwelcome age. However, several metropolitan high schools in the Atlanta, Georgia area adopted the 4 quarter plan of operation for September, 1968.

(*b*) A Voluntary Summer Program: Under this plan the regular school year of from 36–40 weeks is followed by an optional summer program of up to 12 weeks in length. The program in the summer includes some remedial and makeup work but the majority of the offerings are courses designed to go beyond those normally available during the regular school year. These include both advanced courses and en-

---

[4] American Association of School Administrators, *The Year-Round School* (Washington, D.C.: AASA, 1960), pp. 4–5, 10–14. Used by permission of the publisher.

richment offerings. This seems to be the most economical means of providing an extension of the school year for those who desire it.

The National Association of Secondary School Principals sees the optional summer session as a more likely solution than the year-round school, for while the latter sounds good in theory, it does not appear to be gaining in practice. They attribute this to two major factors: (1) many schools do not have sufficient enrollment to schedule equal segments of the school population during each quarter. Since all subjects must be offered in each quarter, a secondary school of at least 1600 students would be required; (2) If an "off-quarter" is not a part of the plan, the current cost per pupil will rise approximately 20–25 percent annually.[5] Parents object to off-quarter plans because the vacation period of ¾ of the students would not match the summer vacation period now common in industry.

(c) Extended School Year: The New York State Department of Education is experimenting with new plans for extending the school year. One of these is based upon a 210-day school year with a traditional but shortened summer vacation. Under this plan each grade of the elementary school will finish the regular year's work in a total of 180 days and then pursue the work of the next grade the last 30 days. Thus, it is possible to complete 7 years of elementary work (k-6) in 6 years. See Figure 8-1. In the senior high school the school year of 210 days is divided into 3 or 4 equal terms. By completing a year of work in 2 trimesters or 3 quadrimesters, secondary students may graduate in 3 years rather than 4. Nova High School, Fort Lauderdale, Florida, is experimenting with the trimester plan.

YEAR	HOW THE 210 DAYS ARE SCHEDULED TO COVER SEVEN YEARS OF WORK IN SIX
1st year	180 days in kindergarten, 30 days in grade one
2nd year	150 days in grade one, 60 days in grade two
3rd year	120 days in grade two, 90 days in grade three
4th year	90 days in grade three, 120 days in grade four
5th year	60 days in grade four, 150 days in grade five
6th year	30 days in grade five, 180 days in grade 6

FIGURE 8-1

EXTENDED SCHOOL DAY

Another approach to modification of the traditional curriculum is the extended school day. In many schools another period (or perhaps two) has been added to the

---

[5] *NASSP Spotlight,* "Summer School vs. The Year-Round School," No. 52 (March–April, 1962), p. 2. Used by permission of the publisher.

school day. Thus, the six period day becomes a seven or eight period day. This approach, though lacking in imagination, does offer more time in school for all pupils. After the appearance of James Conant's books, *The American High School Today* and *Education in the Junior High School,* a number of schools adopted the seven period day. Some have since changed the original plan, either by going back to a six period day, or more often, by going to some other means of achieving the same ends without requiring all students to remain in school for a seven or eight period day.

One of the problems encountered in changing from a six period day to a longer one was that some students could handle a six period day adequately, but not a seven or eight period day. This was especially true when the extra period was filled with an enriched academic diet. At this point, the study hall, which had been eliminated in most junior high schools prior to 1950, made a reentry. The students who would use a study hall did not have one, for they were assigned to a full load of subjects. The pupils who could not handle a full load were assigned more time to study in a study hall, but they were not likely to use it. Thus, the study hall, once eliminated from the junior high school, was back again.

A number of ways for meeting this dilemma have been devised. One approach, as an example, is the optional period or periods. Under such a plan the normal day of six periods for all students has one or more periods added before or after hours. Students capable of handling an increased load may then take these subjects in an extended day. Those who cannot, are not in school at that time. Study halls are eliminated.

Another approach tried in some schools is the Saturday session for the capable student. While this was started with some fanfare in several communities a few years ago, there has not been any recent study to indicate whether it is still looked upon with the hope envisioned by its proponents originally.

Another solution for the study hall dilemma is the extended school day for independent study and laboratory work. This has been instituted in junior and senior high schools, either as an optional or a required arrangement. In some instances it is for the express purpose of providing study time with the teachers involved, thus eliminating homework outside the school. In other cases it is for enriching the opportunities of students through making the school's facilities available during part of the study time.

ACCELERATION AND ENRICHMENT

Other ways of meeting the individual needs of pupils are through various methods of enrichment, or by allowing more able students to proceed at a more rapid pace. Acceleration has not been received enthusiastically in junior high school circles. Until recently the almost unanimous opinion of educators was that because of the many physical and psychological changes that take place in children during the junior high school years, acceleration might be acceptable earlier or later, but not here.

While this is still a widely held view, some are now questioning it. One evidence of this second look is the non-graded school which will be discussed later.

Because most educators have not favored acceleration in the junior high, enrichment has been a popular alternate. Provision has been made for a wide variety of enriching experiences. These have ranged from special classes to special units or supplemental work as a part of the regular class.

In the case of special classes the approach is to cover the basic curriculum and weave in special areas which go beyond the usual coursework. This may include branching out to new areas, or going more deeply into basic areas. Regular classes can use enrichment projects in much the same way. Unfortunately, much that is unimaginative, or "more of the same," is cloaked with the label, "enrichment." With the rapid proliferation of knowledge, there is plenty which can be added to each area of the curriculum to enrich it without replowing the same furrows.

The 28th yearbook of the National Council of Teachers of Mathematics is a collection of enrichment activities for the more capable mathematics student.

It should be noted that enrichment activities should not be thought of as only for use with the more capable student. Murray Polner's *Enriching the Social Studies* is a collection of activities for pupils of all levels of ability.

THE ADVANCED PLACEMENT PROGRAM

The Advanced Placement Program deserves special mention as a means of acceleration in the senior high school. This program is aimed at challenging the college bound students with advanced courses in such areas as mathematics, science and history. Satisfactory performance in advanced placement courses allows selected high school students to receive advanced standing in college. The satisfactory performance is usually evaluated by examination.

For a more detailed discussion of the Advanced Placement Program the reader is referred to Inlow's recent book.[6] It should be noted that participation in advanced placement courses has increased from 1200 pupils in 104 schools in 1955 to 42,000 pupils in 2800 high schools in 1967.[7]

A principal who wishes to evaluate all opportunities to upgrade curriculum, and extend mind-stretching opportunities to his students should carefully consider the advanced placement program.

OUTDOOR EDUCATION

The out-of-doors classroom has received increasing interest in recent years. There are many unique advantages which come from learning outdoors. Some of these have been enumerated as follows: [8]

---

[6] Gail M. Inlow, *The Emergent in Curriculum* (New York: John Wiley and Sons, Inc., 1966), pp. 322–337.

[7] Herbert G. Lawson, "Off to College at 15—Is It a Good Idea?" *The Wall Street Journal* (New York: Dow Jones and Co., Inc., August 9, 1967), p. 10.

[8] Lawrence H. Conrad, ed., *Outdoor Teacher Education* (DeKalb, Ill.: Northern Illinois University, 1961), p. 25. Used by permission of the publisher.

Outdoor education:

1. Provides more opportunity for the social maturation of the student
2. Allows more understanding of the social science concepts; of man in his total environment; of the interrelationship of all the sciences and all the disciplines of knowledge
3. Is not a particular body of subject matter content; it is rather a *body of educational method,* linked with demonstration opportunities generally superior to most of those that can be provided indoors
4. Provides a completely inter-departmental approach to the growth and development of young people
5. Is crowded with glimpses of the aesthetic and the spiritual, and inspirational experiences are encountered in greater profusion in the out-of-doors than inside the classroom
6. Affords rich experience in human values
7. Brings students and teachers closer together

Outdoor education is not a separate discipline with its own objectives, rather it is a climate for learning that furnishes opportunities for direct laboratory experiences in identifying and solving problems found in the real world, for acquiring skills to equip one for a creative life, for developing an understanding of human and natural resources, and for providing a basis for understanding man in his environment.[9] A unit should begin in the classroom, move out-of-doors, and then return to the classroom for the wrap-up.

The relationship of the teacher and the student assumes a new dimension and learning can become a highly personal, very exciting experience. Partridge expresses it this way: [10]

> "Teachable moments" multiply in number, in depth and in meaning in the out-of-doors. . . . The very structure of our schools, the very nature of our schedules, the very way we have to herd people around in numbers and do things mechanically, as it is necessary to do them today, tends to destroy the teachable moments. We have got to create some kind of situation in which the teachable moments arise and do not get destroyed by the sound of the bell that disperses people. We are so far from this in our institutional life that most teachers are not even able to recognize a teachable moment—to see it in the rough and to develop it into something worthwhile.

TEAM TEACHING

Team teaching covers many different kinds of procedures. For this reason it is extremely difficult to define exactly what is meant by the term. One definition which is probably general enough suggests that it is a design whereby two or more teachers

---

[9] Conrad, p. 21.
[10] Julian W. Smith, Reynold E. Carlson, George W. Donaldson, and Hugh B. Masters, *Outdoor Education* (Englewood Cliffs, N.J.: Prentice-Hall, Inc., 1963), p. 19.

cooperatively plan and conduct the learning activities of a group larger in size than the usual class. These learning activities may be conducted as a large group including all the students, as small groups, and individually. Later in this chapter, a slightly different definition of team teaching is presented.

In considering team teaching, it is well to remember that embarking on such a program will be dependent upon the acceptance and capabilities of the faculty involved, facilities and equipment necessary for its success, and appropriateness of the program to the school involved. Without *caveat* pre-planning, "team" teaching can deteriorate into "turn" teaching. This eliminates the advantage of using the best talent of individual teachers. The type of student body, whether it is a junior or senior high school, and whether it is to be an interdepartmental team, a subject area team, or otherwise, must also be considered. It should be noted further that some teachers may well be able to operate more effectively alone and thus should not be required to be a part of a team.

One difficulty with some team teaching projects is that too much time has been devoted to large group instruction. It has been suggested that no more than 20 percent, and preferably 10 percent of the time be devoted to the lecture at the senior high level. The shorter attention span of the junior high student would indicate less than this.

INDEPENDENT STUDY

One of the adjuncts of team teaching is independent study. One of the valuable outcomes of a good flexible schedule including team teaching is a well-integrated program of independent study. The program should be started in the junior high school and gradually increased through the senior high school. As expressed by Bush and Allen,[11] "the time is overdue to recognize that twelfth-grade students may appropriately be treated differently from seventh-grade students insofar as need for supervision is concerned. The emphasis should be on developing students' responsibilities systematically rather than on demanding a metamorphosis at the time of college entrance or vocational employment."

Just as the level in school will cause variation in the amount and type of independent study, so will it also vary with the pupil. Some pupils will require a fairly high degree of supervision during time for independent study, whereas others may assume considerable responsibility for these activities. For a concise discussion about many phases of independent study the reader is referred to the May, 1967, *Curriculum Report*.[12]

"The limited experience students have had with independent study has largely been relegated to after hours' homework when neither the resources of the school nor the assistance of the teacher is at hand to aid the after hours' learner. Independent study, if

---

[11] Robert N. Bush and Dwight W. Allen, *A New Design for High School Education* (New York: McGraw-Hill Book Co., 1964), pp. 72–73. Used by permission of McGraw-Hill Book Company.

[12] National Association of Secondary School Principals, Warren C. Seyfort, editor, "Independent Study," *Curriculum Report* (Washington, D.C.: NASSP, May, 1967), pp. 1–12.

it is to realize its promise, must be a part of, not apart from, the regular school activity."[13]

The ultimate aim of independent study is to develop the self-propelled student in search of learning. For this reason independent study is an integral part of the total program—large group, small group, and the extra class program. It is, therefore, important that when embarking on a program involving these approaches to learning, the staff must have accepted the project to the extent that they are willing to bring their teaching methods into line with the desired outcomes. It must be realized that such a program of team teaching, flexible scheduling, independent study, and large and small group activities requires facilities designed with these activities in mind.

It is likewise important to remember that the decison of whether to use small or large groups or independent activities is based, not upon how it is easiest to schedule, but rather on the basis of how it fits the program of the particular course. In other words, the teachers must ask such questions as: What do I wish to accomplish in this course or unit? In order to reach these objectives, how much time will be required in the give and take of small group discussion? How much in activities which are primarily devoted to showing or telling? How much individual activity will be required for reading, viewing, listening, or in a laboratory, or thinking? From the answers thus supplied will come the proportion of time to be scheduled to the various activities.

THE NON-GRADED SCHOOL

The non-graded school has received considerable attention at the elementary level for several years. More recently this approach has been given serious attention at the secondary level. There are those who believe that the junior high school may be the most appropriate level for non-graded teaching. The Association for Supervision and Curriculum Development suggest that the junior high school of the future should be an ungraded institution.[14]

Brown suggests that "every non-graded plan should meet several criteria: (1) it must make possible an accurate classification of students of near equal achievement; (2) it must provide for frequent re-classification so that students are permitted to move forward on an individual basis as fast as they can go; (3) it must permit the establishment of individualized goals for each student; (4) it must have standards compatible with the varying rates at which students learn." [15] It is a program whereby the student moves at his own pace rather than at a yearly pace per subject course. The student may pursue any course in which he has an interest and has the ability to achieve, regardless of the normal grade level or sequence.[16]

---

[13] David W. Beggs III and Edward G. Buffie, *Independent Study* (Bloomington, Indiana: Indiana University Press, 1965), p. XII. Used by permission of the publisher.

[14] Association for Supervision and Curriculum Development, *The Junior High School We Need* (Washington, D.C.: ASCD, 1961), p. 22.

[15] B. Frank Brown, *The Non-Graded High School* (Englewood Cliffs, N.J.: Prentice-Hall, Inc., 1963), p. 48. Used by permission of the publisher.

[16] Brown, p. 43.

In a brochure describing the program at Nova High School in Fort Lauderdale, Florida, the following explanation of the ungraded program is made:

> The program is designed to meet the critical needs of each student. However, since each level must be mastered in turn, no one can fail and no one will be required to repeat an entire year's work in any subject.
>
> . . . Instead of being 'promoted' a grade each year, students will progress through a series of achievement levels in each subject area. As a student masters one level in a course, he may continue to the next on any day, week, or month of the school year. The speed of his advancement depends upon his capabilities and interest.

Some secondary schools using this approach to a subject have divided the course or sequence into a large number of small segments, each of which must be mastered in turn by all students. For example, the six years of English (grades 7-12) have been divided into as many as 200 separate steps or packages. The student completes one satisfactorily, then moves on to the next.

TECHNOLOGY AND THE CURRICULUM

Several factors handicap school administrators as they attempt to organize educational programs which recognize the importance of individual differences in pupils:

1. Knowledge is growing in scope.
2. The rigid requirement of 55 minute periods, 5 days per week limits the number of subjects students may take.
3. Rate of learning varies with different children.
4. Schedules dominate pupils and teachers.
5. Special competencies of teachers are not fully utilized.
6. Mass study halls do not effectively develop independence in work habits.

Modern technology is being used to remove these handicaps. Some of the techniques will be introduced in the remaining portion of this chapter.

MODULAR SCHEDULING

There is nothing new about dividing the school day into class periods or modules. All schedules are modular, usually ranging in length from 40 to 55 minutes. Flexibility is obtained when periods are shortened to something less than 40 minutes. School officials are experimenting with schedule periods in units of 15, 20, 25, or 30 minutes. For example, a 7-hour school day, with 30 minute modules will have 14 class periods. The benefits are many. By using three or four modules in succession, science classes will have increased time for laboratory work. Students who do not require three or four "mods" to finish their work will be free for independent study or to practice music or to finish an art project. Traditional classes may continue using two modules. However, the benefits of a modular schedule are lost if all classes simply go ahead in the same old way, using two modules of 30 minutes each to replace the traditional class period of 60 minutes.

The modular schedule promotes independent study. When the number of periods in the school day is doubled, pupils will have considerable free time. While development of desirable work habits is a major school goal, many schools have failed to trust students to be "on their own." Herding non-academic students into study halls will not result in developing improved work habits. Self study requires use of such learning materials as films, tapes and tape recorders, reading machines and study carrels.

Before increasing the number of periods in a school day, school officials would do well to make certain that adequate facilities for developing good work habits are available. No pupil can learn to work without tools.

The modular schedule promotes large group instruction and team teaching. Team teaching has been defined as "the continuous functional operation of two or more teachers to plan and implement the curriculum through the development or selection of appropriate materials and methodology. This definition implies a need for time within the weekly schedule so that teams can meet and carry out the all-important planning function." [17] Large group instruction promotes efficient use of teaching films. It conserves teaching time. It frees teachers to meet children in small groups or individual instruction. It makes best use of the master teacher and of resource persons. Large group instruction requires comfortable areas for large groups. Seats should have tablet arm chairs. Electrical outlets and light control are needed.

FLEXIBLE SCHEDULING

The terms "modular scheduling" and "flexible scheduling" are often used interchangeably. They are not the same. Modules relate to periods of time in a schedule. Flexibility relates to modification of schedule patterns. Thus it is possible to break out of the traditional pattern of requiring students to schedule classes daily, five times each week.

The traditional six period, and more recently the seven period, day has come in for much attention from the principal. Earlier in this chapter it was stated that a schedule of six or seven periods, all of the same length, places many restrictions on the school's program regardless of whether the principal starts with curriculum, student activities, utilization of staff, or efficient use of materials, media and facilities, and sooner or later he comes to the schedule, for it is basic to all which goes on in the school.

This idea is expressed by Bush [18] as follows:

---

[17] *Illinois Journal of Education* (Springfield, Illinois: Office of Superintendent of Public Instruction, Ray Page, editor, January, 1968), p. 19.

[18] Robert N. Bush, "Decision for the Principal: Hand or Computer Scheduling?" *NASSP Bulletin*, XLVIII (April, 1964), pp. 141–142. Used by permission of the publisher.

Depending on one's point of view, the most important element in the high school program may be the pupil, the teacher, the principal, the curriculum, the building, the teaching materials, or even the size of the school. Nonetheless, the school schedule lies close to the heart of the matter, for it represents the way in which all of the foregoing essential ingredients are brought together into an effective whole. The schedule can make or break any one of the elements. It frees or fetters, enhances, or enchains the rich potential inherent in any school.

In an effort to break the lock step of a schedule made up of classes meeting daily for 50 minutes each, a number of schemes have been tried. These have included: (1) floating periods, (2) a special period each day or several times a week, to be used for student activities or special "short" courses, (3) a special schedule made up essentially of extra long periods, one day each week, for laboratory and other activities requiring extended periods of time, (4) "parallel" scheduling to provide for combining classes for large group instruction, and (5) differing lengths of periods throughout the day—to mention only a few.

From these have come the more complex schedules which are generally referred to as flexible schedules. The flexibility frequently pertains to the fact that periods of varying lengths may be included in the pupil's day. Except for a few rare instances, however, the flexibility ends at this point, for once the student's program is set it is just as inflexible as the traditional. What takes place within the packets of time, however, is an entirely different matter.

Flexible scheduling fits the program to the subject and the student rather than to the clock. With flexible scheduling it is possible to divide the school day into a number of small units of time called modules. They are usually 15 to 30 minutes in length. A student's schedule is then formed by assigning him to classes made up of large groups, small groups, or independent study sessions, and possible laboratory sessions, each varying in time depending upon whether they are one, two, three or more modules in length. An example of a junior high school student's flexible schedule is shown in Figure 8-2.[19]

In actual operation a junior high school pupil will have the daily schedule illustrated in Figure 8-3.

This program is based upon a 6½ hour day with twelve 30 minute modules and 30 minutes for lunch.

By extending the day to fourteen 30 minute modules, more time might be allowed for industrial arts, home economics, art, etc. It may be necessary to revise the offering in a given school to meet local or state requirements. Example: Physical Education must be taught daily in some states. More opportunities to use the electronic laboratories for foreign language or shorthand are available with 14 modules.

Such a schedule has several advantages not found in the more traditional one. It provides opportunities to use teaching teams and the several advantages which may accrue from this technique. It places additional responsibility on the student for his own learning. It tailors the length of time to the activity and to the pupil's learning ability.

---

[19] From BADEN MAURER LETTER NUMBER TWO: Flexible Scheduling II by Walter Baden and David Maurer. © 1967, Science Research Associates, Inc. Reprinted by permission of the publisher.

FLEXIBLE SCHEDULE FOR JUNIOR HIGH SCHOOL STUDENT

8 A.M.	Day:	A	B	C
Modules	*1	Math-Sci	Math-Sci	Perf Music
30 Min.	2	Math-Sci	Math-Sci	Perf Music
	3	Math-Sci	Math-Sci	Phys Ed
	4	Math-Sci	Math-Sci	Phys Ed
	5	Math-Sci	Sped Block	Eng-Soc St
	6	Math-Sci	(Ind Arts,	Eng-Soc St
	7	Eng-Soc St	Home Ec,	Eng-Soc St
	8	Eng-Soc St	Art, etc.)	Eng-Soc St
	9	Eng-Soc St	Sped Block	Eng-Soc St
	10	Eng-Soc St	Sped Block	Eng-Soc St
	11	For'n Lang	For'n Lang	For'n Lang
−2:30 P.M.	12	Typing	Typing	Typing

FIGURE 8-2

* Twelve 30 min. modules plus 30 min. lunch equals 6½ hour school day

NOTE: Examples of possible A, B, and C and an A, B schedules for senior high schools are contained in the Baden Maurer Letter Number Two cited above.

	1st WEEK	2nd WEEK	3rd WEEK	4th WEEK
Monday	Schedule A	Schedule C	Schedule B	Schedule A
Tuesday	Schedule B	Schedule A	Schedule C	Schedule B
Wednesday	Schedule C	Schedule B	Schedule A	Schedule C
Thursday	Schedule A	Schedule C	Schedule B	Schedule A
Friday	Schedule B	Schedule A	Schedule C	Schedule B

FIGURE 8-3

THE AUTOMATED SCHEDULE

There was a time when most high school scheduling was done by hand. Manual construction of a traditional schedule that calls for little change for even small high schools is a formidable one. The innovative principal who is dedicated to flexible scheduling finds the process well nigh impossible without the assistance of automation. Bush and Allen [20] describe the complexities of the task as follows:

---

[20] Robert N. Bush and Dwight W. Allen, *A New Design for High School Education* (New York: McGraw-Hill Book Co., 1964), p. 5. Used by permission of McGraw-Hill Book Company.

The possibility of developing a flexible high school schedule to serve educational needs of pupils has become a reality with the advent of electronic data-processing procedures and high-speed computers. These machines have been used in a variety of complex industrial, governmental and military applications. They mark a new industrial revolution—freeing men from mental labors more prodigious than the physical labors eliminated by the power revolutions of the past two centuries. As a school schedule becomes more varied to provide for new levels of individualization, the number of schedule alternatives increases geometrically. What is an odious task under current practice becomes an impossible task without mechanical assistance. The magnitude is incredible—if an 80-period week is used for 1,800 students, it would take a computer capable of a million operations a second about twenty-five years to systematically consider all alternatives possible for a single schedule.

Automated scheduling requires careful planning. Its implementation will depend upon (1) administrative approval as well as (2) school board acceptance and (3) complete faculty cooperation. Without all of these, automated scheduling will die aborning. Once an agreement has been reached on these important matters these next steps will follow:

Step 1. Purchase computer time.

This can be secured from (*a*) a nearby University, (*b*) a nearby scientific laboratory, or (*c*) a commercial data processing center. Until the rental price for computer hardware is drastically reduced, it will be less costly to purchase computer time than to rent sophisticated equipment that will remain idle a large part of the time. Commercial data processing centers are being established in most large cities. The cost of computer time varies from $1.00 to as much as $7.00 per pupil depending on the size of the school, the complexity of the schedule, the completeness of the data required and the number of runs required before a satisfactory schedule is developed.

Many schools are now forming cooperatives for purchase of automatic data processing services. The NEEDS, project of the New England School Development Council,[21] is an example. Through a grant from the Ford Foundation, this group (called NESDEC) is using automatic data processing for instruction, file creation, reporting to parents, scheduling, student accounting, and test scoring. In addition to the grant, member schools pay a modest fee based on size and enrollment.

Step 2. Collect input data for constructing the master schedule, including such items as:

(*a*) Names of teachers and subject areas.
(*b*) Room schedule with size and special purposes.
(*c*) A list of all students with subjects requested if fewer than 1000 pupils. Larger schools submit samples.
(*d*) The time pattern and type.
(*e*) A list of all subjects together with number of sections of each.

---

[21] The New England School Development Council, 220 Alewife Brook Parkway, Cambridge, Massachusetts, 02138.

(*f*) Maximum number of students per class (25 in English, 32 in social studies, 22 in shop and laboratories).

(*g*) Number of rooms for each subject. This prevents automatic assignment of 50 history students to the swimming pool and 30 art students to the physics lab.

(*h*) Miscellaneous important information. Example: The high school may be so spread out that the extreme walking time required to go from the gymnasium to the science laboratory is 8 minutes whereas the passing time between classes is only 5 minutes. The computer can be directed to schedule students so that the next class is less than 5 minutes away.

Step 3. Take the information to the data center for a trial run. This run will reveal conflicts, inaccurate and incomplete data.

Step 4. Study the data from Step 3 and prepare corrected input data.

Step 5. Repeat Steps 3 and 4 until an acceptable master schedule results. With good input data, this should not require more than four or five runs. It is well to remember the cost is in direct ratio to the number of runs. The more complete the original data, the fewer the number of runs.

The plan developed by Bush and Allen is an interesting one. The curriculum is divided into six basic areas: mathematics, science, social studies, English and foreign language, physical education, and the practical, visual, and performing arts.

Individualization is achieved by providing that all students spend a minimum amount of time each year in each of the six areas. Since these requirements are minimal, special needs or interests may be provided by scheduling for more modules in those areas. It utilizes ability grouping on the basis of: (1) ability and level of growth in a particular subject area and (2) developable interest on the part of the student.[22]

POSTSCRIPT

Obviously, there are many rough educational nuggets ready for the perceptive principal and his staff to find and polish. The climate is ripe for innovative ideas which improve the education of the youth in our schools. There is really no other justifiable reason for change. He knows that children learn at different rates. Therefore a flexible schedule must replace the cells and bells schedule. He knows that all teachers are not equally talented. Therefore, he experiments with team teaching to make better use of individual talent. He believes that the secondary school should promote independence in work habits. Therefore, he provides facilities for independent study.

It is well to remember, however, that recent studies show that a surprising number of innovations have been abandoned. Johnson expresses the warning clearly.[23]

> We must remind ourselves that overhead projectors can enlarge nonsense as effectively as the truth. Making material more visable does not make it more valid.

---

[22] Robert N. Bush and Dwight W. Allen, *A New Design for High School Education* (New York: McGraw-Hill Book Co., 1964), p. 61. Used by permission of McGraw-Hill Book Co.

[23] Mauritz Johnson, Jr., "The Dynamic Junior High School," *NASSP Bulletin*, XLVIII (March, 1964), p. 125. Used by permission of the publisher.

The pooling of ignorance does not create wisdom, and a team of three incompetent teachers does not add up to one competent one. . . . Unless the purpose is clear, chopping the school day into smaller modules may as easily result in chaos as in flexibility. And no amount of flexibility can make outdated content current or a haphazard program coherent.

SELECTED READINGS

American Association of School Administrators, *The Year-Round School*. (Washington, D. C.: AASA, 1960)

Baden, Walter and Maurer, David, *The Baden-Maurer Letters*. (Chicago, Illinois: Science Research Associates, 1967)

Beggs, David W. III and Buffie, Edward G., *Independent Study*. (Bloomington, Indiana: Indiana University Press, 1965)

Beggs, David W. III, *Team Teaching*. (Indianapolis, Indiana: Unified College Press, Inc. 1964)

Blair, Medill and Woodward, Richard G., *Team Teaching In Action*. (Boston: Houghton Mifflin Co., 1964)

Brown, B. Frank, *The Non-Graded High School*. (Englewood Cliffs, N. J.: Prentice-Hall, 1963)

Brown, B. Frank, *The Appropriate Placement School*. (West Nyack, N. Y.: Parker Publishing Co., Inc., 1965)

Bush, Robert N. and Allen, Dwight W., *A New Design For High School Education*. (New York: McGraw-Hill Book Company, Inc., 1964)

Fraunce, Roland C. and Bossing, Nelson L., *Developing the Core Curriculum*. (Englewood Cliffs, N. J.: Prentice-Hall, Inc., 1958)

Inlow, Gail M., *The Emergent in Curriculum*. (New York: John Wiley & Sons, Inc., 1966)

Morphet, Edgar L., Johns, Roe L. and Reller, Theodore L., *Educational Administration*. (Englewood Cliffs, N. J.: Prentice-Hall, Inc., 1959)

National Association of Secondary School Principals, "Independent Study," *Curriculum Report*. (Washington, D. C.: NASSP, May, 1967)

Shaplin, Judson T., and Olds, Henry F., Jr., *Team Teaching*. (New York: Harper and Row, Publishers, 1964)

Smith, Julian W., Carson, Reynold E., Donaldson, George W. and Masters, Hugh B., *Outdoor Education*. (Englewood Cliffs, N. J.: Prentice-Hall, Inc., 1963)

NINE

Selection and Organization of Learning Materials

Too often a school, by some means or another, finds itself the possessor of a new piece of audio-visual equipment. The teacher is told to use it in his class. He then sets about trying to find some way of "working it in." The equipment thus becomes "gadgetry" rather than an integral part of the learning process.

When learning aids are fused into the work of the classroom, they become an important part of the learning process rather than a diversion or a "plaything." This will help to eliminate such student evaluation of the use of audio-visual equipment as evidenced by the following conversation: "Are we going to have to work in science today?" "No, we're going to see a movie!"

RELATING MATERIALS TO OBJECTIVES

Audio visual hardware and other types of teaching aids are means to an end—not ends in themselves. The teacher who wishes to use them effectively must first establish the goals or objectives he seeks.

One of the frequently voiced objectives of the classroom is to provide for individual differences. If learning materials are carefully selected and skillfully used, this goal may become much closer to reality than is presently the case. After the objectives or goals have been selected, and the means of reaching them chosen, then the media which are most appropriate to each group of students may be selected. Different students require different types of materials and methods if they are to learn most efficiently. A wide variety of learning materials should thus be available in the school to meet the individual needs of its pupils.

GROWING IMPORTANCE OF TECHNOLOGY

Technology has become commonplace. It is invading every facet of life, it brings changes in ways of living, and it produces mental upheaval as well. As the old order changes, relationships change in families between parents and children; in industry between employers and laborers; in schools between teachers and pupils. Despite the braking power of status quo agencies, prospects are that technological change will come faster and faster.

Technology has not ignored education. Its impact is felt in most classrooms in America. The growing list of audio-visual and technical aids to learning reads like a fairy tale. A brief description of some of these is discussed in this chapter.

FILMS, FILMSTRIPS, AND SLIDES

Some of the audio-visual materials which have been available for several years have recently been updated. This has greatly enhanced their use. Others are entirely new to the classroom.

Generally, the motion picture film has been used for clarifying complex ideas. The filmstrip deals with a central theme developed in single frames in sequence. The slide carries a single idea. A tremendous visual impact is possible with the use of slides in multiple-screen programming. The slide has been used for individual study more than the motion picture or the filmstrip. This is due primarily to the slide's flexibility. It is a relatively simple matter for an individual to study slides through a hand viewer. Until recently the use of the film or filmstrip involved bulky projectors, portable screens, and darkened rooms. This restricted their use by teachers in the classroom. "It's more trouble than it's worth," has been too frequently heard.

Projectors now available for the classroom have been greatly simplified, incorporating cartridges or self-threading techniques which facilitate operation. Variable speed projectors having stop and single frame projection, as well as the ability to go back and rerun an important section, give this machine a new dimension. Screens are often a permanent fixture in the room.

One of the most recent advances in the use of films has been in the development of 8mm cartridges. They may be projected on a rear screen unit. A cartridge provides from two to four and one-half minutes of repetitive film devoted to a single concept. It is especially adapted to self-study, allowing the student to take the equipment to a study carrel where he can repeat the short film as often as he feels is necessary to fully understand the concept.

The filmstrip viewer is now being combined with a tape or record player in one unit. The filmstrip is actuated by the tape so that it moves in synchronization with the audio message. This is another device which is useful for individual study. Some teaching machines also combine the use of the filmstrip or slides in conjunction with magnetic tapes.

EDUCATIONAL TELEVISION

Educational television has proven to be one of the most disappointing of the innovations of the past ten years. After numerous studies, the expenditure of several million dollars in foundation grants, and involvement of hundreds of school systems, the results have been short of expected outcomes. These conclusions are voiced by a number of educators and have been reached by the Carnegie Commission on Educational Television.[1]

Educational television has not been used in the secondary school nearly as widely as in the elementary school. In 1965 television was viewed in the classroom by approximately three and one-half times as many elementary as secondary pupils. There are several reasons for this fact. (1) The most obvious is the difficulty of scheduling. In the self-contained classroom, it is a relatively easy matter to use the telecast at whatever time it is broadcast. At the secondary level, however, this is a more difficult matter. Multiple telecasts of a single classroom presentation do not always solve the problem. Relatively inexpensive video tape recorders may be the answer to this problem in the future. (2) Another reason for limited use of educational television is that the television series has often been "too full." The classroom teacher who uses four forty-minute telecasts per week becomes little more than an aide to the television teacher. Very few well-qualified teachers are willing to operate in this manner. (3) A third factor has been insufficient or inadequate supplementary materials to back up the telecast in the classroom. (4) Finally, there has been much duplication of effort by local school systems. Quality of the product has been inferior. Coordination of efforts might have provided funds for making a more effective product. An example of interdistrict cooperation that resulted in better quality educational television is provided by the Winnetka, Illinois, Public Schools.[2]

It is obvious that the quality of the television presentation must be clearly superior to what can be done live in the classroom. A number of telecasts have been described by teachers as "a better way of teaching what should not be taught at all." While this may be a valid criticism of ETV, it can also be a criticism of live practices in the classroom. Another major criticism of the telecast is that the student is removed from contact with the teacher.

Educational television will undoubtedly be used more frequently as costs of recording equipment and tape rentals are reduced. When educational or network telecasts can be recorded and stored for use as needed in the school program, one of the big roadblocks to utilization of open circuit ETV will be removed. Video tapes have many educational uses. The science teacher can use the video tape for recording one carefully planned, well-executed demonstration which may then be shown to many classes. It is

---

[1] James R. Killian, Jr., et. al., *Public Television: A Program for Action* (New York: Bantam Books, Inc., 1967). Used by permission of the publisher.
[2] New Trier Township ITV Council, Office of the Coordinator, "The First Year," *ITV Newsletter* (Winnetka, Illinois: New Trier Township ITV Council, June, 1967), pp. 1–2.

not likely that a teacher will want to use this device for all demonstrations because it will remove some of the excitement which comes from "live" demonstrations.

Video tapes can also be used in physical education classes to enable students to see their needs for improvement in developing skills, posture, and physical stamina.

The possibility of videotaping a class session for replay for the entire class to see or for individual analysis in study carrels offers some distinct opportunities. This is especially true for a class presentation which includes a great deal of detail or a difficult or abstract concept. It also provides the opportunity for the student who was absent from class to see what went on in his absence. Teachers often profit from objectively watching their own teaching techniques.

Nova High School in Broward County, Florida, has a closed circuit system in every classroom. A video distribution system allows an unlimited number of programs to be run simultaneously. Resource centers in several buildings contain study carrels for individual work utilizing video tapes. In large lecture halls a TV enlarger projects the image on an 8' by 10' screen. These are but a few examples of the uses which are possible with this medium.

Even with a slow start, educational television is already a multimillion dollar business. In 1954 there were ten licensed educational television stations in the U.S.A. This number had grown to 600 by 1960.[3] More than 1000 schools were operating closed circuit television systems by 1966. They were reaching 10 million students (both elementary and secondary) in Ohio, Michigan, and Indiana.

M.P.A.T.I. (Midwest Program of Airborne Television Instruction) was one of the privately financed pioneer efforts in television teaching. Beginning in 1961 a program of video taped courses, prepared by carefully selected teachers, was telecast from an airplane flying over Montpelier, Indiana. Approximately five million pupils lived within the area covered by M.P.A.T.I. Rigidity of schedules limited its use, and when private funds were withdrawn the project collapsed.

Several state-wide ETV networks provide source material on film and video tape for use of local schools and for inter-state exchange. The Nebraska Educational Network is an example. This network serves the entire state of Nebraska with nine stations. Nebraska is one of 15 states which used all of its quota ($1 million) of matching grants available under the E.T.V. Facilities Act of 1962. The Nebraska Unicameral Legislature allocated $2.87 million for promoting educational television during the 1967–69 biennium. The nine stations are interconnected by microwave. The network is administered by a 13-member commission.

Instructional programs for classroom use make up a major portion of the daytime schedule. These programs are developed under contract, by the University of Nebraska. Teacher's guides are developed by classroom teachers in university summer workshops. In 1967–68 membership included 238 schools enrolling 112,000 pupils. Membership fee is $2 per pupil or $50 per school, whichever is larger.[4]

---

[3] Lloyd McCleary and Stephen P. Hencley, *Secondary School Administration* (New York: Dodd, Mead and Co., 1965), p. 59.

[4] Information received directly from Nebraska Educational Television Commission, Lincoln, Nebraska.

Thirty-four tele-courses are already developed; more are coming. Senior high school courses are offered in American literature, mathematics, American history and current problems. Junior high school courses are available in art, Nebraska heritage, and Nebraska studies.

Advantages of instructional television are listed by the state's Educational Television Council for Higher Education as follows: [5]

1. It brings outstanding specialists to the classroom.
2. It makes possible integration of multiple instructional resources.
3. Rare and expensive resources can be introduced in class.
4. Multiple instructors are available for team teaching by television.
5. Incidents and events can be clarified by the use of such technical advantages as superimposition, video tape editing, split screen and rear projection.

National Educational Television is a non-commercial, non-profit corporation with a privately financed budget of about $8 million. N.E.T. produces or acquires for distribution five hours of programs each week. The outlet is 140 educational television stations. The programs are about equally divided between public affairs and cultural interests. These broadcasts are available for rerun in the schools.

A report from Educational Facilities Laboratories states the case for E.T.V.: [6]

Of audio-visual tools available, television appears to offer the broadest potential. The teaching image is easily transmissible by air and cable. It is reproducible from magnetic tape. It is viewable at relatively high ambient light levels without the need for darkening a room. It permits viewing of current events concurrently with the occasion. Taped programs, entire courses, or laboratory demonstrations may be banked in libraries for use as required. Such tapes and/or programs for the slow learner or the advanced student may serve to enrich the gifted and help the slow. The viewing and audio instrument itself is relatively inexpensive, easily used, widely available in a variety of sizes and easily maintained. The arts of the industry are rapidly improving and lowering the costs of receiving, transmission, recording, and production equipment.

E.T.V. is probably better adapted for presentation of demonstrations and factual material and less adapted to developing judgment, interaction, and drawing of inferences.

PROGRAMMED LEARNING

Programmed learning and teaching machines have enjoyed all of the fanfare which accompanies a panacea in any field. Their proponents have made uncompromising claims leaving little room for charge of failure. And as with any idea presented in this

---

[5] Nebraska Educational Television Commission.

[6] Dave Chapman and Frank Carioti, "Planning for Schools with Television," revised 1968. Educational Facilities Laboratories, 477 Madison Avenue, New York, p. 22. Used by permission of **Educational Facilities Laboratories.**

way, experienced educators who felt they knew a little about what was going on in the classroom prepared to do battle on the pros and cons of teaching machines and programmed instruction.

Now that the smoke has cleared somewhat, it is possible to take a more realistic view of programmed learning. There is obviously a place for it in the work of the school.

Perhaps one should first look at what opportunities are offered by this medium. Programmed instruction is based on a series of steps—questions, problems—to which the learner must respond. The steps are programmed so that they increase in complexity.

The advantages offered for programmed learning are: [7]

1. It makes the instruction, goal oriented.
2. It organizes instruction into an effective sequence.
3. It presents one point at a time, moving from the simple to the complex.
4. The student must become actively involved in the learning process.
5. It provides instant knowledge of results of choices made.
6. A student may move through the learning sequence at his own pace.

There are three types of programming. Linear programming is a method of breaking down complex responses into a number of simpler ones which are then rebuilt in a complex form. Branched or intrinsic programming uses the technique of inserting a difficult question to determine whether the pupil should follow the regular sequence or bypass material which he may have already mastered. Usually a multiple choice question is offered. If the correct response is selected, he is informed and told why, and then allowed to proceed. A wrong response elicits the reason why and he is directed back to a remedial sequence. Adaptive programs utilize electronic devices which can incorporate factors related to change in human behavior during the learning process. It assumes a certain amount of error in learning. Difficulty of the program is automatically raised or lowered depending upon the error rate.[8]

Utilizing these three approaches, teaching machines are developed in forms ranging from the simple programmed textbook to very complex electronic devices. Some of the latter forms currently being developed utilize a variety of media, such as film, slides, filmstrips, models, records, and written texts. They are controlled by complex computers and can serve over 100 students simultaneously. They are designed to provide feed-in of test data and other information on students to be utilized by the computer in analyzing answers and making decisions on next steps.

Programmed learning has already had an impact upon the classroom and it may have an even greater one in the future. As teachers do a better job of selecting behavioral objectives, and of determining the most effective means of reaching them, programmed instruction should find its proper place of supporting—not replacing—the teacher. Some of the more straightforward concepts, drill, and similar activities could well be relegated

---

[7] Paul I. Jacobs, Milton H. Maier, Laurence M. Stolurow, *A Guide to Evaluating Self-Instructional Programs* (New York: Holt, Rinehart, & Winston, Inc., 1966), p. 12. Used by permission of the publisher.

[8] C.A. Thomas, I.K. Davies, D. Openshaw, J.B. Bird, *Programmed Learning in Perspective* (Chicago: Educational Methods, Inc., 1964), pp. 15–22. Used by permission of the publisher.

to the teaching machine. The teacher could then use his time for those areas the teaching machine cannot handle, such as fostering creativity, encouraging critical thinking, or stimulating experimentation. The teaching machine cannot help the student to develop the ability to work with one's peers, or to present one's ideas, defend them, or to make value judgments. Excessive amounts of programmed learning eliminate the give and take values of class discussion—an important element in good education. Properly balanced programmed instruction should produce more efficient learning. Research is needed to verify this assumption and it is hoped this will soon be forthcoming. Programming has a definite contribution to make to learning. Its most effective use is yet to be determined.

ELECTRONIC LABORATORIES

Spurred by the foreign language-in-the-elementary school movement, the availability of NDEA funds, and the new aural-oral approach to teaching foreign languages at the secondary level, language laboratories became something of a status symbol several years ago.

It appears quite evident that language laboratories do not need to be highly elaborate to be effective. A number of schools have found they get good results with fairly simple electronic setups. Idle, inoperative equipment was an early nemesis for language labs.

Following the Keating Report [9] most schools took a careful look at their use of language labs and ultimately improved their effectiveness. The language laboratory as it was known in the late fifties is obsolete today. The more acceptable idea is an electronic laboratory which will be utilized by several subject matter areas. This facility may be used by the business department for shorthand classes where dictation tapes may be employed both in class groups and on an individual basis. Speech and drama classes can use it for listening to skilled performers and to improve their own presentations. English classes can use the lab for spelling drills. The obvious application to foreign languages and music appreciation courses needs no elaboration.

A school with a laboratory of this type finds many uses for it. Such laboratories will probably become part of most good secondary schools of the future.

OTHER MEDIA

Other mechanical aids to teaching are also enjoying increased popularity in today's classroom. Many teachers have now discovered the advantages of the overhead projector. As an adjunct to the lecture, it has all of the advantages of the chalkboard without its disadvantages, and it has flexibility not obtainable at the chalkboard. The

---

[9] Raymond F. Keating, *A Study of the Effectiveness of Language Laboratories* (New York: Institute of Administrative Research, Teachers College, Columbia University, 1963).

teacher has eye contact with his students continuously. By careful preparation beforehand he can make overlays which are colorful, interesting, and functional. By using them in series or with "flip strips" he can control the presentation of his material in a way which is difficult to duplicate in any other way.

It should be pointed out, of course, that a school making optimum use of the overhead will provide for the services of a full-time or part-time staff artist who can prepare projectuals for the teachers. The teacher can explain to the artist what he wishes to accomplish, and the artist, in relatively little time, can produce highly effective materials which aid the teacher's presentation. The overhead projector is now available in a highly portable lightweight form which significantly solves problems of sharing equipment.

The opaque projector is just coming into its own after gathering dust in the A-V closet for years. When used with imagination, this can be one of the greatest assets to the mediated classroom. Its handicap has been its size and the need for a darkened room. For sharing the work of other students, projecting illustrations from books, or other forms too small to be seen normally throughout a room, and for generally sharing opaque materials which cannot be used on the overhead, this is a valuable asset to the classroom.

EDUCATIONAL COMBINES

Any discussion of educational media today would be incomplete without mention of the latest entry on the educational scene, the newly formed combines (partnerships between textbook companies and manufacturers of the "hardware" of educational media). The impact they are likely to have on what takes place in the classroom may be understood most easily by simply looking at some of the members of these new partnerships. Among the more prominent are:

Random House and RCA
Creative Playthings and CBS
Science Research Associates and IBM
General Electric, Time, Inc., and Silver Burdett
Newsweek and Minnesota Mining and Manufacturing
Xerox, American Education Pubs., University Microfilms, and Basic Systems
Reader's Digest and Sylvania

These combinations represent some of the giants of industry and the leaders of the communications world. Indications are that billions of dollars will be expended in producing educational systems for the schools. The January 1967 issue of the *Phi Delta Kappan* contains one of the most comprehensive collections of articles relating to the many ramifications of this new member of the education colony. The entire issue is devoted to the topic "Big Business Discovers the Education Market." The February 1967 *NEA Journal* also considers this development in a special section. It contains articles on computer-assisted instruction, educational data processing, the school information center, computer-assisted counseling, the systems approach to education, and the relation of industry and education in the new technology.

The combines offer the possibility of providing complete packages of learning materials. These would utilize a variety of media and approaches. Such a package might include paperback books, 8mm film cartridges, 16mm film, filmstrips, tapes, records, programmed materials, transparencies for the overhead projector and even video tapes.

The opportunities which this event offers to schools are exciting to contemplate. The problems which it could provide are likewise foreboding. Educators must be involved in what the combines produce. One is reminded of that comic sign, "Are you helping with the solution or are you part of the problem?" The answer may well rest with the educators.

If educators, perhaps with the aid of the systems analyst, determine what types of hardware and software are needed to reach the goals that have been set for our schools, the outcome could be one of the finest things to happen to education in decades. If industry designs new gadgets to be sold to the schools who then must figure out ways to use them, we will need much larger storage spaces in our buildings to accommodate the unused hardware and software. The charge is a real one.

KEEPING THE MEDIA PICTURE IN FOCUS

All of the various types of hardware and software can be excellent adjuncts to learning when properly used for that purpose. Any experienced administrator is aware, however, that misuse of these devices is frequent, and non-use is just as prevalent. A few suggestions are, therefore, in order concerning the mediated school.

1. Teachers are more likely to utilize these materials when they are readily accessible and create a minimum of confusion.

2. A well-qualified media specialist on the staff (he may but does not need to, be a teacher), who works with teachers to facilitate the use of teaching materials and equipment, may well determine the success or failure of the program within a building.

3. A good, periodic, in-service program for the staff demonstrating ways to use teaching machines is a must.

4. Teachers should have assistance in selecting media and evaluating their merits.

5. The principal can demonstrate his support of and interest in these new aids to learning by using them in faculty meetings, parent meetings, and student assemblies.

THE BUDGET FOR INSTRUCTIONAL MATERIALS

Budgets for instruction should reflect actual needs. The people who are best qualified to determine these needs are the teachers who use the materials and the principal who directs their use. Therefore principals and teachers should be involved in planning the budget for learning materials. This budget will include funds needed for (*a*) textbooks, (b) library books and supplies, (c) audio-visual equipment, (d) teaching machines, (e) language laboratories, (f) supplies and workbooks, and (g) television equipment.

Teaching films can be rented from the nearby university or college or they can be purchased and added to the learning materials library. Films that are used only once or twice a year should probably be rented. In the interest of economy, those that are used five or more times each school year should probably be purchased. Films showing people become obsolete as soon as styles of clothing and hair-do change. Those representing basic scientific principles can be used until they wear out.

The cost of audio-visual equipment is high. For limited budgets overhead projectors, movie machines, and other hardware can be purchased on a carefully considered five-year plan until the inventory is complete. Enterprising teachers are often able to secure free and inexpensive materials from a number of sources. This may ease a tight budget or permit the purchase of an extra piece of equipment. Federal monies are available for assistance in securing many teaching aids, electronics laboratories, and science apparatus. The cost of textbooks and library references is increasing; budgets should reflect this.

Let it be said that educational television, the electronics laboratory, teaching machines or any other mechanical aid to learning cannot replace the teachers. A machine cannot counsel, assist, direct, or provide aid and comfort to students. Properly used, teaching machines free teachers from repetitive tasks and routine. This allows more time for teaching, counseling, motivating, and helping individuals.

A WORD OF CAUTION

The North Central Association Study [10] of innovation in the nation's high schools revealed that much innovation has taken place in recent years. They discovered, however, that a sizeable number of schools have instituted innovations only to abandon them. They concluded,

> Current innovation may be motivated as much or more by the "band wagon" phenomenon than by theories of instruction and learning.
> . . . The high abandonment rate for innovations such as new science and math curricula, television, programmed instruction, and team teaching indicates the need for careful planning before adoption and careful attention while in operation.

This is a warning which any experienced administrator has seen demonstrated repeatedly. The charge is to carefully prepare for them and then put these innovations to work to improve the learning process. Any other reason for innovation must therefore become of secondary importance. In the years ahead, media and the systems approach to learning offer opportunities to improve the learning process. Large sums of money may

---

[10] North Central Association, "Innovation Study of Nation's High Schools Reveals Important Changes in Recent Years," *North Central Today,* XI (March, 1967).

be spent by industry to see that the machine approach to learning will find widespread use in the schools. The principal must devote much thought and energy to assure that staffs are involved in their evaluation and use.

Educators are urged to consider the purchase of teaching hardware and software with considerable caution. Before making total commitment to programmed instruction board members and educators should give careful study to such questions as:

1. *Is the equipment designed around sound theories of learning?* Since all educators do not agree on how learning takes place, hardware and teaching machines that are appropriate in one school may not be acceptable at all in another.

2. *Can the salesman explain his product in terms that are psychologically sound?* In the next decade audio-visual products and communications equipment will be combined into systems which will be "packaged" for sale. Some experts see programmed instruction developing into a billion dollar market by 1980. Industrial giants in electronics, programmed instruction and publishing are developing a dazzling array of hardware. Beware of the ambitious salesman who may be seeking a fast buck in a highly competitive market. He may know more about techniques of selling than about techniques of teaching.

3. *Has the equipment been tested?* It is possible that competition will hasten the production of hardware that is untested. When this happens, the taxpayers' precious dollars are wasted and educators are criticized. The educator should be familiar with the research upon which the particular piece of hardware is based.

4. *Is the software (programmed subject matter) in ample supply?* Hardware is of no value unless the necessary software is available and of good quality.

5. *Can teachers be persuaded to use these new approaches to learning?* Some teachers are fearful that teaching machines will replace them. Unless teachers are reassured that this will not be the case, teaching machines are likely to collect dust in the storeroom. Some educators precede the introduction of new educational hardware with seminars and demonstrations on ways to use the new equipment.

Some securities analysts recommend education as one of the emerging industries. They predict that much of the learning in coming years will probably be done with the aid of some mechanical or electronic device. Clients are advised to invest now in companies that make innovative and creative teaching machines with their accompanying software. Educators, school board members and teachers need to be discerning lest they lose their educational footing and get carried away in the mad rush to surround every child with a host of mechanical gadgets to ease the pain of learning.

TEXTBOOKS

Of course, the most obvious of all teaching aids are the textbook and other printed materials. The recognition of the importance of providing materials with a wide range of reading abilities but with topics of interest to the early and young adolescent is one of the greatest advances of recent years. The recognition of the need to provide reading materials which are compatible with the reader's world is also important. This is a very recent need which is only beginning to be accommodated.

After all is said and done, reading is still the major method of learning in the schools. Therefore, the textbook remains the single most important teaching tool used by classroom teachers for instructional purposes. In many schools the textbook is also the curriculum guide.

METHOD OF SELECTION

Since textbooks are so important, their selection requires most careful consideration. Children in nearly half of the states must study out of state-adopted textbooks. There are both advantages and disadvantages to state-selected textbooks. Advocates of state adoption claim several benefits. First, state committees are better qualified to select textbooks than local groups. Therefore, better selections will be made, free from local pressure groups. Again, it is economical. Mass purchase of textbooks on a state-wide basis results in reduced textbook costs. Finally, because of uniformity, children who move about within the state are not frustrated by changing textbooks every time they go to a new community. Opponents of state control of textbook selection claim that the disadvantages far outweigh the benefits. (*a*) State adopted books may not keep abreast of current changes. As an example, in Illinois,[11] textbooks once adopted may not be changed for five years. Content is often out of date in less than five years. (*b*) Teachers want to assist with the selection of books that fit local needs. Some states encourage local participation by providing multiple lists from which local schools are permitted to choose. This practice is helpful especially for inexperienced teachers. (*c*) Politics sometimes are a powerful and unfair influence in state textbook selections.

In states where state-wide adoptions are not mandated, local textbook selection is the responsibility of local school boards. Wise boards delegate this activity to members of the professional staff under coordination of the superintendent. Effective selection of textbooks and related printed teaching materials requires the leadership of the principal. Desirable practices in textbook selection are listed herewith:

1. Written school policies are needed. They define such matters as length of adoption periods, the need for quality materials, and the amount, if any, to be charged for books and supplies.

2. Committees of teachers should be involved in the selection process. This requires time for meetings with salesmen, for study and for determining the adequacy of materials.

3. A system of textbook accounting is necessary. While free textbooks are provided for secondary school children in most states, this practice is not yet universal. Methods of

---

[11] "Textbooks adopted by any board under provisions of this article shall not be changed within five years and shall be used exclusively in all public high schools and elementary schools." . . . Sec. 28-6, Illinois School Code.

accounting and control procedures will reflect local practices. Where books and supplies are sold to students through the book store, transactions involve many thousands of dollars. Books are returned for credit against next year's texts or for cash at the end of the year. Book stores in many schools have become big business. Their administration demand the applications of good business procedures. Computers can be used to keep records of second-hand books for resale, and of credits to be applied on next year's purchases.

Accurate accounting in schools furnishing free textbooks requires adequate storage space, stamped and numbered texts in each subject, a textbook loan record with spaces for assessing fines for lost and badly damaged books.

4. The budget for textbooks should be realistic. It should reflect both the financial ability of the school district and also the ever increasing cost of printing instructional materials. A recent study of textbook costs recommends higher budgets for textbooks.[12]

> Data prepared by a private statistical agency showed that during the school year 1966–67, the average national per-pupil expenditure for books was $7.25 for grades 1 through 6, and $11.75 for grades 7 through 12.
>
> These allocations are inadequate today and will become increasingly so in the months ahead. School systems must reach for higher levels, so that the terms excellence and quality in education take on real meaning.
>
> The teaching imperatives of modern education suggest that a new pupil enrolling in a school district must be fully equipped with an adequate supply of materials if he is to pursue his education without undue impediments. It has been shown that if the new enrollee is in the elementary grades (1 through 6) it will take $42 to give him what he needs; if he is in the secondary school (grades 7 through 12) it will require $63.
>
> Similarly, to maintain these materials for their normal cycle of two to three years and to keep the student's resources up to adequate standards, it would require an annual figure of $14 for each elementary pupil (grades 1 through 6) and $21 for each secondary student (grades 7 through 12).

LIBRARY

The library has long been considered the center of the secondary school program. Whether the library is thought of in its more traditional form or in the more recent sense as a materials center, this fact still holds. The library should be an integral part of the teaching-learning activity. The use of the library should not be an artificial, separate activity apart from the work of the classroom; rather, the work in the library should be a natural outgrowth of what transpires in the classroom. The natural flow of work from the classroom into the library should make it difficult to determine the line separating the two activities.

---

[12] National Educational Association, "Guidelines for an Adequate Investment in Instructional Materials, 1967, the association, p. 23. Used by permission of the publisher, National Education Association, Washington, D.C.

Some schools have extended the concept of the library to include all resource materials. Various stages in between these two extremes may be found throughout the country. In some schools, such as Nova, in Florida, resource centers have been placed in several buildings. Study carrels, which include facilities for using both audio and video materials are available. The carrels also include typewriters. Students may dial either commercial or educational TV programs, or video taped classroom lectures. Also available are language tapes in Spanish, French, Latin, Russian, or German. The resource centers have such media as microfilm readers and teaching machines.

In some schools, study carrels provide access to enough resource material and media that students may spend a significant portion of their time there. This means a student may do substantial amounts of work without having to go to various places for different materials. A good resource for new ideas in library facilities is Ellsworth and Wagener, *The School Library* (New York: Educational Facilities Laboratories, 1965).

LOCATION

Since the library is the center of learning for the school, it should be located ideally near the geographic center of the building, where traffic converges. If it is to be open to the public evenings, week ends and during vacation periods, the facility should also be easily accessible from the outside. With strategically placed corridor gates and lavatory facilities this unit can be operated independently of the rest of the building. Future expansion may be required as the school enrollment grows. Therefore classroom areas adjoining the library should be convertible for use as part of an expanding library. In multi-story buildings the school library may be located on more than one floor level in such a manner that booklifts can be used for moving learning materials between floors. Circular stairs between floors save steps for busy library employees.

THE LIBRARIAN

The director of the learning materials center is given different titles in individual schools. For simplicity this person will be called the librarian in the following discussion and will be referred to as the modern librarian. The majority of librarians are females; however, men are becoming librarians in increasing numbers. She is something more than a classifier and protector of books, or a strict disciplinarian. The responsibilities of this position increase as new knowledge grows in scope, and as new ways of recording and disseminating information appear on the educational horizon.

In a well-organized secondary school the librarian discharges her duties in a variety of ways. She establishes a close relationship with members of the teaching staff. She is familiar with library materials including books, magazines, films, loops and records that supplement the work in the classroom. She notifies teachers of the arrival of new references. She prepares reading lists for use in classes. Many librarians work with

English teachers in organizing an orientation program for freshmen and others new to the system (including teachers). Classes of students become acquainted with the library organization. They learn how to locate materials quickly as they watch a film, and listen to explanations.

The librarian is a catalyst, getting pupils and books together. Books are of no value unless they are read. She works closely with the reading consultant in selecting materials that are geared to the reading ability of individual pupils. Some American history students, for example, require hero stories while others are able to study original documents. She provides loops, records or films for the student who missed a class.

The librarian makes her center an attractive and inviting place. The bulletin boards are neat and carry a stimulating message. Display cases are filled with jackets from the newest books. Exhibits show local paintings. Coin clubs and stamp clubs are promoted with displays and with hobby books.

With the increasing number of audio-visual materials on the market, the librarian must become knowledgeable about movie equipment, overhead projectors, films, loops, slide machines, microfilm, Xerox duplicators and now computer hardware.

The librarian works with the administration. Realistic library budgets require careful preparation and study. She secures budget lists based on actual need from teachers and from departments. The budget includes requests for books, magazines, newspapers, library supplies, and film rental. Funds must also be provided for purchase of hardware, for repair and maintenance of equipment and for furniture. Periodically she prepares reports showing the extent to which library goals are met.

THE LIBRARY STAFF

The very large and most medium-sized school libraries are well staffed, meeting the recommendations of the American Library Association and the North Central Association. The staff includes clerks, secretaries, para-professional, audio-visual technicians and several certified librarians.

However, the supply of certified librarians is limited. Many small schools are not able to get them. Reference materials are limited. Library space is confined to a few shelves in the rear of the study hall. There is little money for library materials.

In many states mobile units provide a minimum of library services to sparsely settled areas. Federal funds are sometimes available for the establishment of area libraries serving several small schools.

It may be possible to assign an English teacher for library duty one of two periods each day. Boards of education often pay the expenses of such a person to take summer courses or extension training in library science. Many fully qualified librarians started out as part time pioneers in library work. Another possible source of part-time librarians in small communities may be found in housewives who were once librarians and whose children are now sufficiently mature to permit mother to work two or three hours during the day. Full-time secretaries in cooperation with student employees have been known to operate an acceptable makeshift library organization during emergency periods.

If learning materials are to be carefully selected, properly organized and effectively used, the librarian is one of the V. I. P.'s in the school organization.

SELECTED READINGS

American Association of School Librarians, "Standards for School Library Programs." (Chicago: American Library Association, 1960)

Associated Public School Systems, "Eighteenth Annual Conference Report." (New York: Teachers College, Columbia University, 1966)

Austin, David B., and Gividen, Noble, *The High School Principal and Staff Develop the Master Schedule*. (New York: Bureau of Publications, Teachers College, Columbia University, 1960)

Brown, B. Frank, *The Non-Graded High School*. (Englewood Cliffs, N. J.: Prentice-Hall, Inc., 1963)

Bush, Robert N., and Allen, Dwight A., *A New Design for High School Education*. (New York: McGraw-Hill, 1964)

Chapman, Dave, and Carioti, Frank, "Planning for Schools with Television," revised 1968. Educational Facilities Laboratories, 477 Madison Avenue, N. Y.

Conant, James B., *The Comprehensive High School*. (New York: McGraw-Hill, 1967)

Cronin, "Innovations for Time to Teach," Department of Classroom Teachers, National Education Association, 1966.

Educational Policies Commission, "Mass Communication and Education," National Education Association. (Washington, D.C.: The Association, 1958)

Ellsworth, Ralph E., and Wagener, Hobart D., *The School Library,* Educational Facilities Laboratories, 477 Madison Avenue, 1966.

Garner, W. Lee, *Programmed Instruction*. (New York: The Center for Applied Research in Education, Inc., 1966)

Jacobs, Paul I., Maier, Milton H. and Stolurow, Laurence M., *A Guide to Evaluating Self-Instructional Programs*. (New York: Holt, Rinehart, and Winston, Inc., 1966)

Keating, Raymond F., *A Study of the Effectiveness of Language Laboratories*. (New York: Institute of Administrative Research, Teachers College, Columbia University, 1963)

Killian, James R. Jr., *Public Television: A Program for Action*. (New York: Bantam Books, Inc., 1967)

Lumsdaine, A. A. and Glaser, Robert, *Teaching Machines and Programmed Learning—A Source Book*. (Washington, D.C.: National Education Association, 1960)

McCleary, Lloyd, and Hencley, Stephen P., *Secondary School Administration*. (New York: Dodd, Mead, and Co., 1965)

National Education Association, "Guidelines for an Adequate Investment in Instructional Materials," Washington, D. C.: The Association, 1967.

National Council for Educational Television, "In-School Program Schedule." University of Nebraska, Lincoln, 1968–69.

New Trier Township ITV Council, Office of the Coordinator, "The First Year," *ITV Newsletter*. (Winnetka, Illinois: New Trier Township ITV Council, June, 1967)

North Central Association, "Innovation Study of Nation's High Schools Reveals Important Changes in Recent Years," *North Central Today,* XI (March, 1967).

Pellegrin, Joseph, Abstract, *Bloomington's Base Three Plan for Small High School Curriculum Development,* 1966.

Phi Delta Kappan (January, 1967), p. 204.

Suppes, Patrick, "The Computer and Excellence," *Saturday Review* (January 14, 1967).

Thomas, C. A., Davies, I. K., Openshaw, D., and Bird, J. B., *Programmed Learning in Perspective.* (Chicago: Educational Methods, Inc., 1964)

Trump, J. Lloyd and Baynham, Dorsey, *Guide to Better Schools.* (Chicago: Rand and McNally and Company, 1961)

TEN

Planning for Innovations in Educational Facilities

The need for a new secondary school building is usually correctly perceived by a community as a problem. However, this problem is accompanied by the opportunity for the community to reexamine and redefine its philosophy of education in order to construct a building which best meets the needs of its clientele.

While a school is composed of people, we often visualize a particular building when we think of a school. But a school is not just a building, as a house is not necessarily a home. However, the building houses the school and its activities, and can do much either to help or hinder the work of the school.

Psychologists long ago discovered that environment is a powerful influence upon learning, and the pupil is surrounded by the physical environment of the school for the length of the school day. If the environmental conditions are stimulating and satisfying, the energy of the pupil can be devoted to worthwhile learning experiences. If such conditions as the temperature, humidity, noise level, and the visual environment are improper, then the pupil may become frustrated, restless, and disturbed—and under these circumstances energy which could be devoted to useful purposes is expended in attempting to adapt to unfavorable surroundings.[1]

School buildings in the United States are ordinarily of quite durable construction, and consequently often serve for a half century or longer. But the educational programs which most communities desire are not static in nature, and the durable, inflexible buildings have often provided a barrier to the adoption of newer instructional tech-

---

[1] American Association of School Administrators, *Planning America's School Buildings* (Washington: The Association, 1960), p. 23.

Note: This chapter was prepared in part by William R. Wilkerson, Associate Professor of Education, Indiana State University.

niques. Unfortunately, the educational program is dictated by the nature of existing school facilities in far too many communities.

We cannot predict the future nature of the educational programs which must be accommodated by school buildings now in planning, but we can be certain that they will be unlike the programs of today. The primary challenge for school facility planners is to develop plants which are educationally functional today and can be easily adapted for new purposes in the future.

The school building which is capable of furthering the desired educational program is rarely the product of chance. Indeed, the excellent school building usually occurs as the result of careful planning by a team of educators, community participants, and outside consultants. A considerable amount of time and energy must be expended to develop appropriate plans for a school building. When one considers the probable length of time the building will be used, it would seem desirable that the facility not be the result of hasty decisions.

Ovard called attention to the necessity for building the new facility three times: (1) by the educators, in the form of educational specifications; (2) by the architects, in terms of architectural specifications and working drawings which are developed from the educational specifications; and (3) by the contractors, who develop the physical structure as the interpretation of the work of the architect.[2] The educational administrator, while interested in each of the three building processes described by Ovard, is much more intimately concerned with the development of the educational specifications.

McClurkin defines the educational specification as a communication device from school authorities to the design team of architects and engineers. Ideally, they should convey understanding without confusion, be free from educational jargon, and not prescribe solutions in such a manner as to unduly restrict the architect.[3] The educational specifications for a particular building should result from a comprehensive educational plan for the entire school district. Elements of the comprehensive educational plan include sub-plans for curriculum, operations, instruction, school organization, personnel, evaluation, in-service training, and supporting resources and services.[4]

THE PLANNING ROLES

The School Board. The lay board of education is the legally constituted governing body for the local school district, and has the responsibility for formulating policies and providing the human and material resources necessary for the implementation of its policies. The school board must make all final decisions with respect to the planning of school buildings, but the magnitude of the comprehensive planning process makes it

---

[2] Glen Ovard, *Administration of the Changing Secondary School* (New York: The Macmillan Company, 1966), p. 420.

[3] W.D. McClurkin, *School Building Planning* (New York: The Macmillan Company, 1964), p. 75.

[4] National Council on Schoolhouse Construction, *Guide for Planning School Plants,* The Council, 1964, p. 2.

necessary that the board rely upon many other individuals and groups to provide the necessary information upon which to base its decisions.

The School Superintendent. As the chief executive officer of the school board, the superintendent of schools is responsible for advising the board on policy and for execution of policies adopted by the board. Requests, reports, and recommendations concerning all educational matters, including school facilities, should flow through him to the board. Since his job imposes many varied demands, the skillful, prudent superintendent will delegate many of his plant planning responsibilities to his staff so that he can continue to function as the chief educational officer of the district.[5]

The School Professional Staff. The school staff members who will utilize the proposed new school facilities should be intimately concerned with the educational planning. School facilities are a basic instructional tool for the teachers, and will be an important determinant of the nature of the total educational program. Most faculty members today keep up to date with respect to instructional techniques and new knowledge in their teaching fields, and they are usually well informed about desirable physical facilities which are related to the new developments in instruction. Teachers can make valuable contributions to the planning of the new building, and they also can give new insights about the total educational program if their involvement is properly planned and coordinated.

The Principal. The principal, as the chief administrator of the individual school, can play an extremely important leadership role in the planning process. If the proposed new building is to replace an existing building, the principal can lead the existing staff in classification of the philosophy of the school and the determination of the nature of the educational program which must be accommodated by the new building.

When the new school will result in an additional secondary school for the system, many districts are finding it worthwhile to appoint a principal-elect early in the planning stages. Often key members of the instructional staff for the new school are selected from personnel already employed in the district, and the principal-elect and the prospective faculty members work together in the development of the educational plans.[6]

Pupils. Pupils have not often participated in the planning of school facilities, but it is likely that new insights pertaining to instructional programs and facilities could be obtained by their involvement. Pupils could participate in the evaluation of existing buildings and programs, and their suggestions for new buildings should be solicited.[7]

Non-Professional Personnel. Custodians, maintenance workers, cafeteria workers, and the secretarial staff can also contribute to school plant planning. These people are also closely acquainted with the daily aspects of their particular spheres of operation, and can often make worthwhile suggestions which can be incorporated in the plant.

Because the building should be designed and constructed as a tool for teaching and learning, care should be taken that the interests of the non-professional staff members be placed in the appropriate perspective. For example, maintenance and operation factors

---

[5] National Council on Schoolhouse Construction, p. 4.
[6] American Association of School Administrators, pp. 101–103.
[7] National Council on Schoolhouse Construction, p. 4.

are important considerations, but these factors should never receive priority over educational considerations.[8]

Lay Citizens. The ultimate control of all of the activities of the public schools resides in the citizenry, and this control is expressed primarily through elected representatives serving as school board members and as state legislators. Many students of public education believe that participation of lay citizens in problem-solving activities of the schools is a valuable vehicle for gaining public interest in and public support for the schools. Citizen participation has been demonstrated to be of value in fund-raising activities and in conducting studies of the schools.

Citizen involvement in the school plant planning process would seem desirable, if great care is taken to select participants who are broadly representative of the community, and if competent leadership is given throughout the planning process. Ordinarily, lay citizen involvement is obtained through formation of citizen advisory committees, or by appointments of lay citizens to serve on committees with school staff members. It must be made quite clear that all committees are advisory in nature, since the school board cannot delegate its ultimate responsibility. The scope of operations for each of the committees must be clearly delineated, and the necessary resources need to be provided so that the work of the committee may be fruitful.

The Architect. The range of services provided by the architect is often misunderstood. Strevell and Burke note that the services of the architect cannot be introduced too soon in the planning of school facilities. His services are not limited to drawings, specifications, and contract documents as many people assume. The architect, because of his previous experiences, can be of great assistance in program planning and site selection, which occur prior to the actual advancement of the building project.[9]

The Educational Consultant. Educators who are either school plant specialists or curriculum specialists may be employed by the architect or by the school board to assist the local district in its efforts to plan a school plant which will accommodate the desired educational program. The consultant may be on the staff of a university, from the state department of education, or in private business. While a consultant may have a considerable amount of specialized knowledge about school buildings, care should be taken to clarify his role so that he confines his efforts to educational, rather than architectural or engineering matters.[10]

ORGANIZING FOR PLANNING

The preceding description of roles for various participants in the planning process points logically to a committee structure for planning. It is possible for one person to do all of the planning for a particular building, and in many respects this is the easy

---

[8] American Association of School Administrators, *Schools for America* (Washington: The Association, 1967), pp. 161–162.

[9] W.H. Strevell and A.J. Burke, *Administration of the School Building Program* (New York: McGraw-Hill Book Company, Inc., 1959), p. 362.

[10] National Council on Schoolhouse Construction, p. 5.

course to follow. However, since no one person possesses all of the knowledge necessary to develop the best possible educational plans for a building, the cooperative study approach is frequently used.

If it is decided to involve the staff, pupils, and laymen in the planning activities, it is desirable to organize the participants into sub-committees which study the various aspects of the educational program. Coordination of and communication among the sub-committees is necessary in order that duplication of effort is avoided and to assure that omissions do not occur.

The co-ordinator might be a central office staff member, an educational consultant, or the principal or principal-elect. The coordinator should assume responsibility for providing background materials and resources for the sub-committee. He should keep all participants informed regarding major findings and recommendations emanating from the various sub-committees.

Strevell and Burke indicate that the following provisions are necessary if the cooperative study approach is to be of maximum benefit:

(1) Competent advice should be obtained when necessary,
(2) A schedule of jobs should be prepared and the tasks should be assigned to the person, group, or agency best able to complete them,
(3) A system of reporting progress in the various tasks should be devised,
(4) Each person involved should thoroughly understand his assignment,
(5) Participants should be encouraged to be objective, and to obtain all relevant facts before presenting solutions to problems.[11]

MAJOR CONSIDERATIONS IN PLANNING

Existing Program. The first step in planning the new facility is a thorough study of the present educational program. Analyses should be made to determine the philosophy and purposes of the school and the nature of the instructional program as it exists in terms of its effectiveness in meeting the needs of the pupils and the community. Particular care should be devoted to ascertaining the extent to which the present facilities have shaped the existing program.

The Desired Program. The next step is to project the desirable educational program of the future. Due consideration should be given to anticipated societal demands upon education, promising practices used in other schools, and discernible trends in curriculum content and methods of instruction. Since the proposed building will likely serve far into the future, it is essential that the planners look beyond the horizon in order to obtain a facility that can serve the needs of today and yet readily accommodate the progress of tomorrow.

Proposed Enrollment. The projection of the number of pupils to be accommodated by the new plant is basic to the determination of space needs. The projected enrollment and the projected curriculum together are used to ascertain quantitative aspects

---

[11] W.H. Strevell and A.J. Burke, p. 96.

of the facility, such as the desired size of the site, the number of instructional spaces, and space requirements for non-instructional activities.

The Site. The school site is not just a building location. It is part of the total education plant, and it should be selected and developed in view of the functions which it must accommodate. Sufficient area must be provided for the building structure, outdoor physical education activities, outdoor education, and driveways and parking areas. When possible, it is desirable that the selection and utilization of school sites be planned jointly with other community agencies so that optimum utilization can be attained.

Among the factors to be considered in the selection of a site are its size, shape, accessibility, availability of utilities, topography, general environment and beauty, and the costs of acquisition and development. If possible, the ultimate site size should be obtained at the outset as it is usually very expensive to expand the site after the school building is constructed. The National Council on Schoolhouse Construction recommends a minimum site size of 20 acres plus an additional acre for each 100 pupils for junior high schools and 30 acres plus an additional acre for each 100 pupils for senior high schools. It is recognized that the desired minimums cannot always be attained, particularly in cities, but all districts should strive to achieve them and most should exceed them.[12]

Teaching Stations. The number and type of general and special purpose instructional spaces needed can be calculated from analysis of the proposed enrollments and the projected educational program. Consideration must be given to the required and elective subjects to be offered, the average class size in each, which specific instructional spaces may be utilized for various subject areas, the length of the school day, and the number of periods each class will meet each week.

One formula to compute the number of teaching stations for a given subject is given in Figure 10-1.[13]

$$\text{Number of teaching stations} = \frac{\text{Anticipated enrollment in subject} \times \text{Number of periods per week in subject}}{\text{Desired average class size} \times \text{Number of periods per week teaching station can be used}}$$

FIGURE 10-1

To illustrate the use of the formula, assume that the anticipated maximum enrollment in freshman English will be 300, the desired average class size is 25, the class will meet 5 days per week, and the room will be available for use 6 periods per day for 5 days per week. The calculation would be as shown in Figure 10-2.

The formula can be used for each proposed class offering and the total number of teaching stations can thus be determined. It should be kept in mind that it is unlikely that each teaching station will be scheduled for use during each period of the week, and

---

[12] National Council on Schoolhouse Construction, p. 27.
[13] J.H. Herrick et al., *From School Program to School Plant* (New York: Henry Holt and Co., 1956), p. 115.

$$\frac{300 \text{ (pupils enrolled)} \times 5 \text{ (periods per week class will meet)}}{25 \text{ (average class size)} \times 30 \text{ (periods per week room will be available)}} = 2 \text{ teaching stations}$$

FIGURE 10-2

allowances will need to be made for this factor. Some margin will likely exist since the formula will not always yield a whole number of teaching stations. For example, if the calculation for biology yields 1.7 classrooms, then 2 biology rooms will be required.

Gross measures of needed instructional spaces can be obtained by dividing the anticipated total number of pupils by the projected average class size adjusted by a factor to provide for less than 100 percent room utilization. For example, 1500 students ÷ 25 (average class size) ÷ .80 (percent of utilization) = 75 teaching stations. This method of estimating should only be used as a check on the results of the application of the formula to each prospective class offering, as it fails to consider the variety of teaching stations necessary.

 a. General Purpose Instructional Spaces. Classrooms which are used for English, mathematics, social studies, speech, etc., are often termed interchangeable teaching stations. In schools built prior to the last decade, these classrooms were typically designed for the lecture method of instruction and would accommodate from 25 to 40 pupils. Newer methods and media for instruction require variations in the size of instructional spaces for these subjects. Large group lecture and demonstration areas, spaces for small group discussions, and provisions for individual study areas are incorporated in many of the newer educational facilities.

 b. Special Purpose Instructional Spaces.

  1. *Science facilities.* Modern science programs are characterized by increased involvement of the pupils as active agents in the instructional process. A large amount of space is required in order that first-hand experiences can be gained by the pupils, long-term experiments can be conducted, and materials and equipment can be adequately prepared and stored by the instructor.[14]

  2. *Industrial Arts and Vocational Shop Laboratories.* Instructional shop facilities vary considerably from school to school, dependent upon whether industrial arts, vocational trades and industry training, or vocational agriculture are included in the curriculum. The needs of the community and the pupils, the availability of area vocational schools or community colleges, and the local school policies regarding adult education help determine the amount and nature of space which needs to be devoted to these purposes. Among the

---

[14] National Council on Schoolhouse Construction, p. 52.

laboratories which might be included are woods, metals, electricity, plastics, power mechanics, drafting, printing, agriculture, etc. Special planning consideration needs to be given to safety factors, the noise generated by shop activities, storage of equipment and materials, and accessibility to service drives.

3. *Physical education.* Planning for a total program of physical education means that outdoor spaces as well as gymnasiums need to be considered. Functional instructional areas, rather than spectator-oriented areas, should result from the planning. This does not mean that the interscholastic athletic program is not of value, but it should be kept in balance with the total program. In view of the carryover value of swimming, strong consideration should be given to inclusion of a swimming pool in the facility.

4. *Music.* The amount and nature of the space devoted to music education will depend upon the size of the school and the breadth and depth of the music program. The policy of the school toward individual and group lessons taught during school hours will help determine whether special rooms will be needed so that noises will not disturb other classes. Some of the large group music activities may be accommodated in gymnasiums and auditorium, and proximity to these areas may be desirable. Music education classes may be taught in general purpose classrooms, if proper acoustical treatment is provided.

5. *Arts and crafts.* Arts and crafts rooms in secondary schools should accommodate a variety of learning activities. Desirable equipment includes kilns, electric saws, grinders, buffers, sinks, etc. Because of the relationship of art education to homemaking and industrial arts, it is desirable that the art facilities be located in proximity to the shops and the homemaking laboratories.

6. *Business education.* Vocational training and general education progress will need to be housed in the business education quarters. Large group, small group, and individual practice areas are desirable. Adult education use of business facilities is common, and the area should therefore be easily accessible to the community.

7. *Homemaking Laboratories.* Different kinds of learning centers should be considered in planning home economics facilities. Among them are instructional areas for child development, housing and home furnishings, foods and nutrition, clothing and textiles, family health, and a large group area. Multiple grouping of the centers is possible, and the exact space arrangement should be determined according to local needs. Accessibility for community use and ease in delivery of supplies are important considerations in planning.[15]

8. *Exceptional Children Facilities.* Physically handicapped, mentally retarded, and emotionally disturbed children today are educated along with normal children in the regular school setting. This fact has important implications for facility planners, since the instructional program for these pupils will often dictate that special rooms and equipment be provided.

---

[15] National Council on Schoolhouse Construction, p. 40.

Auxiliary Areas. In addition to the general and special classrooms, decisions will need to be made about the amount and nature of space for other areas which are essential or desirable to include in the new plant. Again, the amount of space allocated and the arrangement of the space need to be based upon the functions to be performed.

1. *The Instructional Materials Center.* The development of new media and the movement toward independent study activities have created an expanded role for the school library. Provisions for storage of audio-visual materials, work areas for media specialists, processing rooms, teacher preparation rooms, student carrels, seminar rooms, and listening and viewing areas are desirable. Previous reading room standards of 25 square feet per reader for 10 percent of the school enrollment have been found to be inadequate, as have the standards for the number of volumes, periodicals, and reference works. The emerging concept of the role of the instructional materials center requires that careful attention be devoted to the space arrangements for this area.[16]

2. *The Auditorium.* The nature of the auditorium facilities will depend upon the educational program, the enrollment, possible community use, and the availability of auditorium facilities in the community. In view of the high cost, it is advisable to plan for a high degree of utilization in order to justify the existence of the auditorium. This can be accomplished by utilization for large group instructional purposes, for music, dramatics, instruction, and for community purposes. It is usually recommended that an auditorium should seat a minimum of one-fourth of the ultimate pupil enrollment to a maximum of 500 to 800 seats. Several school buildings with provisions for dividing the auditorium into three or four small areas have been constructed recently. Proper location of the auditorium with respect to accessibility to music, speech, art, and shop rooms is desirable.[17]

3. *Dining and Food Preparation Facilities.* The size and nature of the food service facilities are determined by the projected number of pupils who will use the facilities, the types of lunches to be served, the anticipated school schedule, the school system policy with respect to central food preparation, and other considerations. Only after thorough study of the anticipated functions of the food service area can adequate facilities be planned.

4. *Administrative, Guidance, and Health Service Areas.* The administrative area should be easily accessible to the public, the staff, and the pupils. Adequate space needs to be provided for offices, work areas, conference rooms, storage and waiting areas; and care should be taken to arrange for logical inter-relationships of the various areas.

The guidance program must be clearly defined in order to provide facilities to house it. Many secondary schools locate the guidance areas separate from the general office areas, dependent upon the local philosophy toward the guidance function.

Details of the health service facilities are also largely determined by local policies and practices. Facilities should include a waiting room, examination rooms, isolation areas, and toilets.

---

[16] R.E. Ellsworth and H.D. Wagener, *The School Library* (New York: Educational Facilities Laboratory, Inc., 1963), 143 pp.

[17] National Council on Schoolhouse Construction, p. 64.

5. *Pupil Activity Areas.* Proper facilities should be provided for student activities such as clubs, student government, and social affairs. Many schools incorporate a commons area where students naturally congregate when time and opportunity permit. Many of the pupil activity areas can be planned as multi-use spaces.

6. *Teaching Staff Facilities.* Preparation rooms, relaxation areas, and conference rooms for the use of the professional staff need to be planned. Many secondary schools are providing offices for faculty members, since fully utilized classrooms mean that the classroom cannot serve as the teacher's home base for the entire day.

Space Relationships. It is important to secure the proper allocation of spaces for the various facilities which are included in the school plant, and it is equally important to plan for logical inter-relationships of the facilities. The relationships are determined by the nature of the educational program, and activities which serve related functions should be grouped together when possible.

COMMUNICATING EDUCATIONAL NEEDS TO THE ARCHITECT

After the various study committees have evaluated the proposed program and the total facility needs, one person or a small committee should assume the responsibility for compiling, analyzing, and synthesizing the reports. At this stage of the planning process, the priorities are established. This means that some of the requests from the various sub-committees will need to be denied and some combination of spaces into multiple purpose areas will need to be considered. Such changes should be explained thoroughly to those who developed the requests and, if possible, agreed upon by them.

The board of education must approve the final program of requirements for the new plant. After this approval has been gained, the requirements of the educational program are translated into written educational specifications which serve as a guide for the architect and engineers who will design the structure.

The educational specifications should relate to the architect what is required of the building; but they should not prescribe rigid solutions to the problems. The specifications should include background information such as the philosophy of the school, the nature of the community, the organization of the school, and the teaching methods to be employed. For each type of required facility, the following information should be provided:

(1) The number of rooms required
(2) The desired pupil capacity of each room
(3) The activities to be carried on in the facility
(4) The methods of teaching to be used
(5) The location of the area and desirable relationship to other areas
(6) The type and amount of fixed and moveable equipment needed
(7) Requirements for display and storage areas
(8) Special mechanical and electrical considerations

The educational specifications should be written in clear, concise terminology so that misunderstandings will not occur. Questions will undoubtedly arise, however, and these will need to be answered by conferences with the architect. As the architect progresses, all drawings and specifications should be checked to ascertain that they are in harmony with the educational plans.

SOURCES OF INFORMATION FOR PLANNERS

A wealth of information for school building planners is available. The National Council on Schoolhouse Construction, an organization composed of educators and architects, publishes the *Guide for Planning School Plants* and *Secondary School Plant Planning*. The American Association of School Administrators published volumes in the plant planning field in 1949, 1960, and 1967. State departments of education are also sources of planning information, as is the Education Facilities Laboratory.

Information relative to the planning of specific instructional or auxiliary areas can be obtained from the various professional organizations such as the American Library Association, the National Science Teachers Association, etc. Periodicals such as *Nation's Schools, American School Board Journal,* and *School Management* are additional sources.

INNOVATIONS IN PLANT AND EQUIPMENT

The American secondary school probably has been the subject of intensive professional scrutiny for nearly a century. Remarkable gains are evident. Only a careful problem census followed by specific action can effect substantial improvement without giving up some accumulated long-term gains. A partial listing of the pressing secondary school problems of today follows.

1. Transmitting a rapidly growing body of knowledge.
2. Keeping ahead of the expanding enrollments.
3. Modifying programs and facilities to accommodate new methods and techniques.
4. Recruiting, developing and retaining high quality teachers.
5. Operating within a restrictive budget.

Better plants and facilities for our secondary schools can perhaps contribute to solutions for these problems. If they do so with style, good taste and real economy, education is well rewarded.

Environment for Learning,[18] a research report of a study which compared a school of ten years ago with what is possible today, indicated certain design features and principles which promise to enhance better secondary schools:

---

[18] *Environment for Learning* (Syracuse, N.Y.: The Carrier Corporation, 1960), pp. 6–7.

1. Sound is bridled better than ever before.
2. Light, temperature, humidity, ventilation, air purity and circulation are consistently controlled at optimum levels.
3. Spacious main corridors for multiple use are provided.
4. Provision is made for maximum supervision of traffic control in the building.
5. Areas are zoned to control sound and facilitate school-community use.
6. Flexibility of size and shape is provided in most teaching situations.
7. Provision is made for use of mechanized teaching aids.
8. Travel distances within the building are minimized.
9. It is possible to expand without acquiring additional land.

Among the more recent educational ideas which may affect secondary school plants of the future are:

Educational Parks: A single complex serving an entire city or district. Sarasota and Fort Lauderdale, Florida, have the plan in partial operation and East Orange, New Jersey, and Pittsburgh are committed to it.

Great or Super High Schools: Pittsburgh is well along in its planning.

The Ecumenical Approach: In Franklin County, Vermont, four small towns and a Catholic parish are planning a single joint junior-senior high school.

Increasingly education is viewed as a creative, thoughtful method of learning. Therefore, it is a fluid activity. According to Architect John Lyon Reid, "A fluid might be said to take the shape of its container. If that is true, I think we might also say that the container should change its shape when required." Buildings open to change are opening the eyes of teachers everywhere. School plant design is a "total concept," in which shape is determined by purposes and functions.

Flexible design to acknowledge the fluidity principle affords learners the maximum opportunity to learn to develop in accordance with their individual needs and potential, encourages each child to find his own path to learning, enables teachers to pool their talents and permits greater interaction between teacher and pupil.

SUGGESTIONS TO GUIDE INNOVATIONS IN BUILDING DESIGN

Innovation or adaptation in school building design may proceed with order and purpose resulting in a more functional climate for learning or it may proceed without regard for anything other than dramatic uniqueness.

The following suggestions may serve as guidelines for innovation which will support a purposeful secondary school educational program:

1. Humanize the school buildings in scale and decoration.
2. Decentralize the school building(s) and the administration.
3. Make the school an inviting learning location rather than an imposing monument.

4. Use integral design rather than applied decoration.
5. Incorporate unique shapes if they are functional.
6. Plan the program first with the building design flowing from the program.
7. Use simplicity in detail to enhance the quality of the structure.
8. Isolate noisy areas from quiet areas and from the auditorium. (Areas requiring special notice include shops, music rooms, music practice rooms, listening rooms, language laboratories, and gymnasiums.)
9. Plan the building(s) as an organic whole from the inside out.
10. Plan flexible buildings which can be adapted for a variety of teaching methods and techniques.
11. Plan buildings cognizant of the fact that there will be a continuing explosion of knowledge in subject matter disciplines, in knowledge about how pupils learn, in technological developments, and in knowledge of improved materials for school building construction.
12. Give consideration to the pupil's physical and emotional response to his environment—the tactile environment, and the scale of buildings and furnishings, and the degree of openness or enclosure.

INNOVATIONS AND ADAPTABLE IDEAS IN USE

The square box of previous years has changed into packages of many different shapes.

> One-story schools have fingers of classrooms reaching out for sun and air. Hexagonal, pentagonal, and round clusters of school rooms break up the forbidding massiveness of yesterday's schoolhouse and invite the pupil to enjoy education. Loft plan schools with movable interiors admit our inability to predict the future of education and allow for tomorrow's change. Campus schools with a number of buildings isolating functions within the school are breaking down the big school into units of manageable size so that the identity of the pupil isn't erased in the institution operated, theoretically at least, to develop him as an individual.[19]

As function decrees an innovative change, the development of new building materials and procedures makes the use of new designs possible. Thin shell reinforced concrete is being used for hyperbolic paraboloids. Mass produced elements are used in geodesic dome construction for auditoriums and physical education facilities. Laminated wood arches are being used for auditoriums, field houses, or other large open areas to be spanned by one roof.

The United States may need to adopt more extensively the use of a standard module which can be prefabricated as a cost-saving procedure without sacrificing local autonomy in planning the utilization of these modules in educational structures. The American In-

---

[19] *The Cost of a Schoolhouse* (New York: Educational Facilities Laboratories, Inc., 1960), p. 33.

stitute of Architects and several other important professional and industrial groups have urged the adoption of modular construction. The writers for Educational Facilities Laboratories feel that this procedure will be in use "when school boards demand it, architects urge it, contractors become familiar with it, and manufacturers of components are willing to retool to produce it."[20]

The School Construction Systems Development (S.C.S.D.) project sponsored by Educational Facilities Laboratories has resulted in the development of four components—the structural system, ceiling-lighting system, air-conditioning system, and movable and operable partitions. These components provide for flexibility and for speed in construction. The Barrington, Illinois, Middle School utilized all the S.C.S.D. components except cabinets.

Plastic roof bubbles and the connection of a series of plastic hyperbolic paraboloids are appearing in roof construction. These plastic materials have the advantages of being light and strong. The roofs constructed almost entirely of the plastic also have the advantage of being erected quickly. However, the plastic bubbles for light filtration have not proved to be too successful, primarily because of the difficulty of preventing leaks around the points of installation.

The case for educational parks or plazas seems to be gaining momentum. The arrangement shows promise as a means of combating *de facto* segregation and of revitalizing community interest in the total educational system. Advantages are apparent in the educational value received for the investment made. The plant arrangement is made up of schools-within-a-school with some of the most expensive facilities shared by the various levels—libraries, music rooms, language laboratories, remedial centers, science laboratories, and athletic fields. Research has not yet proved that travel to such a complex will actually be a detriment to pupils. By having small home schools within the complex, the humanizing principle needed for junior high school pupils can still be achieved. The school system in East Orange, New Jersey, has an educational plaza under construction and anticipates the completion of the plaza within 15 years.[21]

In recent years a new concept of educational organization has been expressed through the creation of "middle schools." Middle school refers to the middle organizational unit in the usual 12 or 14 grade program which provides an appropriate learning environment to support the natural educational development of 10–14 year old youth. The crux of the middle school concept is an emphasis on the individual learner. A new middle school in Saginaw Township, Michigan,[22] incorporates a plan based on the concept of gradual transition from elementary school to high school. This middle school begins with the fifth grade in classrooms with the open ends facing each other. The pupils are given visual separation by a raised platform with a dividing partition over a utility core. To make an increasing change from this virtually self-contained type facility for the fifth grade pupils to a more open plan for the sixth grade pupils, the

---

[20] *The Cost of a Schoolhouse*, p. 17.
[21] "The Education Plaza— Death Knell for the Neighborhood School?" *School Management*, X (October, 1966), pp. 102–105.
[22] *Profiles of Significant Schools: Two Middle Schools, Saginaw Township, Michigan* (New York: Educational Facilities Laboratories, Inc., September, 1960).

building designers omitted the dividing partition and placed the permanent utility equipment, such as the sink, near the ends of the open area. The central raised portion serves as a stage and for group activities. The absence of any permanent partition encourages team teaching. The same basic structure is used for the seventh and eighth grades except that two facing classrooms are considered as one open area with study carrels and seminar space provided in the center section. Specialized facilities for exploration and independent study in science, art, mathematics, crafts, and home economics are provided also.

Flexibility is needed in junior and senior high school buildings in order to keep pace with changes in teaching methods and with booming school populations. Flexibility can be achieved within new building shapes or within traditional squares or rectangles. The round school with an open plan probably is the most flexible. This becomes a hub and spoke scheme with the instructional materials center serving both teachers and pupils as the hub. The spoke areas are easily adapted to self-contained classroom activities, to team teaching activities, or to non-graded teaching. The round building has disadvantages in that it has a more expensive exterior wall to be constructed and that it seems to be a shape more difficult to blend into the surroundings.

Movable walls or panels within the exterior walls—whether new in shape or more traditional—permit remaking a building quickly. Educational Facilities Laboratories have explored, in a laboratory setting, a neoprene sealed, woven wall of fabric and lead which has tested well for speech privacy.[23]

Walls held up by air are being used successfully in Lamphere Public School District in Madison Heights, Michigan.[24] The air walls are lightweight wood panels which fit tightly together and are held in place by an inflatable rubber rim running between the ceiling and the top of the panel. When the air is released from the rim, the wall can be moved quickly.

A design element appearing consistently in new junior high facilities is area zoning. This may be achieved by building wings, such as the classroom wing, the connecting wing, and the special class wing. In a junior high school in St. Paul, Minnesota, the special class wing includes those facilities to which the public needs frequent access—the auditorium, the gymnasium, and the administrative offices. In addition, shop rooms, home economics rooms, art rooms and the music suite are included. The connecting wing includes the commons-cafeteria, kitchen, library, and speech classrooms. The commons-cafeteria serves as a dining area with one smaller section serving as a corridor and social meeting place.

The space outside the walls of a junior high school building is economical. For schools built in appropriate climates much noise and congestion has been saved by grouping pupil lockers in a covered, centrally located, outdoor mall.[25] For less inclement sections of the country, the same advantages of sound and space utilization have been achieved by grouping lockers in a central glass-walled locker commons that connects

---

[23] *The Cost of a Schoolhouse*, p. 79.
[24] *Profiles of Significant Schools: Schools for Team Teaching* (New York: Educational Facilities Laboratories, Inc., February, 1961).
[25] "The Nation's School of the Month," *The Nation's Schools,* LXXVII (June, 1966), pp. 75–77.

the basic buildings of a campus plan, giving pupils protection from adverse weather conditions.[26]

Lockers have been a problem in many schools. Most administrators still seem to favor the location of lockers in corridors. However, an educator from New York adds an additional suggestion for the organization of a central locker arrangement. If the lockers are grouped as spokes in a wheel, a custodian can supervise all locker corridors from a station at the hub.

Increasing efforts are made to utilize outdoor space for instructional purposes for junior high pupils. These early adolescents need opportunities and space in which to develop and practice social skills. Many older two- or three-story structures, perhaps hand-me-downs to the junior high schools, have unused center courtyards. Inaccessibility becomes a problem for effective pupil use of the space. Boulder, Colorado, solved this problem by creating "balconades" in the courtyard to provide practical and attractive routing to this area. During the seasons of the year or in sections of the country in which the weather will permit, courtyards are used for pep rallies, outdoor theatrical productions, choral programs, and other student activities. The central courtyard can become a living science area.[27] Enclosing it with a glass roof and supplying sufficient heat to protect plants and birds and to keep water from freezing will be necessary. An elementary school in Utah is utilizing the space for experiments with tropical plant life and pond life by providing heat with infra-red heaters.[28] If the art facilities open onto the courtyard, this space can be utilized for outside classwork.

One of the ways in which costs of school construction may be lowered is through the dual use of space and facilities. Two relatively expensive areas to include in any school—whether junior or senior high—are the auditorium and the gymnasium. Seldom are activities involving the public planned for the same time in both facilities. In the high school in Waterville, Maine, this factor has been considered in building the back of the auditorium adjacent to the side of the gymnasium. A single balcony containing reversible bleachers serves both areas. The bleachers come in 16-foot sections under which dollies with pack attachments are inserted and used to swivel the seats around a full 180 degrees. A back-up wall for the seats and partial soundproofing are provided by movable walls hung on an oval track. These same bleachers can be folded to clear an additional space for physical education activities.

Exploratory experiences in dramatics and speech are important in the junior high program. A theater-in-the-round which can be divided by electrically operated folding doors into two, three, or four sections permits extensive and varied use of the one facility.[29]

In the Griffith Junior-Senior High School, Griffith, Indiana, the old senior high

---

[26] "The Nation's School of the Month," *The Nation's Schools,* LXXVII (August, 1966), pp. 49–52.

[27] William W. Caudill, "Fourteen Ways School Design Has Responded to Modern Education," *The Nation's Schools,* LXXI (January, 1963), p. 55.

[28] "School Design Must Keep Pace with Educational Innovation," *Architectural Record,* CXLI (March, 1967), p. 169.

[29] "New School Has Three Kinds of Flexible Space," *Architectural Record,* CXL (September, 1966), pp. 225–226.

school building was renovated for the junior high school and was joined to a newly constructed senior high building with shared physical education facilities, food service facilities, music rooms, and an auditorium. The auditorium provides a good example of multiple use of space. By closing folding panel doors, the auditorium can be divided into three large group teaching areas. One of the smaller rooms at the rear of the auditorium is equipped with all the connections for a portable science demonstration unit—gas, water, electricity, and drainage. The backs of the folding door sections are permanent chalkboards and bulletin boards so that the tiered instructional area is complete. Screen facilities are also available for the use of projection equipment. This same triad arrangement, without the elevation, is utilized in planning junior high facilities for traditional classrooms.

One procedure to save congestion and to utilize space more efficiently in the library is to provide a window opening into a corridor so that pupils may return books without entering the room. Other schools are experimenting with locating the checkout station for instructional materials in the corridor outside the library in order to leave the librarian free for more educational services than the clerical tasks of handling the mechanics of circulating materials.

Success is being achieved by permitting study carrels to move into all parts of the school halls, foyers, student meeting spaces, classroom corners, and study halls. With the use of either an intercommunication system to the attendant at the central resource center or the use of a random-access electronic system operated by the pupil in the carrel, materials for study can be secured easily. The writers feel some concern as to the kind of study supervision which can be provided with this physical plant arrangement.

With the increasing trend toward summer sessions and with the possibility of twelve-month programs, air conditioning becomes an important feature to be incorporated into the building designs. The increasing use of air conditioning has been a factor in two design innovations—the windowless school above the ground and the underground school. The underground elementary school in Artesia, New Mexico,[30] has proved to be sufficiently successful that plans are underway for the construction of an underground junior high school. The design was planned to cope with the exigencies of dust storms, high temperatures, and the potential danger from atomic attack. The facility has complete air conditioning and light control. In addition to cleanliness and a controlled teaching climate, the advantages include lower maintenance costs. Construction costs were slightly higher; however, the structure does double as a fall-out shelter. Also electrical operating costs are slightly higher because air conditioning is necessary in the underground classrooms whenever the temperature rises above 56 degrees outside because of the heat generated by the physical bodies in the enclosed space.

The same city has an above ground windowless school. This structure affords advantages of cleanliness and lower air conditioning costs than either the underground school or a fully fenestrated school. However, it does not double as an atomic shelter.

---

[30] "The Nation's School of the Month," *The Nation's Schools,* LXXVII (June, 1966), pp. 75–77.

Both structures permit all four walls to become teaching space. Research has not yet been completed on the emotional effects of underground schools and windowless schools on children and on teachers.

The need to control window space is a necessity in order to keep the costs of air conditioning reasonable. Other design features are being tried to offer some control without submitting children to completely windowless schools. These include narrowing the windows, placing the narrow ends of rooms on the exterior room side, and utilizing changes in the overhang of roofs.

The writers propose an innovation borrowed from speech therapists. The use of mirrors has given good results in helping pupils to correct tongue and mouth placement in therapy sessions. Perhaps small mirrored practice areas could provide the same kind of assistance in skill development in physical education activities at the junior high level. Dancing is a good example of the kind of activity for which such an area would be helpful. The need to accept their own physical development and to develop physical coordination and control is recognized as characteristic of early adolescents. For those deficient in such skills, embarrassment tends to be a problem. Individual and small group practice areas seem to have merit in this field just as much as in academic areas.

RATIONALE FOR INNOVATIONS IN SCHOOL BUILDING DESIGN FOR EARLY ADOLESCENTS.[31]

Educators seem to have reached a consensus that a gradual transition from elementary school to senior high school produces less tension for pupils than does an abrupt change. Applying this generalization to the planning of junior high school buildings results in the conclusion that for the first year in the junior high school, the building should be so designed that these young adolescents have a home base for a daily block of time with one teacher who can know each child and his family personally and who will assume a major role in guidance for this child. Specialized facilities will be needed for a part of the day; and, in keeping with the concept of a gradual transition, these specialized facilities will assume increasing importance as the adolescent moves upward through the junior high school years.

Among the techniques of teaching and patterns of administrative organization which are being used to assist in articulation in curriculum from elementary school to junior high school and which affect building design are team teaching, flexible scheduling, and independent study. If these innovations are to result in optimum benefit to pupils, they need to be accompanied by changes in building designs and facilities.

The middle school concept is receiving much discussion in educational circles; however, educators do not agree on the years to be included in the middle school. Many recommend beginning at the sixth grade level; some recommend beginning at the fifth grade; and a few suggest beginning with the seventh grade. If the fifth and sixth grades

---

[31] City school systems in Denver, Colorado, and Kenosha, Wisconsin, have compiled complete educational specifications for junior high schools.

are to be included in the school organizational unit, more emphasis may be placed on the provisions for home base facilities. The need experienced by early adolescents for individual pupil identification is resulting in increasing emphasis on the school-within-a-school concept. This is one means of achieving a human scale in educational building programs.

Ability has long been a term of concept applied to children by educators. Abilities have been categorized as academic or mental abilities, physical abilities, and social abilities or social skills. School buildings, too, need a variety of abilities, meaning capacities to do certain things. School buildings for learners now and in the future need three abilities—flexibility, convertibility, and expandability. The ideas compiled in this chapter represent a number of ways in which these three abilities can be strengthened in existing buildings and provided in new constructions.

NEW IDEAS IN EQUIPMENT AND OTHER FACILITIES

Perhaps the teacher of the early 1970's can do a more effective teaching job than the teacher of any other decade. A wider variety of helpful tools is now available. Education brought this about.

The progressive teacher must be willing to examine what is new. Education implies growth; growth implies change. So, the forward-looking teacher must give the new and sometimes formidable-appearing equipment a fair trial.

Purchasing equipment for a secondary school is a highly complex, many faceted project. Therefore, it should be a cooperative project. Administrators, principals, and staff should plan together. They must concern themselves with the needs of the type of curriculum, the students, the teachers and the immediate community. All should harmonize. Concerned personnel should strive to bear in mind the unique personality of each student, providing for his individual needs as much as possible.

EQUIPMENT FOR LABORATORY INSTRUCTION IN DRIVER EDUCATION

In addition to basic equipment necessary for conducting a quality driver-education program, certain equipment items of a special nature are highly desirable. Among these are the simulator which simulates the auto's interior (Aetna Drivotrainer and Allstate Good Driver Trainer), the Drivometer for training and evaluating driver performance (Driver Corporation), the Auto Trainer for developing basic driving skills and adaptive equipment for the handicapped.

Although the driving range is more a facility than an item of equipment, it is discussed here because of its essential nature in a multiple-car laboratory program. Although there are no national specifications for construction of such a facility, interested principals of senior high schools may contact their respective state departments of education for recommended standards. For further up-to-date information on this topic readers are referred to Chapter 14 of *Driver and Traffic Safety Education,* by J.E. Aaron and M.K. Strasser (New York: The Macmillan Company, 1966).

CONCLUSIONS

Articulation from elementary school to junior high school and from junior high school to senior high school must be planned if the greatest achievements are to be made in the mental, physical, emotional, and social development of early adolescents. Educational psychologists seem to have reached the consensus that the unique characteristics of early adolescents cannot be met adequately in the senior high mold nor can an extension without change from the elementary school be justified. This statement applies not only to curriculum but also to school buildings, equipment, and facilities.

> The school plant at its best is an expression in material form of the community's educational program. And this educational program at its best is an integral part of community life.[32]

SELECTED READINGS

"Air-Conditioning and Windows Too?" *School Management,* XI (April, 1967), pp. 110–113.

American Association of School Administrators, *Planning America's School Buildings.* Report of the AASA School-Buildings Commission. (Washington, D. C.: The Association, 1960)

American Association of School Administrators, *Schools for America* (Washington, D. C.: The Association, 1967).

Baughman, M. Dale, "The Awkward Age," *Educational Leadership,* XVIII (December, 1960), pp. 140–144.

Bossing, Nelson L. and Cramer, Roscoe V., *The Junior High School.* (Boston: Houghton Mifflin Company, 1965)

Caudill, William W., "Fourteen Ways School Design Has Responded to Modern Education," *The Nation's Schools,* LXXI (January, 1963), pp. 52–53.

Chase, Francis S., and Anderson, Harold, eds., *The High School in a New Era.* (Chicago: University of Chicago Press, 1959), Chapter 4, "Housing the High School of the Future," pp. 240–248.

Coody, Ben E. and Sandefur, Walter S., "Designing Schools for Variability," *Educational Leadership,* XXIV (March, 1967), pp. 505–507.

The Cost of a Schoolhouse. (New York: Education Facilities Laboratories, Inc., 1960)

"The Education Plaza—Death Knell for the Neighborhood School?" *School Management,* X (October, 1966), pp. 102–105.

Ellsworth, R. E. and Wagener, H. D., *The School Library.* (New York: Educational Facilities Laboratory, Inc., 1963)

---

[32] American Association of School Administrators, *Planning America's School Buildings,* Washington, D.C., 1960, p. 5.

Herrick, J. H. et al., *From School Program to School Plant.* (New York: Henry Holt and Company, 1956)

"How Districts Shape Up Old Schools," *The Nation's Schools,* LXXVII (June, 1966), pp. 86–88.

The Junior High School Program in Illinois. (Springfield, Illinois: Office of the Superintendent of Public Instruction, 1961)

Leu, Donald J., *Planning Educational Facilities.* (New York: The Center for Applied Research in Education, Inc., 1965)

Lewis, Philip, "Study Carrels Sprout in All Parts of the School," *The Nation's Schools,* LXXVII (June, 1966), pp. 82–84.

Lynch, Howard E., "Equipping a New Junior-Senior High School," *The Bulletin of the National Association of Secondary-School Principals,* LI (February, 1967), pp. 425–426.

MacConnell, James D., *Planning for School Buildings.* (Englewood Cliffs, New Jersey: Prentice-Hall, Inc., 1957)

McClurkin, William D., *School Building Planning.* (New York: The Macmillan Company, 1964)

National Study of Secondary School Evaluation, *Evaluative Criteria for Junior High Schools.* (Washington, D. C.: National Study of Secondary School Evaluation, 1963)

"The Nation's School of the Month," *The Nation's Schools,* LXXVII (June, 1966), pp. 75–77.

"The Nation's School of the Month," *The Nation's Schools,* LXXVII (January, 1966), pp. 66–68.

"The Nation's School of the Month," *The Nation's Schools,* LXXVII (August, 1966), pp. 49–52.

"The Nation's School of the Month," *The Nation's Schools,* LXXVII (October, 1966), pp. 127–130.

"The Nation's School of the Month," *The Nation's Schools,* LXXVIII (November, 1966), pp. 61–68.

"The Nation's School of the Month," *The Nation's Schools,* LXXVIII (December, 1966), pp. 39–42.

"New School Has Three Kinds of Flexible Space," *Architectural Record,* CXL (September, 1966), pp. 225–226.

Ovard, Glen, *Administrator of the Changing Secondary School.* (New York: The Macmillan Company, 1966)

Profiles of Significant Schools: Two Middle Schools, Saginaw Township, Michigan. (New York: Educational Facilities Laboratories, Inc., September, 1960)

Profiles of Significant Schools: Schools for Team Teaching. (New York: Educational Facilities Laboratories, Inc., February, 1961)

Roach, Truett A., "The Loft Plan: Functional, Flexible, Economical," *The Nation's Schools,* LXXI (January, 1963), pp. 68–69.

"School Design Must Keep Pace with Educational Innovation," *Architectural Record,* CXLI (March, 1967), pp. 167–186.

National Council on Schoolhouse Construction, *Guide for Planning School Plants,* The Council, 1964.

"Schoolmen Still Prefer Lockers in Corridors," *The Nation's Schools,* LXXVIII (September, 1966), pp. 86.

"Schools That Look to the Future," *Architectural Record,* CXXXIX (February, 1966), pp. 163–181.

The Southern Association of Colleges and Secondary Schools, *The Junior High School Program.* (Atlanta, Georgia: The Association, 1958)

Strevell, W. H., and Burke, A. J., *Administration of the School Building Program.* (New York: McGraw-Hill Book Company, Inc., 1959)

Sumption, Merle R. and Landes, Jack, *Planning Functional School Buildings.* (New York: Harper and Brothers, 1957)

Tanner, Daniel, *Schools for Youth.* (New York: The Macmillan Company, 1965)

Taylor, James L., *The Secondary School Plant.* (Washington D. C.: Government Printing Office, 1956)

Theisen, W. W., "School Building Past, Present, and Future," *The American School Board Journal,* CLIII (November, 1966), pp. 36–38.

"Underground Abo School Is the Most—in Air Conditioning and Light Control," *The Nation's Schools,* LXXI (January, 1963), pp. 80–86.

VanTil, William, Vars, Gordon F. and Lounsbury, John H., *Modern Education for the Junior High School Years.* (Indianapolis, Indiana: The Bobbs Merrill Company, Inc., 1967)

Wolin, Robert B., "School Features Divisible Theater-in-the-Round," *The American School Board Journal,* CLIII (September, 1966), pp. 8–11.

Part 4

THE STUDENT

ELEVEN

Pupil Personnel Services

The complexities of modern living remind secondary school principals of the growing need to improve services to individual pupils lest they lose their identity. Attention is called to some of these complexities.

It is well known that the emphasis in education shifts away from the child in the elementary school to subject matter in the junior and senior high schools. There are a number of reasons for this. Growth in the scope of knowledge has accelerated the downward extension of subject matter from college to high school to junior high school. In the second place, beginning about 1850 urban living replaced agrarian life, bringing about industrialization. Unemployed unskilled share croppers from the South find it impossible to get jobs after migrating to urban communities where professional and managerial abilities are wanted and where technicians must develop new skills every four or five years in order to keep abreast of the times. Third, compulsory education laws make it necessary for more children to stay in school longer than they did a half-century ago. Finally, college entrance requirements are being raised constantly, limiting admission to only the academically talented. Strains and frustrations result.

These and similar changes in American contemporary life have presented new problems to junior and senior high school principals, superintendents, and boards of education as they try to help youth maintain equilibrium in the modern educational maze.

Fabun [1] gives the reader some notion of the changes that are taking place all about us. He says that rapid change has become radical change. Through innovation, powerful forces have been developed which affect the lives of people. These forces have generated

---

[1] Fabun, Don, *The Dynamics of Change* (Englewood Cliffs, New Jersey: Prentice-Hall, 1967).

leisure time, economic power, concentration of populations, a technological society, huge differences in wealth between the haves and the have nots and racial tensions.

All of these changes affect the individual. They produce stresses and strains. They make it difficult for youth to adjust to a strange and ever changing society. Even more important, youth often loses identity as well as his concept of self. Personnel work in education must forever be concerned with the greatness of the individual. It will always seek to help youth maintain the identity of the ego in the midst of exponential change.

Pupil Personnel Services is a new term in the vocabulary of administrators. It relates to those services in the school that affect the welfare of students. In this chapter the law enforcement aspects of Pupil Personnel Services will not be stressed. The types of services included under this title vary with schools and among the states. The Council of Chief State School Officers in 1960 [2] defined Pupil Personnel Services as:

>   guidance services   social work services
>   attendance services   psychological services
>   school health services

This chapter stresses the importance of the student's cumulative record and its use in schools of various size. It also outlines the duties and responsibilities of the Pupil Personnel Services staff including counselors, attendance officers, the school psychologist, and the school nurse. Finally, the responsibilities of the principal for coordinating and staffing pupil personnel employees are stressed.

ORGANIZING PUPIL PERSONNEL SERVICES

There is no one best way to attack the problems listed above. Secondary school principals are developing a variety of plans to capitalize on the benefits of bigness without losing the values of intimacy, to reduce frustrations, to understand pupils and to help them understand themselves. No two plans are exactly alike. They are tailored to the size and needs of the school. Affluent school districts have more elaborate patterns than poor districts. The different plans reflect the purposes and organizational procedures of the school. The availability of staff must be considered in planning the pupil personnel services organization. Personalities are always a factor. Legal requirements must also be taken into account. Some of the important components of a comprehensive program of pupil personnel services are described next.

CUMULATIVE RECORDS

Basic to any plan for servicing students is the cumulative record. This record starts when the child enters school, and it should follow him all the way through school. When

---

[2] Responsibilities of State Departments of Education for Pupil Personnel Services, Council of Chief State School Officers, Washington, D.C., 1960.

he transfers from one school or community to another, the cumulative folder follows. The record contains information in depth that will be needed by the counseling staff. A folder that fits in a standard filing cabinet contains sufficient space for vital personal and home statistics, test scores, summary of scholastic records, student activities, etc. Exact information items for the cumulative record should be selected by a team consisting of elementary and secondary teachers as well as administrative staff and counselors. Sample records from other schools are helpful when considering items for the folder.

The permanent information to be included on a cumulative folder in dual districts [3] need not differ widely from that which is needed in a unified organization. Because more people are involved, it may be more difficult to secure, but a continuing record is especially important in those high schools where students come from several elementary schools—public, private, and parochial. Recently a suburban high school district joined with supporting public and private schools in the preparation of a cumulative folder that originates in the elementary school and follows the pupil through high school. Representatives of the several schools met regularly for several weeks. They agreed upon the items to be included in the cumulative folder. All also agreed to keep a folder for each child enrolled and to send the record to the junior or senior high school when the child transferred.

The cost of keeping cumulative records up to date cannot be justified unless this data is actually used in helping students. In the small school, much of the information is recorded by teachers or by selected student secretaries who can be trusted not to reveal confidential information. Larger high schools employ competent secretarial assistance for this work. Sophisticated computer hardware for processing information is available in an increasing number of schools. Even smaller schools are forming data processing cooperatives for this purpose.

In addition to the permanent information, the cumulative folder should contain current, temporary information. "Drop in notes" are of great help to the counselor in understanding students. Examples include notes taken during student conferences, the student's own biography of himself, letters from parents, anecdotal statements from teachers, and disciplinary measures taken. Since telephone numbers and addresses may change several times during a school career some schools include this as a "drop in" record. Others provide several spaces on the cumulative folder for it.

The nature and use of the data on personnel records should be reviewed periodically. Unused information should be replaced or deleted. This eliminates useless, time-consuming clerical work.

Location of personnel records is important. This depends upon many factors, not the least of which are (1) the size of the school, (2) the use to which records are put, (3) who will use them, and (4) available funds. Classroom teachers may use such test data as math or reading scores if the information is immediately available as part of the cumulative record. But if they must walk down the hall to the principal's office or

---

[3] Dual districts exist in a few areas of the United States where the elementary and secondary schools are under separate boards and administrations.

across the campus to the personnel office to find the desired information, they will likely get along without it. To be used, information should be in the teacher's room as near her desk as possible. Lockable files or lockable desk drawers are essential for maximum use and safety of cumulative records.

The intimate information which is dropped into cumulative folders periodically probably has little permanent value. Therefore, this type of data need not be saved longer than three or four years after the person has left school.

PERMANENT RECORDS

Permanent records of school marks, credits, attendance and other significant data are of such importance that it is wise to keep them stored inside the principal's fireproof, theft-proof vault. Years after leaving school, adults often need data from their school records for such purposes as establishing date and place of birth for social security records. As automation becomes widespread, school records are being stored in discpacs as well as on microfilm. Regardless of the method used, student records require careful preservation.

RELATION OF GUIDANCE AND COUNSELING TO THE TOTAL PROGRAM

The most complete and elaborate set of cumulative records in the world is of little value unless the information is used to assist pupils in becoming effective citizens. Youth needs personal counsel and guidance. There are almost as many plans for providing guidance to pupils as there are different school systems. However, there are commonalities in most of them.

HOME ROOM

In many schools, the home room is the basis for involving counselors and teachers in pupil personnel services. Small groups make it possible for teachers to become acquainted with each pupil. It is in the home room that roll is taken at the beginning of the day. Announcements are read here. Funds are sometimes collected in the home room. The student council representative reports on the latest council meeting.

Group guidance activities are often conducted in the home room by the home room teacher in cooperation with the professionally trained counselor. Tentative registration for the next semester can be made in the home room. With careful pre-planning, part of the testing program can be reliably handled in the home room. Home room teachers often bring in local citizens to provide vocational advice. Units on developing independent study habits, using the library and reading improvement are often presented and discussed in the home room. Group guidance activities may require a longer home room period periodically. This longer period can be accomplished administratively by shortening regular class periods on group guidance days. To be effective, the long home room period must be carefully planned.

Successful methods used in group guidance have been summarized by Bennett [4] to include (*a*) training in how to study, (*b*) informal discussion, (*c*) role playing, (*d*) case conference, (*e*) dramatics, (*f*) play therapy, and (*g*) group therapy.

The importance of a well-organized, carefully executed program of group guidance cannot be underestimated. Yet in actual practice the effectiveness of the home room organization in many schools leaves much to be desired. Some teachers are unable to handle an effective home room. Others feel that the employment of professional counselors has relieved the teachers from any further need for taking a personal interest in pupils. Unless there is complete cooperation and understanding between counselors and home room teachers, the home room period easily deteriorates to an occasion for roll taking, announcement reading and ticket selling.

ACCOMMODATIONS

In very small high schools (enrollment under 300) where some teachers may not be equipped by training, personality or desire to direct home room activity, class sponsors are assigned to work with an entire class. Carefully selected, properly qualified staff members are sometimes given an extra stipend for the added load. More often they are relieved of one or two classes. The sponsor may remain with the class until graduation.

In junior high schools using a core or block schedule it is possible for core teachers to minister to the common needs and problems of students. The block program permits a teacher to be with one group of students for double periods or in some cases an entire half day. It should be pointed out that plans of organization do not automatically guarantee that guidance and counseling will take place. This requires careful advance planning by dedicated people, able to relate life realities to students who are sometimes neither academically inclined nor vocationally oriented.

Many schools with fewer than 300 pupils will be fortunate to have one qualified counselor on the teaching staff. Most will have none. The school administrators will recognize this handicap and will make the best use of such facilities and talent as are available.

As an example, special emphasis can be placed on group activities. Classroom teachers, especially in the small community, know their students from daily contact. They are acquainted with each child's hopes, needs, abilities, and ambitions. The teachers can furnish vocational information. They are college graduates; therefore, they can talk about college entrance requirements. They can also describe college life on at least one campus. In addition to group guidance, teachers can make use of faculty meetings to pool and share their experiences in guiding students. Teachers can use the cumulative records in working with individual pupils. They can interpret test data. Those who are familiar with graduation requirements will advise students in educational planning.

---

[4] Margaret E. Bennett, "Personnel Services in Education," National Society for Study of Education, Yearbook 58, Part II, 1959, pp. 131–32.

The small school can furnish some of the necessary guidance functions by making use of such outside agencies as local youth councils, the welfare agencies, churches, scouts, and YMCA's.

Impoverished schools may be forced to settle for inexperienced staff having little or no special training. Lack of funds and space may limit the time available for group counseling. Individual guidance may not be possible. But the dedicated principal in the small secondary school will make every effort to bring the benefits of as much counseling as possible to every child in school. In doing this he will:

a. Plan and coordinate the testing program.
b. Involve staff in cooperative development of a cumulative record and of plans to use it.
c. Involve students in preparing their own autobiographies to become part of the cumulative record.
d. Develop guidance materials for use in regularly scheduled home room periods.
e. Plan case studies for use in seminars on problems affecting youth.
f. Relate pre-opening staff meetings to counseling matters.
g. Make plans for registering the incoming fall class during the spring semester.
h. Arrange meetings with parents at time of registration.
i. Plan "open house" for parents early in the school year.
j. Arrange for "career days" and "college nights."
k. Join with other schools in planning a cooperative organization for:

   (1) sharing specialized staff including counselors, psychologists, case workers, speech correctionists.
   (2) organizing special education rooms in the area for the deaf, blind, crippled, educably mentally handicapped, the trainable, etc.

THE NATURE AND EXTENT OF PUPIL PERSONNEL SERVICES

There is considerable controversy concerning how large a secondary school should be before it can be called a comprehensive school. Conant [5] states that a comprehensive high school can be developed with an enrollment of 750 if sufficient financial support is available. He defines the comprehensive school as follows:

> The comprehensive high school is a peculiarly American phenomenon. It is called comprehensive because it offers, under one administration and under one roof (or series of roofs), secondary education for almost all the high school age children of one town or neighborhood.

---

[5] James B. Conant, *The Comprehensive High School,* 2nd edition (New York: McGraw-Hill Book Co., 1967), p. 3. Used by permission of the publisher.

Dr. Conant's recommendation of one full-time counselor for every 250–300 students in high school has been generally accepted as a target toward which school administrators should strive. He finds that a vast majority of the schools have not yet reached this goal.[6]

PUBLIC LAW 85-864

The 85th Congress, in enacting P. L. 85-864 found that "the security of the Nation requires the fullest development of the mental resources and technical skills of its young men and women." In effect, Congress declared that improved guidance programs are urgently needed. It re-enforced this policy position by appropriating funds for strengthening programs of guidance, counseling, and testing, as well as mathematics, science and foreign language, through the several states. The combined stimulus of P. L. 85-864, Conant's proposed 300-1 ratio and of leadership from the American Personnel and Guidance Association [7] has resulted in stepped up counseling and guidance programs in the nation's elementary and secondary schools.

QUALIFICATIONS OF COUNSELORS

The general qualifications of counselors are being upgraded. Many administrators seek, as counselors, experienced successful teachers who show a warm interest in and love for young people. It is unwise to transfer unsuccessful teachers into counseling. Other "poor risks" for counseling positions are people who (a) are easily emotionally upset, (b) like to meddle in the personal affairs of counselees, (c) cannot relate well with members of the teaching staff, or (d) fail to follow through assigned tasks.

In addition to successful teaching experience, counselors need professional competencies that are not common among classroom teachers. These include (a) thorough knowledge of counseling techniques, (b) ability to administer and evaluate standardized tests, (c) familiarity with college entrance requirements, (d) knowledge of vocational opportunities for the non-college bound students, (e) acquaintance with opportunities provided by area trade schools and junior colleges, and (f) the ability to interpret cumulative record information. The successful counselor should know when and to whom students with abnormal problems should be referred. Graduate study leading to the master's and doctor's degrees in guidance and counseling is becoming generally accepted.

Many educators believe that counselors should not only be trained, but should also be certified by the state. Some would go so far as to withhold state and federal funds from school districts whose counselors fail to meet minimum standards.

---

[6] Conant, p. 26.

[7] American Personnel and Guidance Association, "A Statement of Policy Concerning the Nation's Human Resource Problems." *Personnel and Guidance Journal*, XXXVI (March, 1958), p. 454–55.

ORGANIZING AND STAFFING PUPIL PERSONNEL SERVICES

In staffing for pupil personnel services the secondary school principal must indulge in the risky business of looking to the future. He, with the advice and assistance of others, will "guesstimate" future enrollment trends and will determine the components of an adequate program of pupil services on a long-range basis. He studies budget limitations. Physical space and clerical staff will be required.

The relation of the counseling staff to punitive discipline requires consideration. Will guidance staff administer punitive disciplinary measures or will punishment and counseling be separated? A summons to the counselor's office in some high schools causes classmates to wonder what they are "in for this time." In other schools this connotation does not exist. Although it is difficult to completely separate these two functions, it should be done.

Some schools stress the importance of specialists. College counselors work only with college bound seniors. Vocational counselors work with seniors who will enter vocational or technical schools. They also aid with job placement, assisting drop-outs as well as graduates. Specialized people sometimes work only with one class. The student thus has a different counselor each of the years in high school. With the house plan, the counselor has an equal number of counselees from each class the entire time the group is in school. He loses the seniors and gains an equal number of new students (ninth graders in a four-year high school and tenth graders in a three-year high school) each year. This has the advantage of providing the benefits of intimacy and smallness in a setting of bigness. Evanston, Illinois, Township High School has this type of plan. There is a possible disadvantage here. The house may get "saddled" with an incompetent counselor for the three or four years the student is in high school.

STAFF QUARTERS

The principal may be required to use inadequate staff quarters for pupil personnel services. On the other hand, he may be fortunate enough to be asked to assist in remodeling old quarters or in planning a new guidance program and facilities from scratch.

Recently, a committee of administrators and counselors prepared the educational specifications for the use of the architect in designing the Pupil Personnel Services at Maine Township High School North.[8] A study of this description clearly delineates the plan of organization for guidance and counseling in that new high school.

SOCIAL WORKER

A truant officer is sometimes needed in cases where absence from school becomes habitual. This person will visit the home of the truant child, inform parents of the re-

---

[8] Educational Specifications for Maine Township High School North, Short, Wells, and Others, Board of Education, February, 1968.

quirements of compulsory attendance laws and when necessary serve summons for court appearance. The concept of "truant officer" is currently being replaced with the more supportive term "visiting teacher," "case worker," or "social worker."

Social workers are not very plentiful. The accepted ratio is one social worker for every 2000 students. Small schools often join together in employing one case worker to serve several communities. To be qualified, the social worker should have a master's degree in social work. He should also be experienced in making home contacts.

While enforcement of school attendance laws is no longer the major responsibility of the social worker in most states, he still contacts parents in resolving difficulties which children experience in school with teachers, playmates, and with school progress. Teachers ordinarily have neither the time nor the training to do this type of work. The social worker also works directly with secondary school pupils, resolving attitudes and helping students understand themselves.

Working with teachers is the third responsibility of the visiting teacher. Through contacts with the home and with the individual pupil, the case worker is able to supply the child's teacher with background information that can be used to help the child stay and progress in school. Briefly stated, the social worker is a catalyst.

PSYCHOLOGICAL SERVICES

An adequate department of personnel services should include a psychologist. This person is a specialist in learning theory. He will give attention to mental and psychological conditions that interfere with learning, assist with selection of educable mentally handicapped children, and counsel emotionally disturbed students referred directly to him by teachers or counselors. The psychologist may be the only staff member who is able to interpret test results. Therefore, he may at times serve as a psychometrist in administering individual tests as well as interpreting group test results. Because of his training, he probably knows more about research than most of his peers. Therefore, he may serve as a staff consultant and as a director of local research.

Psychologists are scarce—only a few large schools have them. Until they become more plentiful, many schools will be fortunate to get psychological services even on a part-time or private base. County superintendents often provide the services of a psychologist for all of the schools in the county. Through joint agreements, and with federal funds, school cooperatives are being organized that cut across county lines. By pooling their funds, these educational co-ops are sometimes able to secure psychological and other services that members cannot get individually.

Psychological services are needed to assist modern youth in adjusting to social and emotional stresses. The emotionally disturbed need special therapy. So does the social delinquent, as well as the extremely immature child.

SCHOOL HEALTH SERVICES

Few principals will ever work in a school system large enough to require the services of doctors and dentists. Yet the medical and dental health of secondary school students must have special attention. This is usually provided by the school nurse. In very small schools her services may be shared with other schools within the system or even with other neighboring school districts. Very large schools may require several nurses.

In some schools, the nurses work in cooperation with the local medical association. In others, they may become a part of the pupil personnel services of the secondary school. But in all cases the nurses work under the direction of the building principal, not under the direction of doctors and dentists.

In promoting the health program the nurse will work with public health officials, the local medical and dental associations, the homes and local welfare agencies. She should be properly licensed and certified to work as a public health official. Competence is required in four areas.

(1) *First aid.* First aid kits are needed not only in the nurse's office but also in laboratories, shops, and the gymnasium. Accidents often occur before school or on the football field after school, when the nurse is not around. She can initiate instructions for procedures to be followed in such emergency accidents.

Since school districts have lost their immunity in law suits, reports of accidents must be complete and accurate. They may be used by parents, doctors, or lawyers as evidence in damage claims or in court.

(2) *Communicable diseases.* Nurses are available to check children with sore throats and symptoms of colds. They are called upon to prevent the spread of communicable diseases. Promotion of immunization programs and tuberculosis X-rays for school employees are examples. They stress cleanliness in toilets and showers as well as among the food handlers.

(3) *Health instruction.* While health education is the responsibility of many staff members, nurses are especially qualified to assist with many specialized areas such as sex education and venereal diseases.

(4) *Health records and physical examinations.* Earlier in this chapter reference was made to the child's cumulative folder. The periodic health examinations become a very important part of this record. Entries should show height and weight as well as immunization dates. Vision and hearing records are needed. The results of periodic physical examinations given by doctors and dentists will become part of the cumulative health record.

The health card should contain a space for recording corrected defects. Nothing is accomplished by discovery of physical defects unless they are corrected. This calls for follow-up. Unfilled decayed teeth still ache, interfering with learning. Discovered defective vision is only the first step in clearing up fuzzy print. The child whose impaired hearing is discovered will not hear the "ss" until auditory acuity is improved. Nurses have the responsibility of promoting a corrective program based upon the findings as revealed by the physical examinations. It is especially important to have a good working relationship with local welfare agencies when funds are needed to assist with indigent cases.

THE PUPIL PERSONNEL COORDINATOR

In large school systems pupil personnel services may be coordinated by a director, who is responsible to the principal. He needs the support and confidence of his superior. He also must have authority to synthesize the entire pupil personnel services program within the school. He should be an administrator—not a specialist in one or two of the services. He must be sensitized to the concerns of his staff and should be able to relate well to teachers. It helps if this person can write well. He should also be an effective public speaker. He needs at least a master's degree in the area of pupil personnel services.

THE PRESENT STATUS OF PUPIL PERSONNEL SERVICES

A survey of the existing status of pupil personnel services throughout the United States was completed in May, 1968, by Dr. Glenn Waterloo, Director of the Department of Pupil Personnel Services, Office of Public Instruction, Springfield, Illinois. The findings: [9]

> The present trend is towards developing a Pupil Personnel Services concept with the counselor, psychologist, and social worker as the core working with children, teachers, administrators, and parents. The state of development varies from district to district with small ones concentrating on counselors and in joint agreements with other districts to co-hire the other two professionals. Medium sized districts tend to employ both the counselor and the psychologist, and large districts all three. The combination teacher-counseling assignment is not the trend. Just the opposite! More and more counselors are being removed from teaching assignments and from discipline responsibilities and other administrative functions. This is a trend, but not a full reality since many schools still use the counselor as a quasi-administrator.

Waterloo's study reveals the types of pupil services that are offered in 13 selected states. These are shown in Figure 11-1. The four services most commonly provided are counselors, social workers, psychologists and nurses. There does not yet appear to be nation-wide agreement as to just what constitutes Pupil Personnel Services.

Eight states issue Pupil Personnel Certification.[10]

California	New York
Idaho	Ohio
Kentucky	Utah
New Jersey	Wyoming

---

[9] Permission to use granted by Dr. Glenn Waterloo.
[10] Dr. Glenn Waterloo.

PUPIL PERSONNEL SERVICES OFFERED IN SELECTED STATES

1968

SERVICES	Arizona	California	Delaware	Idaho	Kentucky	Nevada	New Jersey	New York	Ohio*	Rhode Island	So. Dakota	Utah	Wyoming	TOTAL
Counselor	X	X	X	X	X	X	X	X	X	X	X	X	X	13
Social Worker	X	X	X	X	X	X		X	X	X		X	X	10
Psychologist	X	X	X	X	X	X		X	X	X	X	X	X	12
Psychometrist	X	X		X							X	X	X	6
Pupil Appraisal					X									1
Rehab. Counseling		X												1
Pupil Accounting					X	X		X		X		X		5
Health			X	X	X	X		X	X	X		X	X	9
Guidance Coordinator													X	1
Speech-Hearing				X					X	X	X		X	5
Special Ed.**				X	X				X		X		X	4
Food Services														1
Librarian												X		1
Occupa. Therapist									X					1
Physical Therapist									X					1

* Proposed
** Includes Specialties in Special Education

Note: Pupil Personnel Services are increasing rapidly. Since this study was completed, New Jersey has developed a comprehensive plan.

FIGURE 11-1

THE PRINCIPAL AND PUPIL PERSONNEL SERVICES

Not all of the pupil personnel services outlined in this chapter exist in every school. The principal will decide which components are needed in a given school. His decision will include such factors as (*a*) size of the school, (*b*) availability of personnel, (*c*) requirements of law, (*d*) funds available, (*e*) community setting, (*f*) needs of the students, and (*g*) attitude of the teaching staff.

Since group decisions are usually better than those made individually, he will seek the assistance and advice of his co-workers in determining the elements to be included in the Pupil Personnel Service program.

Facilitation of communication between teachers and specialists in pupil services is a third responsibility of the principal. Communication is faulty when teachers feel that the appointment of a counseling staff relieves them from the need for taking a personal interest in students.

Finally, the principal will make a periodic assessment of the school's pupil personnel services. This evaluation will consider to what extent the program is and is not achieving its goals. The evaluation requires more than conversation. It will consider soul searching questions. Are the facilities and clerical service adequate? How effective is the testing program? Should counselors teach? Who manages punitive discipline? Do students feel that guidance is effective? To what extent is it used voluntarily? Do parents suggest any changes? Should the information on the cumulative folder be changed? Can the home room be improved? Should it be abandoned? What does the Pupil Personnel Services program cost? Is it worth it? And, do the answers call for a re-definition of philosophy, goals and objectives of Pupil Personnel Services?

SELECTED READINGS

Arbuckle, Dugan S., *Pupil Personnel Services in American Schools.* (Boston: Allyn & Bacon, Inc., 1962)

Conant, James B., *The Comprehensive High School.* (New York: McGraw-Hill, 1967)

Downing, Lester N., *Guidance and Counseling Services—An Introduction.* (New York: McGraw-Hill, 1968)

Fabun, Don., *The Dynamics of Change.* (Englewood Cliffs, N. J.: Prentice-Hall, Inc., 1967)

Fedder, Ruth., *Guidance in the Homeroom.* (New York: Columbia University, Teachers College Press, 1967)

Hill, George E., *Management and Improvement of Guidance.* (New York: Appleton-Century-Crofts, 1965)

Miller, Carol H., *Foundations of Guidance.* (New York: Harper and Row, 1965)

Miller, Van., *The Public Administration of American School Systems.* (New York: Macmillan, 1965)

National Society for the Study of Education, "Personnel Services in Education," *58th Yearbook,* Part II. (Chicago: The University of Chicago Press, 1959)

Ohlsen, Merle M., *Guidance Services in the Modern School.* (New York: Harcourt-Brace, 1964)

Shertzer, Bruce and Stone, Shelley C., *Fundamentals of Guidance*. (Boston: Houghton-Mifflin, 1966)

State Department of Public Instruction, *Guidance Services for Illinois Schools*. (Springfield, Illinois: the Department, 1967)

Wrenn, C. Gilbert, *The Counselor in a Changing World*. (Washington D. C.: The American Personnel and Guidance Association, 1962)

Zeran, Franklin and Riccio, Anthony, *Organization and Administration of Guidance Services*. (Chicago: Rand McNally & Co., 1962)

TWELVE

Developing and Maintaining Effective Disciplinary Policies and Procedures

Discipline is an emotionally packed, highly controversial word. To some, discipline connotes the "bad" things youngsters do to scuttle the efforts of a teacher in the classroom. To others it means a set of rules, which by their existence should somehow provide the magic means of maintaining order. A more productive approach is the feeling that a mentally healthy teacher aids in developing a respect within his pupils for other human beings and all that such respect entails. This means that the teacher begins by respecting each pupil as an individual. This atmosphere permeates the entire school. Upon this base, disciplinary policies and procedures are built.

FOUNDATIONS OF GOOD DISCIPLINE

Even a cursory search of studies related to problems of beginning teachers, reasons for persons leaving the field of teaching, and reasons for leaving the inner city schools to go to the suburbs, will spotlight discipline as a prime factor in each case. Interviews with beginning teachers regarding their area of poorest preparation in terms of relating the work in the college of education to life in the classroom on the first job overwhelmingly indicate the area to be disciplined. Talks with teachers regarding opinions of their principal frequently hinge on their view of his ability in the area of discipline. What constitutes a good disciplinarian in the principal's office in the mind of a teacher will vary, of course, from the feeling that "when I send a pupil to the office I want him straightened out," to the teacher who is primarily interested in being "backed up" by the principal.

Because of the extremely personal nature of discipline, and the wide variety of personalities involved in the discipline business, any discussion of the subject will automatically encounter many frustrations. It must be understood at the outset, however, that there are no pat answers, no easy sure-fire rules. The handling of discipline within the secondary school is one area which is not likely ever to be handled by a computer.

One of the basic goals of the secondary school is the development of self-discipline on the part of its students. This goal is not only important for adult citizens of our society, it is necessary for accomplishing the other tasks of the school.

Good discipline and good teaching go hand in hand. It is extremely difficult to have one without the other. This leads to one of the most important elements in good discipline—the classroom in which young people find work which is interesting, within their reach of accomplishment, and for which reasonable returns are to be expected for the effort expended. When young people see these possibilities, problems of conduct are less likely to be found. The teacher who devotes a lot of time to preparing such lessons is automatically preparing for reducing discipline problems.

CHARACTERISTICS OF THE ADOLESCENT

It is worthwhile for every member of a school staff to remind himself periodically of the characteristics which are normal for the adolescent. This is important because in the day-to-day give and take of the classroom, especially as the school year begins to wear on, it is understandable that teachers often forget that some of the exasperating activities of young people are expected and predictable. They are just being themselves. It is in ignoring this fact that teacher behavior often is such as to invite, in fact to promote, poor student behavior.

The following list is not an exhaustive one, but rather is selected to highlight some of those characteristics which affect classroom behavior. First consider the 13–15 year old, the age range normally found in the junior high school.[1]

Physically, these pupils are experiencing rapid physical growth which frequently results in awkwardness, they tire easily but are reluctant to admit it, girls reach sexual maturity from one to two years earlier than boys, and thus girls are usually taller, heavier, and more well developed physically, mentally, and socially than boys of the same age.

Socially, the youngster of this age is likely to show drastic behavior; to be daring, aggressive, critical, boisterous, argumentative, and defiant, and they are slavish to gangs. They act ashamed of home and family, yet they are likely to be hiding their real feelings in so doing. They display fads and extremes in dress, speech, mannerisms and handwriting. They show extreme devotion to a particular boy or girl friend but are likely to transfer that devotion to a new friend overnight.

Emotionally they are unstable, restless, and moody. They resort to fantasies, have crushes, and evidence feelings of persecution. They are beginning to assert themselves

---

[1] Charles Young, Junior High School Workshop Report, *Behavior and Development of Adolescents in Contemporary Society* (DeKalb, Illinois: Northern Illinois University, 1963), p. 6. Used by permission of the publisher.

better as individuals. For the first time, they begin to show interest in the future, feel a keen pressure to succeed and may even use dishonest methods to win recognition. This is the start of devaluation of parents and turning to other adults. They feel inadequate if their maturation differs from that of their friends.

In their learning activities, they are at war with time; they never begin things soon enough. Their attention is easily distracted, they flit from one subject to another, and have difficulty in concentrating. They are inclined to ignore adult help in planning, resent adult interference in their activities, and interpret criticism by teachers as personal feelings directed against them. They have less energy to put into lessons because of the energy drain caused by rapid physical growth. They are intrigued by mechanical gadgets. They are experiencing a steady widening and deepening of the capacity to think and reason.

The high school student is usually in the 16–18 year age group. A similar selective collection of characteristics is worth noting.[2] High school students go through a series of emotional highs and lows. They are sensitive to criticism by their peers, though they can be brutal in their criticism of others. Boys enjoy ribbing and can be unmerciful in this activity. Girls love slam books—about others.

Vacillation is a common characteristic of the high school age pupil. Girls can change from laughter to tears almost instantly. Boys can go from exhaustion to feverish activity upon the appearance of a fellow sports enthusiast.

Daydreams have an important place in the lives of adolescents. This explains the popularity of teenage magazines, movies, comic books, and other fantasy devices. It also accounts for much forgetfulness by the adolescent.

While the high school student has increased intellectual capacity, he is, nevertheless, a highly emotional and physical being. Thus, motivation is an important element in determining whether or not this intellectual capacity is released.

"Adolescence is an age that requires much patience, understanding and love, for in the final analysis, there is nothing wrong with 97 percent of today's teen-agers that their parents didn't outgrow. In other words, the apples don't fall very far from the tree." [3]

While there are many similarities between today's adolescent and those of recent generations, there are some differences which have direct bearing on their attitudes and actions. For one thing, they are more sophisticated than their parents were at the same age. Their social and dating activities are several years advanced as compared to those of their parents.

Today's youth is a mobile generation. Not only does the family move from neighborhood to neighborhood frequently, but it even changes states with regularity. Furthermore, today's youth is on wheels. Distances which today's parents walked or rode on a bicycle as a junior high student, are traversed by car, thanks to mother's willingness to be a chauffeur.

The high school youth often has his own car or access to one belonging to a friend.

---

[2] John M. Gran, *How To Understand and Teach Teen-agers* (Minneapolis: T.S. Denison and Co., 1958), pp. 37–40. Used by permission of the publisher.

[3] Gran, p. 40.

The ability to thus move out-of-sight of the home neighborhood has important implications for his activities.

The young person of today is the product of an affluent society, and he is recognized as an important part of the buying market. Because he seldom has a paying job but is furnished ample spending money, he has good reason to feel that "it's a marshmallow world" and that someone will take care of him. Correspondingly, pressures seldom experienced by youth of other generations are his birthright. He was born and grew up in a world of tension. This includes everything from having never known a world truly at peace, to pressures passed on to him by the world of affluence and its resultant demands.

The teenager of today has been taught to question and be critical. He uses this skill with painful results to adults whom he questions and of whom he is critical. Double standards and conflict between what he is told to hold as important and what he observes these same adults doing, generate confusion in his mind.

Trying to cope with all these problems while going through the painful process of growing up causes today's secondary school student to often be a difficult individual with whom to live. This does not mean that one must resign himself to the fact that nothing can be done to make him a better growing citizen. It simply says one can do a better job of helping him to achieve "livable" status by trying to understand some of the things which cause him to react as he does. So, an understanding of the adolescent and the world in which he lives is a proper start toward any program of good discipline. The school must never make it illegal to be an adolescent.

GENERAL PRINCIPLES

The management of boys and girls in the school situation is a complex problem in human relations. As the various personal, social, and environmental factors which influence their behavior in the classroom are understood and preventive measures are brought to bear which take these factors into account, many problems of discipline will be eliminated or minimized. This will enable routine control measures to be developed. While this approach does not give specific answers for immediate specific problems of discipline, it does hold much greater promise for successful discipline practices over the long haul.[4]

This approach includes the idea of building into the process the gradual shifting of responsibility for one's action to the individual by the steady removal of restraints. The aim is a mature adult who functions in a responsible manner. This evolves throughout the years in school, from kindergarten through high school. Adolescents like the security which comes from an awareness that there are certain bounds within which they are expected to operate. The restraints, however, must be removed as rapidly as the student is self-reliant enough to handle them. It is not reasonable to allow the high school senior very little responsibility for his own actions and then send him out to the

---

[4] Louis Kaplan, *Mental Health and Human Relations in Education* (New York: Harper & Brothers, 1959), p. 402. Used by permission of the publisher.

adult world, suddenly removing all restrictions, and expect him to operate in a responsible manner.

It is well to remember that while some general principles of discipline are applicable throughout the secondary level, there are also several distinct differences of which one should be cognizant. The differences in physical, mental, and emotional characteristics have already been noted, and these differences are significant. There can be no doubt that the junior high pupil is much more likely to exhibit extreme and rapidly changing behavior than the senior high pupil.

Another difference is related to the compulsory school age. In most states a student may legally drop out of school during the early high school years. Even in states where the age limit for school attendance is 18, there are usually escape clauses which reduce this to 16 with parent consent, "when it is in the best interest of the pupil," "when deemed appropriate in the opinion of the school authorities," etc. This means that by one device or another many of the most incorrigible pupils have been removed from the high school. For those who remain there is always this threat which may be employed as leverage.

Likewise, requirements in course offerings are much less and the chances to elect subjects of one's own choosing are increased as one moves toward the senior year of high school. Since students are more frequently in courses they elected, there is more chance of a built-in motivation factor to reduce discipline problems.

On the other hand, the pupil in junior high school who has become a severe discipline problem must remain in school. Except for suspension, usually limited to two weeks, he cannot be removed from school. Legally, a Board of Education does have the right to expel a pupil from the junior high school, but rarely is a board willing to do so. The problem is compounded because this student has probably had a long history of failure to succeed in any of his classroom activities. He has become well known to the entire teaching staff as a troublemaker. The counselors, assistant principals, principal, truant officer, guidance director from the central office, perhaps the local juvenile bureau of the police department, are all familiar with his frequent brushes with trouble.

With this background, he has probably given up on any possibility of ever liking school, or finding any way to be successful there. He has set his sights on that magic age of 16, and while he must by law be physically a part of the school, he probably dropped out psychologically at about the seventh grade. From that point on he is just "serving time."

Another handicap of the junior high school is that most of the courses are required. Electives are few, even at the ninth grade. For the majority of pupils this is not a problem, because the characteristics of curiosity, enthusiasm, energy, transfer of adult models from home to school—all combine to make this youngster susceptible to being motivated. This, of course, is the surest deterrent to discipline problems.

However, the youngster previously described, the psychological dropout, is the very pupil who is further "boxed in" by a full program of requirements. He doesn't like school, academics least of all. At that point when he might have been salvaged, or at least made possible to live with, by providing some areas in his program to do something he liked and in which he could be successful, this door is usually shut in his face. The program has no room for electives. For this student in particular, the flexibility provided by a program of requirements, variables, and electives described in Chapter Seven is recommended. It offers much promise for not only meeting his learning needs more realistically, but also reducing at least one of the factors contributing to his inability to live within the expected bounds of good school citizenship. With these factors underlying the approach to good discipline procedures, a sound program can be built.

HELPING TEACHERS WITH DISCIPLINE PROBLEMS

In helping teachers with behavior problems the principal should recognize the importance of being a good listener as well as a dispenser of advice. Kaplan[5] states: "The school administrator must make himself available to teachers and be a willing listener. He should encourage not only verbal communication, but also the communication of feelings which often are more important than the words expressed. He must have the patience and insight to refrain from offering hasty solutions, and encourage people to reach their own decisions."

The principal also needs to remember the importance of supporting his teachers. Nothing breaks down morale in a faculty so fast as the feeling that the principal will not back you up in disciplinary problems. Teachers must be confident of the principal's support. If they are not, a good program of discipline in the school is impossible.

DISCIPLINE POLICIES

By the time a youngster has reached junior high age, he has become quite adept at sizing up adults, especially teachers. He, furthermore, has developed certain skills at playing one parent or one teacher against another. For these reasons, the efforts of maintaining good discipline within the classroom and throughout the school will be most effective when integrated into a well-formulated, well-administered school-wide, or even system-wide, policy on discipline.

ESTABLISHING POLICY

One of the most important reasons for establishing a school-wide policy on discipline is to present a united front to the offender. It takes the fun out of seeing how much more a pupil can get away with in one class as opposed to another. It furnishes the security which comes from knowing where the bounds are located. Finally, it provides the opportunity for more rational and intelligent behavior in situations involving discipline cases.

Discipline policies should be established in cooperation with the faculty. It is a

---

[5] Kaplan, p. 414.

good rule of administration to involve those people in the formulation of policies which they will be responsible for carrying out. This is especially applicable to discipline policies. The use of hall passes, handling of classroom tardies, "to chew or not to chew"—all of these are policies which could be formulated by the principal and passed on by administrative bulletin to teachers. There are plausible reasons for not doing it this way. If the policy doesn't fit the feelings of the individual teacher, he will probably ignore it. One good reason for his feeling this way is that he sees the problem from a different vantage point than that seen from down the hall in the office. Since the problem will be lived with in his classroom, he will probably choose to do it his way.

For these and other reasons, the wise principal will involve the staff in facing the problem and agreeing on steps which all will promise to support. The policy should then be written, distributed, and publicized. Periodically it should be reviewed to see if it is relevant and if it is effective.

Involving the Staff. As indicated in the preceding, the administration of the school discipline policy is an all-staff effort. The principal is responsible for the overall administration of the policy, but it functions or fails according to whether the other members fulfill their roles. When an individual staff member does not uphold the policy, it is the principal's job to work with that person to remedy the situation. When large numbers of the faculty fail to support the policy, it is time to have another look at the policy.

Records are imporant to the discipline program. Of course, the guidance department will keep records of its activities. Some of these become a part of a student's cumulative folder. Others become a part of separate files, according to how the particular guidance office is organized.

There are other records connected with discipline which are also of importance. A good policy followed in some schools is a card file maintained by each person who has contact with a student having behavior problems. This includes, among others: the principal, assistant principals, counselors, and nurse. The first time a student makes a contact with one of these people, a card with his name, grade, and home room is placed in the file. Each time that person contacts him, he makes a simple notation on the card. Usually this will only include the date and the nature of the situation, such as: "Oct. 10—sent to office by Brown for fighting in hall."

This file can prove quite valuable in those instances where concrete information is needed, such as a parent conference, or more serious instances such as a court case. It is a helpful device to have the secretary type a chronological listing of these contacts with names, dates, and the nature of the contact, and have copies available for a parent conference. After the usual amenities have been dispensed with, this summary can be presented to the parent with the suggestion that it might be helpful to the discussion for him to read over this summary first. This approach is useful for starting the conference with all parties possessing an understanding of the extent of the problem. It is much faster than a verbal summary, and it is likely to be more to the point. It then provides the parent with an opportunity to question points about which he is uncertain and does not waste time with those he readily accepts.

It also is very useful for starting a conference with the parent who comes in with the attitude, "I'm tired of this school picking on my son." After reading over such a list, the parent is usually more susceptible to talking about the problem.

The extent of other records will depend upon the particular school situation. It is important that when the discipline problem becomes serious enough for conferences or court action, one does not base his case on the collective memory of the staff that "he has been in trouble continuously." Many parents, and certainly a judge, will follow this statement with, "Specifically what has he done?"

This points up the importance of similar records by teachers. Specifics committed to memory have a way of fading away from one in a conference, especially when "under the gun" of a perceptive, interested parent who really wants to know just what has been occurring. Such a brief record as described above is all that is needed in those cases. Its absence can often cause the parent to leave the conference frustrated and convinced that his son or daughter has really done very little wrong and that the teacher just does not like him.

If the central guidance office is likely to eventually be called into the picture, it is also good policy to begin feeding information to this office ahead of time. The purpose is quite similar to the reason for a teacher to furnish the principal with information about a possible visitor to his office. In each case the person, principal or central guidance officer, can make initial moves with some degree of knowledge while gaining the time for contacting the person with more information. The way this is likely to happen in the case of the central guidance officer is when the pupil becomes involved with some external agency in the community, such as the police or a youth agency.

Involving the Students. The most successful discipline policies are those which are adopted by giving everyone involved a voice in them, and then utilizing their efforts in making them work. This means the student body should also be heard. This assumes careful guidance by the staff, however, to assure that they have sufficient information to see all sides of the problem. It is also essential that they are helped to keep the picture in focus. Young people are often much more harsh in the judgments they make than are adults.

Involving students can be most helpful in establishing codes of conduct and dress. Schools which have followed this policy of involvement have voiced great pride in the caliber of such codes and the degree of student cooperation in their administration. One point to be remembered in this respect—the type of student who is most likely to be the "breaker" of the code should be represented in the group drawing it up. As wonderful as they are to work with, a group of academically oriented, well-adjusted, school-loving students does not reflect the views of all students in the school. The code they draw up will please the heart of the principal. He needs to remember, however, that it is probably too restrictive for many of the pupils. Those most ready to adhere to this code really do not need one at all. They will follow it automatically for they are oriented to operating this way. Their self-discipline is superior! The wise principal will, therefore, assure that code writing groups are selected to represent all elements of the school population. The code thus developed may not be exactly what the principal and staff would like, but they will be able to live with it—and it will probably work!

DRUGS, SEX, AND RIOTS

There are several problems, somewhat related, which are becoming more prevalent each year and which carry with them a whole new set of headaches for the administrator, the staff and the community. The first of these are problems related to sex education, or a lack of it, drug abuse, narcotics, and related areas. Many states have had long standing laws which require that schools teach about alcohol, tobacco, and narcotics. The teaching about sex has had a more hesitant acceptance in many communities, feeling this belonged in the realm of the home and the church.

Many educators and community leaders have now come to feel that all of these subjects, along with such things as race relations, for example, should be made part of a larger area: guiding youth in gaining the ability to make value judgments. As adults, we are faced constantly with the need to face up to situations which require making such judgments. As our youth face the situations involving such things as civil rights, sex, and drugs, they need to be able to make such choices with an understanding of the elements involved in the choice, including the consequences that accompany each possible choice. Thus, the handling of these areas in this way seems to offer the greatest return on the effort we have to expend in the secondary schools.

Of course, young people cannot make reasonable value judgments without adequate knowledge of the subject involved. Because of the special concern in the areas of sex education and drugs, there have been a number of recent additions to the literature concerning these problems. For your considerations, only a few are mentioned here.

In the area of sex education, the Bureau of Research of the U. S. Office of Education published a bibliography on the subject in 1966 which lists references according to the possible area of the curriculum in which it might be taught, i.e., science, health and physical education, home economics, guidance, etc.[6] Another source worth considering is *Planning a Program of Sex Education*.[7]

The use of drugs among teenagers is known to be growing at an accelerating rate, and law enforcement officers indicate that no community is immune to the pressures of the dope peddler. A good beginning source to gain perspective on the problem is "Straight Talk About the Drug Problem."[8] Included in the article is a "Schoolman's Guide to Illicit Drugs." Among the recommendations offered are: (1) students must be educated to the dangers of drugs and narcotics, (2) include materials on drugs and narcotics in basic materials, and (3) make sure that school personnel are realistically informed on the subject.

---

[6] Lois B. Watt, Myra H. Thomas, *Family Life and Sex Education* (Washington, D.C.: U.S. Office of Health, Education & Welfare, November 15, 1966).

[7] National Association of Independent Schools, *Planning a Program of Sex Education* (Boston: NAIS, April, 1967).

[8] "Straight Talk About the Drug Problem," *School Management* (May, 1968), pp. 52–60, 96–100.

Two other references which can be quite helpful are: *Drug Abuse: Escape to Nowhere*,[9] and *Drug Abuse: A Call to Action*.[10]

Of course, it cannot be emphasized too strongly that the parents and community leaders need to be brought into the efforts of the schools in such areas. Secondly, these problems need attention prior to secondary school. The secondary school personnel need to work with those in the elementary school to assure a well-integrated program to continue through the grades.

Lastly, the whole area of student protests, student riots, and police in the schools must receive at least a brief mention, for it would certainly appear that this is to be a problem in many schools for quite awhile at least. This is a new area of concern for school administrators and to offer "tried and proven" methods is just not possible. It has not been a secondary school problem long enough for that. It certainly would appear, however, that several facts related to the problem are known and should be used by any administrator as he approaches the problem and seeks to develop his own solution.

1. Student protests and riots are a symptom. Any real solutions, therefore, will come from searching out the cause and treating it rather than the symptom. Of course, much of this is a re-reflection of society's problems, not just the school's. It then requires getting at those the school can rightly expect to have some responsibility for, plus helping the student understand those for which the school cannot assume the responsibility. The previous discussion of value judgments is relevant here.

2. The administrator and staff that has worked to build up the respect and understanding discussed before, as a basis for good self-discipline in the school, have a firm base from which to launch any further understanding which will prevent such student protests from reaching the "boiling point," or restore order if they occur.

3. Students are going to seek continually greater involvement in the school's functioning. The administrator and staff must find ways to make that activity meaningful and to provide understanding and respect for those areas of the functioning of the school in which the student might rightfully become involved.

4. The staff must be well informed of the relationships of students, staff, and community. There must be a solidarity of effort on the part of the staff toward the meaningful involvement described above. This means there must not be "maverick teachers" feeding militant students with sympathetic support. Actually this closely relates to the whole problem of the understanding by all involved in the school with the appropriate areas of operation for each.

5. In the event of disorder, especially when police are brought into the schools or onto the grounds, as has now happened enough to suggest it may become much more common than we would hope to believe, this too, requires some careful work with the students on the part of the entire staff. Responsible students must

---

[9] Smith, Kline, & French Laboratories and the American Association for Health, Physical Education, and Recreation, *Drug Abuse: Escape to Nowhere* (Washington, D.C.: National Education Association, 1967).

[10] American Social Health Association, *Drug Abuse: A Call for Action* (New York: ASHA, 1967).

be given every opportunity to exercise positive leadership and to earn the respect of their peers so that they may make a positive contribution in this area. They can be of great help in promoting the understanding of the relationship of one freedom to another. It makes little sense to demand the freedom of dissent in a way and with methods which deny the rights guaranteed by freedom to one's fellow students. It is hoped that those administrators who find themselves gaining unique experience in this area will write of these experiences for the benefit of their puzzled colleagues.

6. The responsibility for the administration of the school rests with the school board and its delegation of this responsibility to its administrators. The courts have repeatedly upheld this fact and as long as school boards and administrators act in a reasonable manner, their actions have received the support of the courts. Nowhere has there been any indication that the courts would pass any part of this responsibility to a group or an individual minor in the secondary school. When the fire gets hot the principal and superintendent must keep this in mind.

This area is probably going to be one of the most difficult with which to cope in the months ahead. It is strongly urged that the school staff lay the groundwork rapidly to provide the strong basis of self-discipline which will provide the base from which to meet the problem positively.

KEEPING THE PROBLEM IN PERSPECTIVE

The essential element in working in the area of behavior problems is that they must be kept in perspective. It is human for the teacher to become so bogged down with a few students in the class who are constantly "in his hair," as to lose sight of the other 25 who are trying to do the right thing. It is not surprising that an assistant principal in a school of 1500 students who devotes 20–30 percent of his time each day to a small handful of trouble makers decides that most kids are at war with the school. One of the most important jobs which the principal has is to assure that he does not fall into this trap and that he opens doors to help all of his staff see the total picture also.

He does this by assuring that none of his teachers spends his day with only problem students. Put a bright spot somewhere in every teacher's schedule. The assistant principal who works with discipline cases should have the opportunity to work with some of the top students too. Success of pupils, particularly those who are not habitually successful, should be given visibility, for the benefit of the staff and the students.

There are times when drastic action is necessary for the good of the pupil and the school. The principal must be prepared to act at those times when suspension or similar action is warranted. As Wilson notes: "A boy's life is important to all of us and especially to him. Sometimes desperate measures are needed to save it for him." [11]

It is likewise important to recognize that there are those incorrigibles in some second-

---

[11] John A.R. Wilson, "Corporal Punishment, Sometimes Yes," *NEA Journal*, LII (September, 1963), p. 20. Used by permissioin of the publisher.

ary schools whom we are failing to serve with programs as currently constituted. There can be no doubt that for these few pupils, the schools have not been even remotely successful and their attendance has been a demoralizing influence on students and staff alike. Spinning states: [12]

> The genuine psychopaths and true incorrigibles should not be kept in schools that have no program adequate to their condition. For their own sakes and the protection of the rights of others, they belong in another type of institution, though one that on the educational side is still school-associated. To it would go for what rehabilitation is possible those whose conduct is nowhere acceptable—the knife and gun toters and the criminally disposed.
>
> A society that requires schooling through the sixteenth year must take the responsibility for creating such institutions. Until we have them, exclusion from the regular school is the only course open.

The level of the mental health of all in the school is the principal's concern. When this level is high, coping with discipline cases is viewed as a need to help the offenders get back on the track—the approach is one of seeking out causes to problems. Symptoms are used as indicators of where problems lie, and, therefore, are used, not treated. Teachers, administrators, and counselors all know the limits of their abilities to treat problems and make proper referrals when that point is reached.

The school which recognizes that discipline is a part of the total program of the school, that it is woven into the curriculum and the extracurriculum, the methods of instruction, the understanding of adolescents by the staff, the involvement of every member of the school population in formulating and understanding policies and assuring adherence to them and in which each staff member helps to maintain a mentally healthy atmosphere which permeates throughout—this is a school which has a proper perspective on discipline. This school has a faculty which probably solves many of its discipline problems before they occur because it is concerned with the broad aspects of learning, rather than a symptom of some of its weaknesses. It is not quite so difficult to get right answers when one asks the right questions. Such a faculty has learned to ask the right questions.

SELECTED READINGS

Johnson, Mauritz, Jr., *American Secondary Schools.* (New York: Harcourt, Brace, and World, Inc., 1965)

Kaplan, Louis, *Mental Health and Human Relations in Education.* (New York: Harper and Brothers Publishers, 1959)

NEA Journal of September 1963. Articles by John A.R. Wilson and James M. Spinning on Corporal Punishment.

Santa Barbara City Schools, *Policies For Student Control: A Guide For Junior and Senior High School Personnel.* (Santa Barbara, California: Santa Barbara City Schools, 1961)

Young, Charles, Junior High School Workshop Report, *Behavior and Development of Adolescents in Contemporary Society.* (DeKalb, Illinois: Northern Illinois University, 1963)

---

[12] James M. Spinning, "Corporal Punishment, Considerably Less Than Seldom," *NEA Journal,* LII (September, 1963), p. 20. Used by permission of the publisher.

THIRTEEN

Pupil Activities

The title of this chapter may produce semantic confusion; therefore, clarification is in order. The curriculum has been defined as "all learning experiences that are provided to students under the influence of the school." Thus, extra-class activities are a part of the curriculum. Frequently, they are referred to as the extra-curricular or the co-curricular program or just student activities. In this chapter all four terms will be used interchangeably to mean those school activities approved, organized and sponsored by the school and voluntarily engaged in (usually without credit) by the students.

In the early nineteen hundreds secret organizations, composed of high school students, existed outside the high school. For a number of years school officials ignored them. These unsupervised secret fraternities and sororities were eventually banned by law. School authorities, recognizing the shortcomings of traditional academic programs, acknowledged the values of some of the activities supported by such clandestine groups. Gradually, these values were incorporated into the school program first as extra-curricular and later as co-curricular activities.

The extent and nature of the student activity program can be determined by a study of the student handbook of any high school. The number of activities listed will be in direct relation to the size of the school. The high school in St. Charles, Illinois,[1] with a student enrollment of 1250 in grades 9–12, offers 25 student activities. The list:

Student Council	Career Club
Halo	Latin Club
Camera Club	Girls Athletic Assn.
Radio Club	Library Club

[1] Student Handbook, St. Charles High School, St. Charles, Illinois.

X-ray (newspaper)	Hi-Lo Club
"C" Club	National Honor Society
Pep Club	Modern Music Masters
Cheerleaders	Dramatics Club
Drill Team	Projectionists Club
French Club	Science Club
Future Farmers of America	Senior Girls Club
Future Homemakers of America	Athletic Team
	Intra Mural Club

A study of extra-class activities offered in 27 Missouri and Illinois high schools was made by Rollins & Unruh.[2] It provides additional evidence of the wide variety of extra-class activities that are to be found in the public secondary schools. Of 93 activities listed in the study, 43 were mentioned more than once. Most common extra-class activities are athletics, dramatics, newspaper, yearbook, G.A.A., and Student Council.

Despite the rapid growth of extra-curricular activities in the secondary schools, the movement is not universally approved. This is clearly indicated in the following quotation: [3]

> The contribution of student activities to the education of youth is perhaps the most questionable feature of secondary education. . . .
> Few would question the power of student activities to attract and hold students' loyalty, to command their time and talents, and to motivate them to unusual effort. What is questioned is whether or not these activities serve educational purposes.

VALUES OF EXTRA-CLASS ACTIVITIES

Burrup[4] outlines the values of student activities under four headings: (*a*) contributions to students, (*b*) contributions to curriculum improvement, (*c*) contributions to more effective school administration, and (*d*) contributions to the community.

Many writers have advocated the need for strong student activity programs in the schools. Among them are E. K. Fretwell, the father of the activity program, Harold Spears and Harry C. McKown.

A well-organized and properly administered program of student activities brings many benefits to the secondary school student. A few of them are indicated below:

LEARNING BY DOING

While it is becoming more difficult to distinguish between the curricular and the extra-class programs, Dewey's basic philosophy that children learn by doing is best il-

---

[2] Sidney P. Rollins and Adolph Unruh, *Introduction to Secondary Education* (Chicago, Ill.: Rand McNally & Co.), p. 72, Table I.

[3] Lloyd E. McCleary and Stephen P. Hencley, *Secondary School Administration* (New York: Dodd, Mead & Co., 1965), pp. 235–36.

[4] Percy E. Burrup, *Modern High School Administration* (New York: Harper & Bros., 1962), pp. 192–93. Used by permission of the publisher.

lustrated in the extra-class activities. Football and basketball plays are executed over and over in practice until they are satisfactorily refined. Errors are corrected at once. Stage acting is perfected by correcting errors as they happen—not later.

FEELING OF SECURITY

School activities provide a feeling of security that results from identification with a small group having like interests. The stamp collector meets with other stamp collectors. Baton twirlers twirl together. The extra-class program promotes a feeling of personal worth and satisfies the ego. People want to feel that they count.

SOCIAL VALUES

Satisfactory relationship with others is a third benefit. In order to work with others the individual learns to relate to them socially and courteously in small groups. Pure recreation is promoted through dances and card games.

LEADERSHIP

Successful living in a free country requires that the individual must learn to lead as well as to follow. Leadership opportunities are offered as students become class officers, club presidents, the newspaper editor or treasurer of the modern music masters.

CIVIC RESPONSIBILITIES

Good citizenship is promoted as athletic teams learn to win and lose graciously. Well-organized campaigns for class officers help in establishing the importance of voting and of becoming active in current politics. The Student Council offers rich and varied opportunities for the development of democratic citizenship, where both civil rights and civil responsibilites are taught.

EXTENSION OF KNOWLEDGE

Clubs in the subject matter areas often offer opportunities for students to go deeply in a single area beyond what is studied in the regular class. One student may explore high frequency sound waves in Physics Club. Another may report to the English Club on the private life of Alfred Lord Tennyson. Horseback riding and hiking clubs grow out of physical education classes.

TYPES OF ORGANIZATIONS

Space will not permit a description of all the student activities that exist in the modern junior or senior high school. It goes without saying that extra-class activities are now generally accepted in most communities and that they contribute to the development of youth. Extra-class activities most commonly found in secondary schools can be divided into seven groups as follows:

        Student Council   Performing Arts
        Assemblies   Athletics & Intramurals
        Clubs   Home Room
        Publications

THE STUDENT COUNCIL

The most frequently found and oldest student organization among junior and senior high schools is the student council. This organization makes it possible for students to participate, with a minimum of guidance from teachers and administrators, in the governance of the school. This is not student government. It is participation in government. There is a difference. Citizenship is learned through practice.

Successful student councils operate under the provisions of a written constitution. This document defines the way members are elected to the council; outlines responsibilities and duties of members; designates the number of officers, their qualifications and manner of election. It indicates the relationship that exists between the council, its sponsors and the principal.

Council members are elected in a number of ways. In some schools this is done by home rooms, and in others by classes or other school organizations. It is important that all groups should be represented. The size of the Student Council varies. When the number of elected members exceeds 25 or 30 as it usually does in very large high schools, two branches can be established, similar to the federal and state governments. It is sometimes necessary to use committees in doing the work of the council.

Student councils are most effective in those schools where the principal takes a personal interest in the organization. While he must reserve veto power over council actions, the wise principal uses it very rarely. Seldom should the principal become the council sponsor. Usually a faculty sponsor is available who can work with and advise student leaders. This person must be neither too strict nor too lax. Leadership of the first order is needed. If council members are made to feel that they are stooges of the administration, the effectiveness of the organization is lost.

The student council must have prestige in the school. This results from successful promotion of desirable school projects. The following activities are examples of excellent student council projects:

1. School parties and dances. After school "sock hops," after game dances, between semester parties and receptions for teachers are examples. One student council stages a special day for teachers, at which time each teacher is given a large red apple together with an appropriate original poem.

2. Approval of Clubs. In a growing number of schools, clubs are chartered periodically by the student council. Before a new organization is approved, application must be made showing its purposes, potential number of members, meeting dates, dues and other pertinent information.

3. Guide and ushering service. The student council at one school plans a conducted tour of the school building for visitors. Part of the tour includes a memorized description of the school's $250,000 art collection. In several schools costumed council members handle ushering for all plays, musicals and operas.

STUDENT ASSEMBLIES

Assembly programs are often sponsored by student councils with the assistance of faculty members. Student enrollments have outgrown the auditorium in many communities. In such cases either several assembles are scheduled or the entire student body is assembled in the gymnasium. Inter communication systems have eliminated the need for calling students together daily for "chapel" type convocations.

Carefully planned and well-executed assemblies constitute a vital element in the learning experiences of junior and senior high school youth. Poor ventilation, bad acoustics and noisy circulating fans should be corrected. Their presence encourages inattention, disrespect, and disorderly conduct. In some schools, advance instruction concerning appropriate conduct at assemblies is given in the home rooms. Where microphones are needed to amplify weak, thin voices, training in their use is necessary. Well-planned assembly programs serve a variety of educationally sound purposes.

1. Athletic assemblies promote school spirit and build morale. They are often used to teach courtesy. School songs and yells are practiced here.

2. Honors programs recognize individual performance. In many schools awards are given to students who have done outstanding work in art, music, shop, debate and dramatics. Properly planned, scholastic excellence can be stressed with an assembly announcing newly elected members of honor societies.

3. Assemblies are used to observe such state and national holidays as Veterans Day, Presidential birthdays, and Memorial Day. They develop a respect for great leaders and perpetuate local culture.

4. Moral and spiritual values are developed in school programs. Inspirational speakers build enthusiasm and develop determination to succeed.

5. Commercial programs provide wholesome entertainment. These are losing popularity in many of our larger junior and senior high schools. There is not much time during the school day for entertainment—especially since sophisticated television programs are viewed nightly by most secondary students.

CLUBS

School clubs appeal to large numbers of students. They are especially popular with pupils who lack sufficient talent to participate in athletics, music or dramatics; however, athletes and musicians often are members of other school clubs. The National Association of Secondary School Principals has endorsed school clubs as a vital part of the school program.[5]

Club groups can be classified as follows:

1. Subject matter clubs. The activities of these groups grow directly out of the academic subjects. Spanish clubs plan fiestas. Latin clubs have Roman banquets. The Science Club builds an electron microscope. Students in economics organize an investment club for the purchasing of securities. The Neptune Club prepares a water ballet. Girls in Physical Education organize G.A.A.

2. Hobby Clubs. Creative use of leisure time is promoted in hobby clubs. Coin Club members meet to discuss and exchange coins. Stamp Clubs promote individual stamp collections, some of which are very valuable. Radio Clubs develop amateur announcers. The Camera Club helps young shutterbugs to take unusual pictures.

3. School Related Clubs. There are many national organizations that sponsor activity units in junior and senior high schools. The Hi-Y is allied with the YMCA. The Girl Scouts and Boy Scouts are supported by national organizations. The Key Club is related to Kiwanis. Junior Red Cross, Campfire girls, Future Farmers of America and Future Teachers of America are additional examples. Properly organized and locally sponsored, these clubs are an important part of school activities.

4. Miscellaneous service and honor groups. Most schools have clubs organized to provide a special service to the school. The Pep Club is an example. Big Brothers Club is another.

Honor societies are sponsored by many secondary schools. Members are selected by teachers. Standards of scholarship, citizenship and service are high, so competition for membership is keen. Principals often find it difficult to explain to parents why Mary was selected and Jane was not. Modern Music Masters is designed to promote excellence in music. There are more than 1000 chapters of M.M.M. in local high schools.

TYPES OF PUBLICATIONS

Nearly every public junior and senior high school issues some kind of school publication. They vary in type from the mimeographed weekly newspaper in the small junior high school to the multi-color slick paged annual selling for $5.00 or more in the affluent high school. School publications have become big business.

---

[5] National Association of Secondary School Principals, "Vitalizing Student Activities in the Secondary Schools," *NASSP Bulletin*, No. 102 (December, 1941).

The four most frequently found school publications include the school newspaper, the annual, the school magazine and the student handbook. Each is discussed briefly:

1. *The School Newspaper*. The newspaper serves many purposes. It interprets the school to the public. It assists in molding school unity. Through its columns, students learn of coming school events for it publishes and interprets school news. It also provides an outlet for students' suggestions for improvements. The newspaper provides a variety of valuable vocational experiences to members of the newspaper staff. They learn to write news, sell advertising, take usable pictures, and write headlines. Such national student press organizations as Quill & Scroll and Columbia Scholastic Press Association are beneficial in setting standards.

Two perennial problems are related to the effective administration of the newspaper—finance and censorship. The mounting costs of printing and the demand for larger or more frequent issues have produced a strain on the activity budget. The cost of the paper can be financed in a variety of ways: Subscriptions can be sold; many schools allocate a percentage of the activity ticket sales to the newspaper.

A budget must be made indicating the number of publications to be issued, the number of pages of each and the amount to be allocated for each. Such fund raising events as candy sales and concession receipts at ball games are used to increase the budget for the paper. In schools where it is approved, the sale of advertising helps finance the school newspaper. The sale of advertising is not permitted in many high schools because some merchants look upon it as "buying good will."

Even with best laid plans, deficits often occur in the newspaper budget just as they do in athletics. Such deficits should be absorbed by the board of education as part of the cost of a good education.

By insisting on a yearly budget for each publication and by holding students and sponsors to the limitations of the budget once it is made, the principal will have solved one of his publication problems—finance.

The second problem, censorship, is equally as important as finance. Supervision of the content of a student newspaper requires judgment and tact. Poorly written articles containing misspelled words indicate careless editing and cannot be tolerated. Tirades on the prison-like atmosphere of the school may be as much a criticism of students as of the administration. College humor may not be appropriate for the high school paper. Some administrators have been known to forbid the release of a school paper because of objectionable writings and criticisms.

Authoritarian censorship can be replaced with self-imposed censorship. The principal should lead in this by developing with the sponsor and student staff a written policy covering deadlines, careful proofreading, guidelines for considering fair and honest criticisms, gossip, harmful small-talk, personal tirades against teachers, etc.

2. *The Yearbook*. The school annual is considered by many students as the most important school publication. It contains pictures of students together with a record of honors received and activities in which they were engaged. This publication becomes nostalgic with the passing of the years.

In many schools, the cost of the yearbook to the individual is becoming prohibitive, thus ways to reduce costs are constantly being sought. Printing costs can be reduced by (1) limiting the number of pages, (2) replacing fancy covers with a stock cover, (3) reducing the number of pictures, (4) limiting (or omitting) color pages, and (5) requiring competitive bids. Some annual staffs hold bake sales or operate the concessions at athletic contests in order to reduce the annual cost to the student. Sale of advertising to local merchants is not recommended as a means of financing the yearbook. Merchants look upon it as a donation. Such advertising confined to the back pages of the annual has little or no value.

With modern methods of reproducing printing and pictures, even the very small school is able to produce a respectable "home made" annual at reasonable unit cost.

3. *The Magazine*. Much creative writing is done in English classes. The best of these are often collected, edited and published annually or semi-annually by a magazine publication staff of English students. The school magazine can be reproduced inexpensively in the school print shop or by mimeograph. Some schools have the booklet printed commercially. It is usually sold to students at a nominal fee. If it is not self-supporting, the cost should be absorbed in the school budget.

4. *The Student Handbook*. The student handbook is usually prepared under the direction of the student council. It contains important information that every student should have; therefore, it should be issued to every student without charge. The cost of preparation can be a part of the student council budget.

THE PERFORMING ARTS

Music, speech, drama and debate are growing in importance. As technology reduces the length of the work week, more time is available for leisure. Thus, the performing arts are coming into their own. Symphony orchestras, barbershop singing groups and community theatres are examples. While academic credit is given for most of the school time devoted to the performing arts, part of the activities are carried out after school and on Saturdays. Hence, they have some of the characteristics of extra-class activities.

The need for inter-school and inter-state contests in performing arts activities involving transportation of large groups of pupils is on the wane. Tax money spent on these junkets might be better used for the purchase of musical instruments or stage equipment. Excellence in performance can be developed through well-organized groups in school. A superior performance of the marching band at football games provides more satisfactory public listening than a music contest with its strain and confusion. Stage productions like *Oklahoma* or *Sound of Music* develop local pride as they provide groups and individuals with opportunity to strive for excellence in performance.

Speech activities—debates, forensics, plays, dramas, radio and television announcing—are getting increased recognition in most schools. Well-qualified teachers are attracting increasing numbers of pupils into speech activities. Limited inter-school activities in debate, forensics and one-act plays are still quite common. But, local debates on current issues before the Rotary Club and presentation of a "theatre in the round" for the Women's Club are to be preferred to inter-school contests.

INTERSCHOLASTIC ATHLETICS

Americans love competitive sports. Millions watch baseball games either at the ball park or by television from their favorite chair in the living room. Ice hockey is a growing sport. College football stadiums are filled every week end during the autumn season. Basketball crowds are limited to the capacity of the field houses. The football season in Chicago closes with a high school contest at Soldiers Field. Every seat is sold—100,000 of them. In most states the basketball and baseball seasons are climaxed with state tournaments, entry to which has been gained by a series of elimination contests.

The enthusiasm of the populace for competitive sports has filtered down to the junior high school where coaches have been permitted and even encouraged to organize and schedule interscholastic athletics for pupils. When the emphasis is focused on winning, to the exclusion of the physical and emotional needs of the boys and girls, an evaluation or re-evaluation of such a program should be made.

Arguments for and against competitive athletics fluctuate with the success of the teams. Sooner or later, contradicting points of view toward athletic contests will be expressed in every community. The following are typical:

FOR COMPETITIVE ATHLETICS

1. Athletics develop healthy, wholesome competition which is an important part of free enterprise.

2. Athletic teams represent the "gifted" group in physical education in the same way that science seminar classes in physics represent the gifted in science.

3. Team membership is determined by ability only—family status, wealth and race are not determining factors.

4. Competitive athletics keep potential dropouts in school, motivating school attendance.

5. Team travel broadens the students' outlook and develops desirable social behavior.

6. Well-coached teams develop pride in the school on the part of the community as well as the student body.

7. Athletics promote self-discipline and clean living habits, thus developing physical fitness.

AGAINST COMPETITIVE ATHLETICS

1. The country needs less competition —more cooperation.

2. Overenthusiastic desire to win often causes coaches to enter boys in competition too soon after injury.

3. Athletics cost too much money.

4. Competitive practice takes a disproportionate amount of time, interrupting the family dinner hour.

5. Night games promote gang fights, vandalism and other types of poor citizenship.

6. Afternoon and week-day games interrupt the regular school program.

7. In competitive athletics, only the best are members of teams. Those who need athletic training most are neglected.

FOR COMPETITIVE ATHLETICS	AGAINST COMPETITIVE ATHLETICS
8. Athletes may secure scholarships, making college education possible.	8. Competitive athletics disrupt the school faculty. *Example*—coaches often ask teachers to give extra tutoring to athletes in order to keep them eligible.

Adequate control of competitive athletics will tend to stress their benefits and reduce their shortcomings. This control is exerted in a variety of ways:

1. State associations determine eligibility rules for inter-school competition. These relate to scholarship, age, residence, physical examinations and participation in summer athletic camps. They have placed inter-school competition on a high level by licensing officials and by disciplining schools for violating regulations.

In most states, the high school athletic association has taken over other inter-school activities, including music, forensics, and debate. The name has been changed to high school activities association, or to a name that involves more than just athletics.

2. Groups of neighboring schools of similar size often form associations to promote effective inter-school relations. School officials of member leagues meet periodically to (*a*) arrange schedules, (*b*) agree on number and fees of officials, (*c*) consider applications of new members, (*d*) settle disputes between schools, (*e*) establish regulations for good sportsmanship, and (*f*) determine the length of pre-season practice period, etc.

3. An effective program of athletics can only be developed at the local level in each individual school. The board of education, upon recommendation of the superintendent, sets the policy. It determines the budget, approves accident insurance, authorizes purchase of adequate equipment. It employs the coaching staff and determines their salaries.

Administration of the local athletic program is the responsibility of the principal. This requires his constant attention. No other aspect of the school's program is as dear to the hearts of the people. The principal must be completely familiar with the athletic policies of the state and of the league to which the school belongs. He is responsible when an ineligible player is discovered. He will be blamed for outbursts of poor sportsmanship at games. When school sidewalks are smeared with red paint the night before a game, the principal must seek the culprits.

The principal must keep proper balance between competitive activities and the academic program as well as among the activities themselves. He protects the coaches from community pressure for a winning team year in and year out. When the coach tells his star player not to take part in the school play, the principal adjudicates the issue. He works with the Dads Club to neutralize the unreasonable demands of the spectator public.

Fortunate is the principal who can establish friendly relations with the local sports writer. Athletic events, both favorable and unfavorable, are likely to get fair treatment by the press when a feeling of mutual trust and understanding has been established between the school principal and the sports editor.

There are important routine matters that require administrative attention. Eligibility lists are a weekly chore. Assignment of game responsibilities must be made. Arrangements for broadcasting games are sometimes a problem. Referees will be required. Complimentary tickets are to be issued. Student tickets must be sent to the competing school for home games. After game brawls must be prevented. Pep rallies are to be planned; tickets sales directed. Buses for out-of-town games are needed. Standards for rooting sections must be set. Many of these details can be delegated, but the principal is responsible when things go wrong.

INTRAMURAL SPORTS

No student should be denied the benefits of competitive sports. Therefore, a strong intramural sports program for the masses should be promoted. It should be open to all, both boys and girls. The goals of the national physical fitness program should undergird the school's intramural program. Junior high schools should give major attention to the intramural sports program and de-emphasize inter-school competition.

No intramural program is complete without activities for girls. There are a variety of extra-class intramural activities for females from which school officials may choose. Among them are:

Badminton	Swimming	Softball
Archery	Fencing	Golf
Bowling	Field Hockey	Tables Tennis
Tennis	Basketball	Volleyball

Whitten [6] in 1950 proposed that the need for competition among Illinois high school girls can be satisfied better through intramural sports than through competitive inter-school contests. That state, therefore, limits inter-school competition for girls to golf, archery and tennis. The state encourages a series of play days. The use of a point system enables girls in small schools having limited equipment to get award. The extra-class sports program for girls is often sponsored locally by the Girls Athletic Association (G.A.A.).

The extent to which high school pupils participate in sports is revealed in a National Sports Survey reported by *School Activities Magazine*.[7] The results are shown in Figure 13-1.

FINANCING EXTRA-CLASS ACTIVITIES

The management of student activity funds has become big business. While exact data is not available, it is safe to say that millions of dollars annually go to finance extra

---

[6] Charles W. Whitten, "Interscholastics—A Discussion of Interscholastic Contests," Illinois High School Association, Chicago, Illinois, 1950, pp. 120–126.

[7] *School Activities Magazine* (September, 1967), p. 19. Used by permission of the publisher.

NATIONAL SPORTS PARTICIPATION SURVEY (1967)

High School

Sport	Number of Schools	Number of Participants
Badminton	339	3,181
Baseball	13,277	372,535
Basketball	20,191	687,261
Bowling	574	8,907
Cross Country	6,907	131,760
Curling	769	7,405
Cycling	1	8
Decathlon	17	98
Fencing	20	200
Field Hockey	56	1,167
Football (6, 8, 9, 11, 12 man)	15,448	1,037,813
Golf	7,361	81,853
Gymnastics	1,317	28,678
Ice Hockey	689	17,051
LaCrosse	88	2,000
One-mile Team Race	89	445
Pentathlon	7	100
Riflery	338	5,163
Rowing	23	298
Rugby	6	180
Rugger	22	390
Skiing	451	7,866
Soccer	1,602	42,443
Softball	431	9,010
Swimming	2,405	71,710
Tennis	5,811	86,879
Track & Field	16,650	569,041
Track (indoor)	1,519	30,938
Volleyball	3,033	55,234
Water Polo	3,147	5,044
Weight Lifting	13	125
Wrestling	5,882	187,074

FIGURE 13-1

class activities in the secondary schools of a large number of states. The 1967–68 budget for managing high school activities from the state level in Illinois was $374,191.[8] Approximately two thirds of this amount ($243,831) represented income from the state

---

[8] *Illinois High School Association,* "The Illinois Interscholastic," Vol. 40, No. 1 (Sept., 1967), p. 11.

basketball tournament. The size and complexity of these accounts demand that they should be managed according to recognized business procedures. Too often in the past, student funds have been poorly handled. Money has not been banked in a separate account. It has been kept in a fruit jar in the teacher's desk or in a box in the vault. Receipts have not been issued. Activity account bills have been charged and not paid. Sponsors have mingled activity funds with their own personal checking accounts. School administrators have been found guilty and sent to jail for mismanagement of activity funds. The secondary school principal should not forget the need for adequate financial safeguards as he develops the activities program in the school.

LEGAL STATUS

In many states, school activity funds are considered to be public funds and therefore are subject to control by the board of education. This seems to be a reasonable assumption. The responsibility of the board for control of activity funds was established in Pennsylvania. In 1942, the German Township decision made it illegal to spend athletic or extra-curricular funds without board approval. Five years later the Hatfield Township decision [9] declared that all activity funds were under the control of the board of education. The school statutes in Oklahoma point the way even more clearly than the court decisions in Pennsylvania:

> Section 70. Control—Rules and Regulations: The board of education of each school district shall exercise complete control over all funds on hand or hereafter received or collected from all student activities conducted in such school district, including all funds received or collected from students and others as admission charges to athletic contests, school plays and any and all other school activities and from the sale of student activity tickets.

It is safe to conclude that there is a gradually developing legislative concern over the importance of extra-class activities and over the use of funds generated from them.

Administrative Responsibility. Regardless of statutory requirements, the principal is responsible for the total educational program in his school, including activity funds.

A Central Treasurer. Usually some faculty member other than the principal is designated as the activities treasurer. This person should have free time during the school day to do his work. The treasurer should be bonded, since he receives and disburses all activity funds, keeping individual records for all school organizations.

ACTIVITIES BOARD

All budgets of anticipated receipts and expenditures should be reviewed by an activities board consisting of the activities treasurer, selected activities sponsors and stu-

---

[9] Hatfield Township School District 161, Pa. Super, 54A (2d) 833. (1947).

dents. Other responsibilities that can be assigned to this group are (*a*) promotion of fair allocation of receipts from activity ticket sales, (*b*) approval of funds for financially deprived organizations such as debate, and (*c*) assistance in keeping organizations within their budgets. The activities board can advise business firms not to open charge accounts with individual groups.

Activities boards can study hidden educational costs, which often show up in excessive admission prices, exorbitant class dues, costly class rings, towel fees, laboratory and shop fees and corsages for dances. It is well known that student activities involve more pupils from the upper and middle economic levels than from those in the lower economic status. Periodic review of these conditions may result in recommendations for "standard" class rings or cloth backs for the annuals. Schools are not truly free until students from every socio-economic level can have the same educational opportunities.

Another concern for the activities board is the extent to which funds earned by a given activity should be the sole possession of that group. It seems educationally sound to allocate some activity funds to areas of need, regardless of the source. The activities board will face this debatable issue at the time budgets are approved.

STUDENT TREASURERS

The treasurers of each organization should keep individual financial records of receipts and expenses. These should be verified monthly with the books of the central treasurer. Purchase orders and authorization for payments should be signed by the student treasurer and the sponsor. Actual purchases and payments are made by the activities treasurer. Banks prefer one large account to large numbers of small accounts involving frequent overdrafts and service charges for handling checks. While at times restrictions on expenditures may be necessary, members of school organizations generally should be free to decide how their funds are to be collected and spent.

GUIDING PRINCIPLES FOR ADMINISTERING SCHOOL ACTIVITIES

Organizing and directing an effective program of extra-class activities are two of the secondary school principal's major responsibilities. He works for a wholesome balance between the extra-class activities and the academic program. Size of the school as well as availability of sponsors will determine the nature of the extra-class program. The general suggestions which are made here may be of assistance in establishing an effective extra-class program.

1. Select sponsors carefully. Teachers should not be coerced into assuming leadership in activities in which they have little or no interest. Teachers should be consulted before appointments are made. In some cases the administrator will have to decide whether to continue the pep club under a poor sponsor or to abandon the club entirely.

2. Justify extra-class programs on the basis of their contribution to the wholesome development of youth. At times the principal will resist public pressure to build a stadium for night football when it means postponement of an auto shop. In riot ridden communities night football may have to be abandoned entirely.

3. Compensate teachers for extra-class assignments. This can be done either by reducing the daily class load or by paying them for the extra time and energy spent with activities. Teachers were once expected to assume these extra sponsorships as part of their regular teaching job. In many schools today teachers accept club and class sponsorships without extra pay when they require no more than one hour per week.

Schedules of extra pay for extra duty are quite numerous. Figure 13-2 is an example:

Audio Supervisor	$100–$200	H. S. Newspaper	$200–$300
Class Sponsors	100– 200	Stage Director	300– 400
Drama	100– 200	Speech Activities	200– 350
Girls' Intramurals	25– 100	Student Council	200– 300
Music	250– 500	Yearbook	200– 300
Clubs	No		

	HEAD COACH	ASST. COACH
Baseball	$700	$350
Basketball	800	400
Cross Country	500	300
Football	800	400
Golf	450	275
Gymnastics	700	400
Intramurals (boys)	700	300
Swimming	700	350
Tennis	450	300
Track	800	400
Wrestling	650	325

FIGURE 13-2

The question of whether or not teachers should be compensated for extra assignments is no longer an issue. But the best way of doing it is still controversial. Regardless of the plan used, classroom competence should be maintained.

4. Encourage wide participation in student activities. Where this is not done, a few aggressive leaders take over all the activities. The captain of the football team gets the lead in the senior play, is president of the senior class, and is a member of the student council. Some schools limit participation in extra-class activities by designating major and minor activities. Participation is then limited to one major and two minor activities. A better plan is to delegate activity assignments to the counselor, who is familiar with the students' strengths and weaknesses.

Wide participation implies equal opportunity for participation. While criteria for membership in school activity groups are needed, secret balloting on members implies racial or social discrimination. This is not desirable. Social cliques often result. There is no place in the American public high school for secret fraternities or sororities. They are illegal in most states. Where these self-perpetuating organizations exist, they should be eliminated. This will require support of the board of education, the students in school and the parents.

Exorbitant dues often prevent wide participation in various activities. The result is that extra-class activities are filled with members from the upper and middle economic levels. Hollingshead [10] found that the students from the upper economic class in extra-curricular activities outnumbered students from the lower class by 4 to 1. Children from the lower class seldom attend school dances. When music students are required to purchase their own band uniforms, talented musicians from poor homes cannot participate in public performances.

Clubs with little or no source of revenue in one high school are permitted to take their turn at operating the concession stand at athletic games and to keep the profits for club expenses. Students who cannot pay reasonable dues are permitted to earn the dues by doing useful work around school.

School-wide support of school activities is encouraged through the sale of activity tickets. Purchase of the activity ticket at a nominal fee admits the student to all games, plays, debates, assemblies (commercial) and musical programs. Subscription to the school paper is sometimes included. The activity treasurer is responsible for the receipts from the sale of the activity ticket, and they are distributed to the benefiting groups as needed. In some junior and senior high schools, boards of education subsidize all or part of the extra-class costs.

5. Recognize extra-class activities as a regular permanent part of the school program. This requires planning and supervision. For example, bus and plane trips must be officially approved and carefully supervised. They should have parental permission. Adequate liability insurance must be secured. Approval should be decided upon the basis of educational values to be derived from the trip. Parents often offer to take children for school sponsored trips in their own cars. This precipitates problems for the principal.

Responsibility for the entire activities program must remain in the firm hands of the principal and his staff if it is to be a significant and integral part of the educational program.

6. Secure an extra-class activities planning board to assist in giving direction to the program. This group should include teachers, students and parents.

7. Provide a simple system of accounting for extra-class funds. This will require a central bonded treasurer with school time for his work. The treasurer will handle

---

[10] August B. Hollingshead, *Elmtown's Youth* (New York: John Wiley & Son, 1949).

funds and write checks. He will build a budget. He will assist student treasurers with their budgets and records. He will work with other agencies in developing a uniform system of bookkeeping for student activities.

8. Finally, arrange for continuous evaluation of the activities program. Rollins & Unruh [11] *have developed 12 criteria that may assist in evaluating the activity program.*

SUMMARY

Extra-class activities are generally accepted as an important part of the educational program of the modern secondary school. The distinction between "class" and "extra-class" is gradually disappearing. Any activity sponsored by the school becomes the responsibility of the principal. He should apply the same administrative practices to the extra-class program as he uses with other aspects of the school program. They should be administered in the interest of developing students physically, socially, mentally, and emotionally so that members of student organizations may learn to become good citizens in a free country.

SELECTED READINGS

Johnson, Edgar and Faunce, Roland, *Student Activities in Secondary Schools.* (New York: Roland Press Company, 1952)

Kilzer, Louis R., and others, *Allied Activities in the Secondary School.* (Englewood Cliffs, N. J.: Prentice-Hall, Inc., 1956)

National Association of Secondary School Principals, "Relationship Between the Student Council and the Secondary School Principal," *Bulletin,* The Association, XXXIX (Dec., 1955).

Rollins, Sidney P. and Unruh, Adolph, *Introduction to Secondary Education.* (Chicago: Rand McNally)

Tompkins, Ellsworth, *Extra-class Activities for all Pupils,* Federal Security Agency, U. S. Office of Education (Washington, D. C.: U. S. Government Printing Office, 1950).

Whitten, Charles W., *Interscholastics.* (Champaign, Illinois: The Illinois High School Association, 1950)

Willis, Albert, editor, "The Illinois Interscholastic." (Glen Ellyn, Illinois: The Illinois High Association, 1967)

Willis, Albert, editor, *Official Handbook.* (Chicago: The Illinois High School Association, 1967–68)

Youngert, Eugene, "The Contribution of Athletics to the Education of High School Youth," *Bulletin,* National Association of Secondary School Principals, XXXVI (Dec., 1954).

---

[11] Sidney P. Rollins and Adolph Unruh, *Introduction to Secondary Education* (Chicago, Ill.: Rand McNally & Co.), pp. 90–91.

Part 5

SCHOOL-COMMUNITY RELATIONS

FOURTEEN

Understanding the Problem

The education of the whole child is a cooperative enterprise in which the school is but one agency, even though it often assumes responsibilities in directing that education; both the home and the community have their inescapable roles and responsibilities. Elected and appointed representatives of the people make policies for school management. Since education is lay controlled, there exists a relationship between the equity of the public in its public schools and its investment in them. In turn this investment is usually related directly to recent or present impressions of education.

In early times citizens closely controlled the education of their children and they possessed a keen awareness of the role of the school in the triad of home, school and community. Such an awareness was possible in view of the boarding teacher and the simplicity of community life and school size and organization. It was not uncommon for laymen to examine both teacher and pupils as evidence that public interest and control in education were accepted as the responsibility of the community. Activities of lay supervisory committees provided continuous public participation. Consequently, the practice of lay supervision, in addition to the many teacher-community contacts and the use of the schoolhouse as a community center, precluded the necessity for an organized program of public relations.

The status of close citizen-school cooperation was influenced considerably when public education became a state function. Reliance on the state for the determination of the organization, program and personnel brought about somewhat of a separation of the people from their schools. Since that time, according to Jones,[1] four concepts of

---

[1] J.J. Jones, *An Analysis and Summary of the Significant Research Findings Concerning Some Problems and Issues of School-Community Relations,* doctoral dissertation, School of Education, Indiana University, 1952, p. 17.

school-community relations have developed, each of which may be found in practice somewhere even today: (1) indifference, (2) school publicity, (3) educational interpretation, and (4) cooperative endeavor. While publicity and interpretation are essential elements of an effective program of school-community relations, it is the last of the above concepts, cooperative endeavor, which provides the basis of the remainder of this chapter.

There is much agreement among educators today that the concept of the interrelationship of school and community is continually expanding. Since past experiences have shown that most social institutions tend to fragment the community unless a specific organization is functioning to prevent such an undesirable process, the school has been singled out in many instances as the logical coordinator of the forces of these community social institutions.

THE ROLE OF THE SCHOOL IN THE COMMUNITY

Having established that in school affairs the people are stockholders, that schools are precious public possessions, and that they are created, patronized and maintained by citizens, it is appropriate now to examine the strategic position of the school in the community. First it is clear that since schools are an investment in youth, they ought to be the business of the citizens of the community.

One high priority function of the school is to help communities help themselves. As a catalytic agent the school works in and with the community, or to put it in another way, the school is a vital agency in promoting the synergism of disparate community forces so that the total effect is greater than the sum of independent elements. Such a concept implies that home, school and community are basic components of society and that school-community relations are reciprocal. In maintaining the mores of American culture the secondary school is a social institution intimately related to most of the families and other social agencies in the community.

Typically, the junior high school, for example, is in the community and frequently serves as a center of community life. There are situations, however, where junior and senior high schools serve more than one community. The authentic community school [2] serves as a laboratory which, through the educative process, relates the resources of people and communities to the problems of people and communities for the purpose of raising the standard of living.

A CORPORATE IMAGE OF EDUCATION IN THE JUNIOR HIGH SCHOOL [3]

The world of business and industry spends considerable time, effort, and money in the task of developing and maintaining its "corporate image." The world's largest cor-

---

[2] National Society for the Study of Education, *The Community School,* 52nd Yearbook, Part II, University of Chicago Press, 1953.
[3] Adapted from *The Junior High School in Illinois,* p. 63.

poration, American Telephone and Telegraph Company, with more than 725,000 employees and upwards of 2,000,000 shareholders, established its Public Relations Department in 1908 for the express purpose of systematically explaining its policies. According to Golden,[4] AT & T in 1962 had 78, and its associated companies 390, people working in public relations, not including supporting clerical aids. In Golden's words, "It would be hard to find an important executive, or any employee for that matter, from the long distance operator to the repair man, who is not conscious of the importance of the general public's good will toward the company." Just having a good company is not enough. The role, function, and value of the services or products—the corporate image—must be understood and accepted by two groups: those who produce them and those who use them. Success goes to that organization whose employees understand and believe in the product or services rendered, and who in addition are willing and able to assist the consumer public in understanding, accepting and supporting the products or services offered. Essentially, the above message may be capsuled in the following terse verse:

> He who whispers down the well
> The things he has to sell
> Will never make as many dollars
> As he who climbs a tree and hollers.

Just having a good school is not enough. Sympathetic and accurately informed publics, properly synergized, are essential to desirable present and projected corporate images of secondary schools. Abraham Lincoln's statement on public opinion is appropriate and pungent:

> Public sentiment is everything; with public sentiment nothing can fail; without it, nothing can succeed. Consequently, he who molds public opinion goes deeper than he who enacts statutes or pronounces decisions.

Reality, however, forces us to recognize the fickleness of communities and their citizens who intermittently surge and regress in their associative role of providing quality education. At different times apathetic, supporting, and meddling, communities inevitably exhibit all the human traits of their component individuals.

The challenge of school-community cooperation at the secondary level lies in the development and acceptance of a clear corporate image, the role and value of the school, by two groups, professionals and the lay-public. The concept of "Partners in Junior High School Incorporated" can be strengthened only when local, state and national professional groups representing all levels of education and well-informed citizens accept and support the purposes and plans of our peculiarly American creation, the junior high school.

Barriers to this kind of acceptance and support are well known to every junior high school teacher and principal. The fact is, unfortunately, that far too many teachers and

---

[4] L.L. Golden, "Public Relations," *Saturday Review* (June 9, 1962), p. 49.

principals themselves are inadequately prepared through training for their positions. How, then, can they be expected to serve effectively as interpreters and agents of sound public relations? Theoretically at least, the junior high school introduces pupils as well as many parents to secondary education; it is recognized that a considerable number of parents of today's early adolescents did not reach the junior high school grade level. An even greater number successfully progressed through high school and were graduated without ever having experiences in the kinds of programs found today in modern junior high schools. It is imperative that the unique contributions of quality junior high school educational programs be made known to such parents and others with imaginative and durable techniques.

Although the junior high school movement, in the minds of some educators, is on the "cloverleaf," it does have some inherent advantages to assist in the building of a favorable corporate image. Reference is made to the late development of the junior high school as a unit in our educational ladder and to the fact that such a school usually enjoys the position of being a neighborhood school. As a latecomer to the educational scene, the junior high school has escaped most of the fetters of conformity and standardization. One great blessing of this newer school has been its freedom from the educational tourniquets of Carnegie units and rigid accreditation from state and regional agencies, although the latter is now a reality. Practitioners especially are hopeful that accreditation procedures applied at this level will eventually be nurturing and stimulating.

The principal of the modern secondary school assumes that public participation is here to stay and that church, recreational and other community agencies will continue to maintain and perhaps extend their programs for early adolescent youth. Moreover, he is mindful of the fact that the junior high school is the one institution through which pass nearly all members of the community. If the symbiotic relationship described earlier is to flourish, experiences for citizens, teachers, pupils and other educational personnel of the kind called "interaction education" by some writers are imperative. In the school as in any other social enterprise the values and understandings of all partners constitute success. Assuming the validity of the foregoing premises, it is easy to establish the classroom as the focal point of home-school-community relations.

Practitioners undoubtedly have noted that much more is written about problems than about solutions. Indeed, the title of this chapter is "Understanding the Problem." In Chapter Fifteen, however, the authors make an honest effort to be positive, although the emphasis is on prevention of problems rather than on solutions.

In the training of both teachers and principals there is far too little emphasis on the importance and maintenance of healthful home-school-community relations. The implication for secondary school principals is quite clear. Thoughtfully conceived and carefully organized in-service education for teachers in this area of the school's role is a necessity. Although the authors favor the inclusion of study of school-community relations in the preservice education of teachers and principals, they realistically are more optimistic about the potential effectiveness of the in-service approach. Therefore, it is also urgent that the principal chart his own path of self-development in this crucial aspect of administrative leadership. The principal who believes strongly enough in the cruciality of the trinity of home-school-community to emphasize it in his self-growth program as well as in his staff growth plan has to have a basic belief in youth and community. It is this: maturity and commitment to democratic values are cultivated in youth when the home, school and community function truly as "Partners in Junior High School Education, Inc." through combining resources and understandings.

THE TRINITY OF HOME-SCHOOL-COMMUNITY

Symbiotic interaction describes the most desirable situation for the school-community relations program. Symbiotic is a biological term which means the living together of organisms of different species, each helpful to, or dependent on, the other. Although individuals of the home, school and community are of the same generic species, they do exhibit obvious differences in religion, politics, economics and racial backgrounds. That school leaders recognize the interdependence and mutual help possibilities of these widely differing individuals is of the utmost importance. Since there are so many different kinds of homes, schools and communities, no attempt is made to compound a recipe or model for the interaction of home-school-community.

In any school community there is a web of social relations. Depending upon the size and complexity of communities, that web is more or less extensive and more or less intricate. Of great concern to parents and principals alike is the question, "How can the school and the home function helpfully in a particular community setting?" Certainly, the school fails when it becomes no more than a cultural isolate, sealed off from the main street of community life, as silent and uninformative as the Sphinx.

No secondary school stands alone. The concept of "town and gown" is out; the concept of the partnership approach is in. Sumption and Engstrom [5] emphasize four principles essential to fully effective home-school-community cooperation. They are:

1. A recognition that the school is a public enterprise.
2. An understanding that the public school in America has the unique function and moral responsibility to seek out truth and to teach people how to live by it.
3. A realization that there must be a systematic, structured and active participation on the part of the people of a community in the educational enterprise.
4. A recognition that there must be a clear and effective two-way system of communications between the school and the community.

In the above essentials one readily discerns the expectancy that lay citizens will participate in education, individually and in various sized groups. In view of urbanization and more complex communities such a concept is strengthened, in theory at least, since diverse competencies possessed by the heterogeneous population may be applied toward improvement of existing educational practices and procedures.

Those same rapidly developing urban centers mentioned above, as well as thickly populated suburban areas, also pose a rather prickly problem in that some schools,

---

[5] M. Sumption and Y. Engstrom, *School-Community Relations: A New Approach* (New York: McGraw-Hill Book Co., 1966).

particularly senior high schools, now serve many diverse communities. Reorganization and consolidation movements also add to this confusion. The two-way communications essential listed above may be insufficient as a model of communication. The public is plural, and multiple-way communications are becoming more essential as the necessity grows for communication among communities. Where the school is concerned, mere outward bound and inward bound communications lines are insufficient to build the triad of home, school and community.

The difficulties encountered in building a durable and mutually sensitive trinity of home-school-community are compounded by research, experimentation, new knowledge and change. Increased complexity adds up to a distinct challenge of maintaining a relationship of sensitive awareness and direct communication among units of the total enterprise. Only the inept principal will wither in the face of a task of such magnitude for many are those who see clearly that our capabilities as well as the task are without parallel.

One of the latest and best books attending to the problem at hand is that of McCloskey [6] who in the light of present social change discusses lucidly such matters as citizen participation, what citizens need to know about schools' long-range programs, and staff personnel and public understanding. Another penetrating piece of writing coming to grips with the problem of education and community was authored by Newmann and Oliver,[7] the focus of their statements being on the individual within the community. Their working definition of community omits residence, political units, occupations, etc., as valid factors in determining the identity of communities. Rather, they defined community with a greater tolerance for diversity of conceptions describing the "good life." A community is a group

(1) in which membership is valued as an end in itself, not merely as a means to other ends;
(2) that concerns itself with many and significant aspects of the lives of members;
(3) that allows competing factions;
(4) whose members share commitment to common purpose and to procedures for handling conflict within the group;
(5) whose members share responsibility for the actions of the group;
(6) whose members have enduring and extensive personal contact with each other.

In the modern world, write Newmann and Oliver, ". . . community (as defined above) is missing." They suggest that perhaps American society will rediscover and reactivate this "missing community" when we realize that education, most broadly conceived, is the interaction between reflection and action and "should arise from real needs and issues within community, not from the drawing boards of distant national planners."

---

[6] G. McCloskey, *Education and Public Understanding* (New York: Harper and Row Publications, 1967), 662 pp.
[7] F.M. Newman and D.W. Oliver, "Education and Community," *Harvard Educational Review*, Vol. 37, no. 1 (Winter, 1967), pp. 61–106.

Although cooperative school planning is a goal to be sought, some elements of citizen participation are neither effective nor desirable. When such participation contributes to excellent human relations, rights and privileges of various individuals and groups are considered, and positive attempts are made to solve problems, it is likely to result in a success story.

OBJECTIVES OF THE COOPERATIVE APPROACH

It should be quite clear that a major purpose of cooperative action and mutual understanding of home, school and community is that of telling the school story. Kindred pointed out 11 objectives in fulfilling that purpose:

1. . . People should understand the purposes of education in a democracy.
2. The story should seek to develop a broader and deeper understanding of the instructional program. . . .
3. Reports should be made periodically on the accomplishments of pupils.
4. Changes in the nature and number of the pupil population should be emphasized and repeated often. . . .
5. It is highly important that explanations be made of financial management of schools in the local district.
6. Citizens should become acquainted with problems facing the local school system.
7. Popular confidence in the worth and value of the educational system should be increased.
8. Citizens should understand more fully the duties and responsibilities of those who direct and carry on the work of the school district.
9. The special services that play a vital part in the education of children should be explained.
10. Citizens should be induced to assume greater responsibility for the quality of education provided. . . .
11. The final objective should be that of establishing a strong partnership between school and community.[8]

It is proper to emphasize that effectively telling the school story does not guarantee the strong partnership suggested in objective 11. Nor does a strong cooperative relationship between school and community always insure that the school story will be told dramatically, accurately and completely. Both tasks need to be accomplished, however.

It is not within the purview of this chapter to illustrate cases where successful school-community cooperation has resulted in stronger communities and improved educational practices and procedures. Such success stories are multiple and are reported in many books devoted entirely to the topic of school-community relations.

The Community School. One major objective of home-school-community rela-

---

[8] L. Kindred, *How to Tell the School Story* (Englewood Cliffs, N.J.: Prentice-Hall, Inc., 1960), pp. 12, 13, 14. Used by permission of the publisher.

tions is the community school. The secondary building principal, particularly the junior high school principal, must have clear direction in fulfilling the desired role of the school in the community.

Characteristics of recognized community schools throughout the country, as well as the wishful thinking of leading proponents of the community school idea, have been crystallized into patterns and recommendations for moving nearer to the desired role of the public school in community life.

The public school as an institution is unique because in reality it belongs to the people. Since elected representatives of the people manage schools, the students of school-community programs must become acutely aware of community sentiment. School policies not in harmony with community ideals and beliefs often result in community resentment of increased costs, significant changes and proposed reforms in school management.

Generally speaking, most social institutions operate to fragment the community unless a specific agency is functioning to prevent such an undesirable effect. The school seems to be a logical coordinating agency, operating to unify the efforts of various community social and civic institutions.

Yeager [9] listed four philosophic steps in the progress of improving school-community relations; his fourth step, cooperative endeavor in the interests of complete child welfare, seems to be the basis of the community-school movement.

The *52nd Yearbook* of the National Society for the Study of Education, devoted entirely to various facets of the community-school idea, proposed this definition of the community school:

> Today, the community school to many educators and laymen is a *good* school, an *effective* school, combining many desirable features of past educational emphasis with those of the present to form a concept of education that is sound and permanent, not a fad of passing fancy.[10]

Most school people are aware of the increased tendency toward the more extensive use of lay people and citizens' advisory committees in helping to solve some of the more complex school problems. Other worthwhile activities receiving added emphasis in the forward-looking schools of today are school-sponsored recreational activities during out-of-school periods and camping experiences. Perhaps an insignificant number of training institutions make serious efforts to educate teachers for community leadership, although such practice is highly desirable and probably will receive more attention as schools expand their community-participation programs.

It is inevitable that the school must have some kind of relations with its community; less is known about the nature and number of these relationships. All schools, however, must be on a scale somewhere between the traditional school, in terms of school-community relations, and the community school.

A list of community-school characteristics was compiled from the educational

---

[9] William A. Yeager, *School-Community Relations* (New York: Dryden Press, 1951).
[10] National Society for the Study of Education, *52nd Yearbook,* Part II, 1953.

literature of ten authorities on school-community relations. Characteristics mentioned by seven or more authors include:

1. Uses community resources when possible.
2. Acts as a true community center.
3. Provides learning experiences for adults and out-of-school youths.
4. Maintains a comprehensive and flexible curriculum.
5. Cooperates with community agencies.
6. Implements democratic methods.
7. Staff members are active in community life.

As a result of these findings, four phases of school-community relations were developed. Such a process resulted in an instrument which can serve, to some extent, in placing a school somewhere on the scale between the traditional and the community school.

The four phases in a school's development in the area of school-community relationships with appropriate activities at each level are illustrated in Figure 14-1.

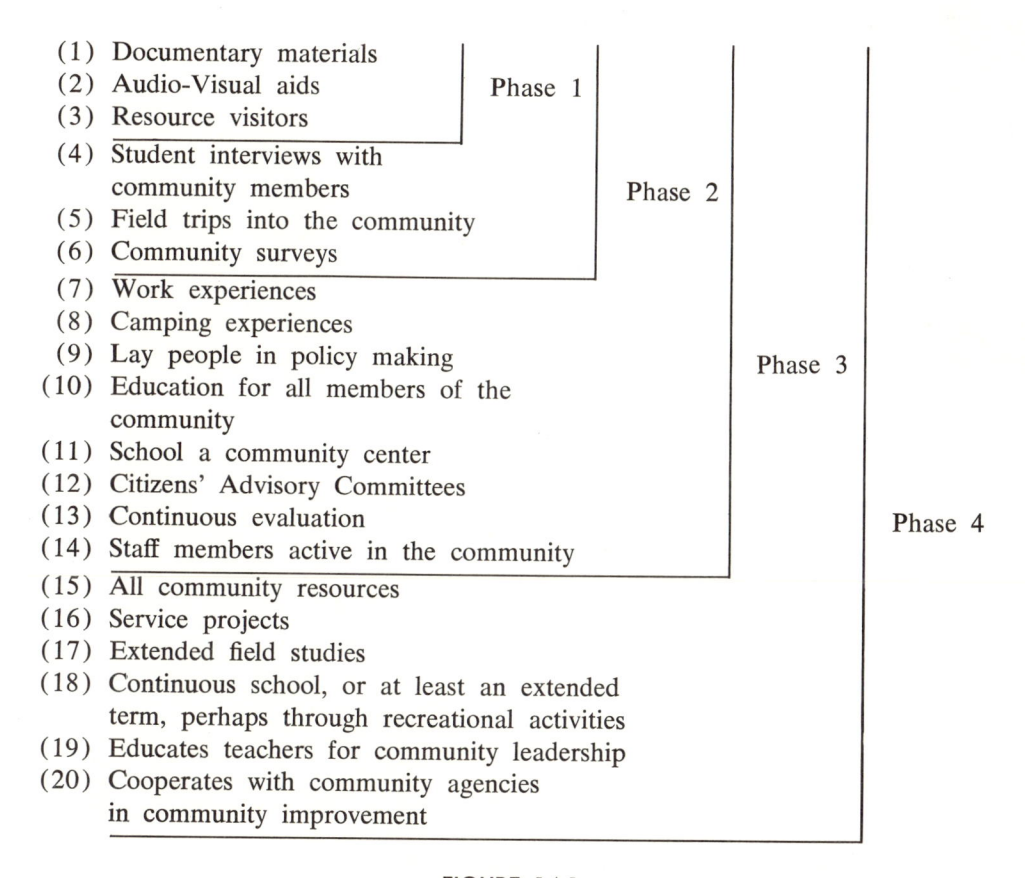

(1) Documentary materials
(2) Audio-Visual aids — Phase 1
(3) Resource visitors
(4) Student interviews with community members
(5) Field trips into the community — Phase 2
(6) Community surveys
(7) Work experiences
(8) Camping experiences
(9) Lay people in policy making
(10) Education for all members of the community
(11) School a community center — Phase 3
(12) Citizens' Advisory Committees
(13) Continuous evaluation
(14) Staff members active in the community
(15) All community resources
(16) Service projects
(17) Extended field studies
(18) Continuous school, or at least an extended term, perhaps through recreational activities — Phase 4
(19) Educates teachers for community leadership
(20) Cooperates with community agencies in community improvement

FIGURE 14-1

Phase 1 represents the traditional school while Phase 4 represents the community school. Phases 2 and 3 mark progressive points between Phases 1 and 4. Phase 1 describes the traditional school with its indifference to community sensitivity and its policy of isolation for the most part; Phase 2 suggests a level at which school policy provides for classroom study about the community as well as student field observations of the community. In such cases the school often has selfish reasons; the door is open for community assistance but not for aid in policy making. Phase 3 goes a step further, allowing students occasional direct participation in community activities for community improvement. This phase signifies an expedient school, lacking philosophical guidance and catering to the whims of certain public sentiments; Phase 4 is characterized by substantial teacher-pupil contributions to the improvement of community living. In this phase, education is a cooperative endeavor in matters of policy making as well as otherwise, with school officials taking an amount of leadership proportionate to their training and knowledge. This developmental level in school-community relations seems to fit the qualifications of a community school. It might be wise to point out the fact that certain schools, by virtue of extrinsic factors, could not reasonably be expected to adhere strictly to certain of the activities listed in the chart.

There are two possible points of departure for attempted reorganization and redirection of emphasis. The areas of organization and administration could include external control, internal control, and internal organization. Respective examples are school-lay group interaction, administrator-teacher-pupil relations and staff-pupil relations. The second area of reconstruction involving content and method is to be found in the practices of pupil participation in community life and community participation in school life.

Basically, a true community school operates democratically in its organization and administration. There should be a two-way movement of ideas and services. For certain purposes, the school would rely upon lay people as sources of direction; in turn, the school's chief concern would be with the underlying principles and conflicts facing its community today.

Authorities are more or less in agreement that the first step should be a thorough and accurate survey of the community. In the process of conducting the survey, which is a school-community project, it is possible to discover the real community leaders. Since the procedure of activation depends more upon leadership than upon leaders, it is necessary that leaders be brought to the fore who can exercise the necessary leadership without calling undue attention to themselves. The more nearly a situation becomes genuinely democratic, the more difficult it is to point out a leader.

A continuous flow of information to the people is a necessity. This can be accomplished successfully through the newspaper, newsletters, word of mouth, leaflets, student publications, local study groups, various meetings, speeches and the community council. The latter is definitely not a panacea but it can be helpful. It is a successful technique to guide public sentiment away from the idea that any meeting is just another meeting to be avoided like the plague. Speakers must accept as their challenge the stimulation of the audience to "take the next step."

As yet very little has been done in the vital area of scientific evaluation of associations of home, school and community. Another area in this whole matter which seems to need careful study is the nature and value of the administrator's leadership in all phases of the processes of interaction. Still another point which requires practical consideration and study is the question of who initiates and originates the processes leading to full cooperative enterprise.

SPECIFIC RECOMMENDATIONS

Administrators should seek a partnership role of community citizens by:

1. a program of educational interpretation simple enough that all citizens can comprehend.
2. exercising educational leadership sufficiently effective to stimulate in people the will to have good schools and assist in their support by energizing all community agencies.
3. a profound knowledge of the nature and intricacies of the community served by the school system.
4. consistency in the use of tact, patience and helpful guidance with individual citizens and their organizations when they offer suggested changes.
5. sympathetic and appreciative attitudes toward, and cooperation with, the efforts of voluntary agencies purporting to improve the schools.
6. constant awareness of education in other areas and inquiry into the methods and techniques employed by others in enlisting citizen participation in the school program.

Teachers should materially assist citizens in their services by:

1. showing courtesy and genuine pleasure toward all visitors.
2. actively participating in parent-teacher organizations and other community affairs.
3. seeking, through invitation, use of the community's human resources both in curriculum planning and in instruction.
4. emphasizing the unique value of citizen contributions.

An address delivered by William G. Werner to the Schoolmasters Club of Cincinnati offers suggestions for other justifiable objectives: [11]

1. Ascertain what the public thinks about the school.
2. Up-to-date evaluation of public attitudes by the school is a necessity.
3. Draw on the public for help and advice.

---

[11] W.G. Werner, *The Schoolmaster and His Publics*. An address to the Schoolmasters Club of Cincinnati on September 8, 1956. (Mr. Werner's talk suggested implications for applying public relations techniques and principles of business to education.)

4. The school must recognize limitations imposed by deep-seated public beliefs, habits and prejudices.
5. Handle complaints and troubles ethically and effectively.
6. Translate news about the school into news about people.
7. Since the school is constantly in the white light of publicity, always remember that at any moment any school can become headline news.

THE NEED FOR INFORMATION AND INTERPRETATION

The larger team of home-school-community, as well as the school's internal team of school-community relations leaders, are admonished to keep in mind that the pressure of public opinion may be compared with the pressure of the atmosphere; you can't see it but it's there, just the same. Public pressure on the school varies, depending on a number of complex factors. The necessity for having accurately and completely informed publics which are sympathetic with the school and motivated to take action is heightened today by such complex variables as social change, increased enrollments, research and innovation, the federal role, finance, and the knowledge build-up. Citizens who compose the many publics which impinge upon the schools will vote, participate in determining local policies and affect the educational climate. It is essential that they be enlightened through appropriate messages which inform and interpret.

Lack of home and community good will toward and cooperation with the school does exist and it is caused. The human element is at the core. Everything that happens in the school affects and involves human beings and has either a negative or positive net effect on the educational climate. Since usually the common problems of a community are educational problems, cooperative considerations and collective action for insuring that all children live happier and more creative and satisfying lives is a necessary function of any modern junior or senior high school.

SELECTED READINGS

The Bulletin, National Association of Secondary School Principals, 44 (September, 1960), pp. 7–16.

Dale, Edgar, *Can You Give the Public What It Wants?* (New York: Cowles Education Corporation and World Book Encylopedia, 1967)

Golden, L. L., Public Relation, *Saturday Review* (June 9, 1962).

Jones, J. J., *An Analysis and Summary of the Significant Research Findings Concerning Some Problems and Issues of School-Community Relations,* Doctoral Dissertation, School of Education, Indiana University, 1952, 246 pp., typed.

Kindred, L. W., *How to Tell the School Story.* (Englewood Cliffs, N.J.: Prentice-Hall, Inc., 1960), 500 pp.

Kindred, L. W., *School Public Relations.* (Englewood Cliffs, N.J.: Prentice-Hall, Inc., 1957), 454 pp.

McCloskey, G., *Education and Public Understanding.* (New York: Harper and Row Publications, 1967), 622 pp.

National Society for the Study of Education, *The Community,* 52nd Yearbook, Part II, University of Chicago Press, 1953, 292 pp.

Newman, F. M. and Oliver, D. W., "Education and Community," *Harvard Educational Review,* Vol. 37, No. 1 (Winter, 1967), pp. 61–106.

Pierce, T. M., et. al., *Community Leadership for Public Education.* (Englewood Cliffs, New Jersey: Prentice-Hall, Inc., 1955)

Stearns, H. L., *Community Relations and the Public Schools.* (Englewood Cliffs, New Jersey: Prentice-Hall, Inc., 1955), 354 pp.

Sumption, M. and Engstrom, Y., *School-Community Relations: A New Approach.* (New York: McGraw-Hill Book Company, 1966), 238 pp.

Werner, W. G., "The Schoolmaster and His Publics," An address to the Schoolmaster's Club of Cincinnati on September 8, 1956. (Mr. Werner's talk suggested implications for applying public relations techniques and principles of business to education)

FIFTEEN

Basic Principles of Communication and Human Relations

The school is a social institution. The ideal relationship is a partnership of the home, the school, and the community. The partnership exists regardless of the level of the school in the total educational program; however, perhaps a greater need exists for improving and strengthening the relationships existing among the partners at the secondary level than at any other level. In *The Junior High School Program in Illinois,* the following factors are identified as reasons for the special importance attached to home-school-community relations at the junior high level:

(1) The junior high school has been the last of the levels of education to develop. (2) Many, if not most, of the adult citizens of today have not attended a junior high school. (3) Developmental tasks and needs of the preadolescent and early adolescent are not as clearly defined and recognized by the public and the profession as are those of earlier and later periods of life. (4) Pre-service education of teachers has not been adequate for this level. (5) The reshuffling of society's values and the reflected pressures on the schools made it imperative that each level of the school system knows and makes known to the public its particular functions and responsibilities.[1]

Home-school-community relations can be considered from a variety of aspects. Human relations are basic to any analysis of the topic. Educators seem to have reached a consensus that adequate communication is the key to any good public relations pro-

---

[1] *The Junior High School Program in Illinois* (Springfield, Illinois: Office of the Superintendent of Public Instruction, 1961), p. 23.

gram. The ideas to be communicated are unlimited; however, appraisal and evaluation are universal for all school systems.

HUMAN RELATIONS

The constant relation of human beings with human beings is so completely universal that one cannot move away from it. However, if one wants to appraise the quality of this vital phenomenon, he must narrow the field. This we shall attempt to do by taking a look at human relations in the secondary school.

Responsible parents consider it their privilege and duty to create and maintain a warm, congenial atmosphere in and about the home. Quite naturally this is a highly desirable climate for the adult world. If a relaxed, tension-free atmosphere is helpful for the mental and physical world of the adult, isn't it much more so for the young teenager? And does it not logically follow that the same sympathetic climate is equally desirable and helpful for a classroom of 30 or more young adolescents? We can say that a calm atmosphere is needed especially in the junior high school for this is where the restless youth spends five or more hours of his day. These human beings are restless because they are looking for answers. Their inquisitive minds are encased in a rapidly changing body which they do not fully comprehend nor always know exactly how to handle. These adolescents rightly resent being termed children, yet they realize they are not part of the adult world.

The adolescent does want to be considered adult. Sometimes he will behave in a manner quite grown-up. Half an hour later he may revert to a manner quite childish. He may become unduly angry at the slightest provocation. The parent and teacher should not be too surprised. Rather, these significant adults should assist this usurper of the peace by providing a tranquil atmosphere in which the young person can think. He needs to think, for he is searching for many answers that concern him.

He wants to know who he is. Name and street number are no longer sufficient identification. This emerging adult wants proper status as a unique individual. Now that puberty has made some physiological changes, the youthful boy and girl realize that they have a significant role to play in the world. They may not be sure what the role is, but they know a few things they want. These strongly felt desires include an urge to be independent of the family, but not alienated from it. They want to be free from parental authority, but in no way disowned by the family. The adolescent wants to be able to cope with himself at all times, and he is surprised to learn that sometimes he cannot. If the boy stumbles over a chair or breaks a dish because he seems to have such long arms and legs all of a sudden, he is only embarrassed further if the teacher reprimands him. A teacher may find it hard to be tranquil if this happens very often, but tranquility will help the lad more than a reproach.

What exactly is the role of the school with regard to human relations within this particular age group, the adolescents? Quite clearly, the school is expected to create and maintain an atmosphere of relative quiet, but in a constructive way. These so-called noisy individuals need a time and place to think. They have problems.

Leland P. Bradford asks the pertinent question: "If money were no object and there were a surplus of good teachers would we eliminate the class group in favor of individual teaching?" [2]

His reply is clearly negative. Teachers are well acquainted with group dynamics. Teachers are also extremely conscious of the adolescent's need for peer group approval. One could hardly evaluate the true worth of the stimulation for learning where there is an adolescent group and a competent teacher. True, the teacher is all too frequently reminded of the negative effects of the group force. The teacher must be able to cope with the unforeseen, with regard to persons and to the unpredicted changes in schedules.

When one or a few students learn a lesson well, recite it, or in some other manner display their accomplishment, more often than not, there is a great inclination for the remainder of the class to follow the good example. Not all the class will do as the teacher hopes, but an encouraging number will. In this way the group stimulates individual learning.

It is possible and necessary for the teacher to impress on his students that the learning situation of the group is an individual enterprise. The teacher's goal is for each student to learn to his fullest potential for that particular class at that particular time.

The importance of the teacher's role could scarcely be overestimated in this matter of human relations in the secondary school. Students want to admire and respect their teachers. They will be more apt to imitate and respect one whom they feel is keenly interested in them as individuals. They will usually respect the teacher who is predictable, prepared, orderly, and well versed in the subject matter. Impressionable students are disappointed when they do not find these qualities in their teachers. Above all, the students want their teacher to be interested in them as individuals. A friendly, relaxed climate is highly conducive to growth in the academic and social worlds. Earnest study is a prerequisite for academic achievement. Good student-teacher rapport cannot be maintained if the teacher constantly hovers over the class in an authoritarian role. It would help if the teacher would move freely about the room rather than remain in the center front of the classroom. There are many times when the class can be broken up into groups for discussion. At this time it is well for the teacher to move from group to group, even sitting in a student chair for a time with each group.

Each student has a certain capacity for learning which is different from that of all other members of the class. The perceptive teacher is aware of this, and will adjust his approach and techniques to fit the needs of each student. This is, at least, a goal for which a teacher should strive.

When the students are permitted a reasonable amount of active participation, more and better learning can be expected. Very often it is possible to permit students to make suggestions as to procedures in problem solving, play acting, the choosing of teammates for contests, room decorations, or appropriate designs or posters pertinent to a project, choosing winners, or electing a student for a certain honor. Students are often content in the classroom in proportion to the amount of leadership activity they are permitted.

---

[2] Leland P. Bradford, "The Class Is a Group," *The High School Journal*, XLIV (May, 1961), p. 270.

This in no way detracts from the teacher's role as the one invested with authority. His dignity will more than likely be enhanced because he will be more enthusiastically accepted by the class.

These activities serve to unite the group. And what is more important to a normal teen-ager than his peer group?

It is also the school's responsibility to impress upon each student the knowledge that learning is each one's own responsibility. If the teacher is to maintain good human relations, he should try to see that no individual is rejected by the crowd. This takes skill and diplomacy. The teacher will probably fail occasionally in his efforts to keep the crowd united, but it is possible for him to be highly successful as a unifying force.

If a student is to respect other persons, he must find some reason to respect himself. Teachers cannot afford to overlook a tired or worried student who sees himself as a failure. If continued, this negative attitude toward one's self leads to further failure, perhaps hostility toward society in general, then delinquency.

The secondary school years are important. These are the years when the adolescents are doing more soul searching than an adult might suspect. These are the years when our young teen-agers daydream constructively. They think generously and altruistically. A great deal of helpful hero worship takes place.

Parents should be informed of what their adolescents are doing in school, what the particular strengths and weaknesses are. A report card which is sent home about four times a year is usually not considered sufficient. Parent-teacher conferences can be scheduled. This is one of the best means that a teacher can have if he is to be of adequate service to the student. Knowledge of the home background of each child is essential. Very often a teacher will take on an entirely new and different attitude toward a student after he has met the parents. Talking with the parents is extremely helpful for the teacher. It need not be regarded as a chore, but rather an opportunity to meet new people and make new friends. The parents of many of our students are struggling financially, physically, socially. The importance of knowing the home situation can scarcely be over-rated. When a teacher does a service for a student, he is certainly helping the family of that student also.

Along with knowing the student's parents, the teacher should be well acquainted with the neighborhood in which the members of his class are spending their free time. It is helpful for the teacher to know about the jobs available in the neighborhood for both the boys and the girls. He should be aware of the recreational facilities available. If adequate recreational parks and areas are not available, the teacher could be a strong force in having them made available or at least, find a way to transport the class to an amusement park of some sort. This can often be done two or three times during the school year.

Maintaining good human relations, no matter what level of school life we are referring to, is extremely important. We never stop needing people, so the teacher's task of setting the example of warm friendliness is probably uppermost in his scale of values.

COMMUNICATION

The key to an effective program of home-school-community relations is communication. A dictionary definition of the word reveals such meanings as the following: "(1) an imparting; (2) the act of making oneself understood; an expression of thoughts or opinions; (3) means of passing, or of sending, information from one place to another; (4) news; intercourse." [3]

Frequently educators refer to communications as a two-way system. An illustration of this view appears in the following statement by Sumption and Engstrom:

> . . . there must be *a clear and effective two-way system of communication between school and community*. Communication which limits itself to telling the people about the school is doing only one-half the job. Equally important is telling the school about the people who support it and are served by it. It is important that the community knows what the school is doing, but it is equally important that the school knows what the people are doing. In brief, the community should know its school and the school should know its community.[4]

A thoughtful analysis of communication as it applies to home-school-community relations reveals that a more adequate definition than the preceding ones can be formulated. First, the term implies a multi-dimensional system rather than a two-way system—multi-dimensional in contacts and multi-dimensional in procedures. As messages follow a circuitous route in returning to the source, the two-way system has been lost. With this kind of communication, the original meaning may be altered, perhaps incorrectly.

Miller's definition adds still another connotation. He writes, "In the main, communication has, as its central interest those behavioral situations in which a source transmits a message to a receiver(s) *with* conscious intent to affect the latter's behavior." [5] His idea varies from the other definitions because of the emphasis on *conscious intent*. Perhaps a lack of conscious intent on the part of secondary school personnel has been a major factor in those situations reflecting poor communication with the homes and the community. Too much may have been left to chance or accident. Cognizance of this view should help to channel the major efforts of those working in communication toward greater productivity.

Education can receive much stimulation for thought and many ideas for application from the general principles and theories utilized in business enterprises. Likert [6]

---

[3] *The Winston Dictionary* (Philadelphia: The John C. Winston Company, 1947), p. 193.

[4] Merle R. Sumption and Yvonne Engstrom, *School-Community Relations—A New Approach* (New York: McGraw-Hill Book Company, 1966), p. XI., and p. 7. Used with permission of McGraw-Hill Book Company.

[5] Gerald R. Miller, "On Defining Communication: Another Stab," *The Journal of Communication*, XVI (June, 1966), p. 92.

[6] Rensis Likert, *New Patterns of Management* (New York: McGraw-Hill Book Company, Inc., 1961), p. 59.

suggests that high performance goals as well as favorable attitudes must be present if an organization is to achieve a high degree of productivity. Secondary school pupils and personnel, including administrators, teachers, and para-professional workers, must assess their roles very carefully to determine what performance goals are appropriate at this level. If teachers and administrators are functioning without a personal commitment and/or without special preparation in cognizance of the characteristics of early adolescence, their effectiveness in communicating with pupils and with the community will be limited.

Educators seem to have reached the consensus that schools should change to meet changing social conditions. The recognition that the local community will be affected by changing conditions which should be reflected in the secondary school program emphasizes the need for more effective dialogue between experienced educators.

The concept of communication all too frequently is limited to the practical aspects —the techniques utilized to convey meaning. DeFleur states clearly the limitations to this view:

> The problem of communication is not actually a "transfer" of meaning. In the communication act, there is no essence, spirit, or invisible "something" that leaves the central nervous system of one person and travels to that of another. . . .
> . . . it takes place through the operation of a particular set of components in a theoretical system.[7]

Robinson emphasizes the importance of theory in communication as follows:

> Theoretical knowledge of communication will contribute to a better understanding of *why* he is communicating and help provide the public relations practitioner with guides as to what form his pratical communications should take.[8]

Techniques and procedures of communication have been given considerable attention in educational literature; however, the theoretical perspective does not seem to have received the consideration warranted. The business world has been much more cognizant of the importance of theory than the educational world has been. The components of the communicative act can be formulated into a theory model. The advantages of such a model for a secondary school lie in the fact that public relations problems can be translated according to the model resulting in a more systematic analysis and solution. The point has been made already that communication is multi-dimensional. If a theory model is formulated for the local situation, then all the participants in the communicative act have a common basis for strengthening and coordinating efforts.

A variety of communication theory models has been formulated. The writers propose to suggest a very simple model favored by Borosage. The complexity of the model and the variations in components do not represent the most vital issue. The most im-

---

[7] Melvin L. DeFleur, *Theories of Mass Communication* (New York: David McKay Company, Inc., 1966), p. 91.

[8] Edward J. Robinson, *Communication and Public Relations* (Columbus, Ohio: Charles E. Merrill Books, Inc., 1966), p. 23.

portant point is that some structured theory model, understood and accepted by the local school system, is essential for optimum communication.

Borosage [9] identified the essential components in a communication theory model as S-M-C-R. These letters represent components present in every act of communication—S for source which initiates the communication, M for the message, C for the channel or means of communication, and R for the receiver.

In considering this theory model for use by the junior or senior high school, personnel need to be aware of their own limitations and of the factors which may hinder communication. The social-cultural context of school personnel may differ from the social-cultural backgrounds of the homes and of the community. The communication probably will never bear fruit if the social-cultural context of the receiver is ignored. The multi-dimensional concept becomes especially important relative to the receiver in school communities incorporating more than one cutural or sub-cultural group. Children may not even want to live in the same social-cultural context as their parents.

The terms, attitudes and opinions appear frequently relative to both the source and the receiver as determinants of whether communication will be received or will meet with interference. Chaffee [10] objects to the use of these terms on the grounds that they are not precise in meaning. He prefers *salience,* defined as psychological closeness, and *pertinence,* defined as the degree to which the people involved possess the same attribute.

The level of knowledge about the subject displayed by both the source and the receiver affects the outcome of the communicative act. The trust and respect held by the receiver for the source is of paramount importance. School personnel must be aware of the level of knowledge of the community members in order to be within the group's frame of reference without phrasing the message beneath the capability of the group to comprehend.

One of the reasons why many junior and senior high school communication programs have failed is that the starting point was the content of the message rather than the relationships among the people involved. Every message must have content, but this content must be coded or replaced in terminology and treated in a manner which will be understood by the intended receivers.

The channels by which people receive information are the five senses—hearing, seeing, touching, tasting, and smelling. The chances of communicating increase as the number of channels used increases. The staff perhaps will be able to utilize media stimulating to more channels than lay community people will be able to do because of the fact that school staff member(s) may have specialized training in the area of communication media.

The writers have approached the use of the S-M-C-R theory model primarily as outward communication. However, any school personnel who utilize the model in de-

---

[9] Presented by Larry Borosage for a Workshop: Teaching Procedures in Home Economics Education at the Purdue University Calumet Campus, Summer, 1964.

[10] Steven H. Chaffee, "Salience and Pertinence as Sources of Value Change," *The Journal of Communication,* XVII (March, 1967), pp. 25–28.

signing outward communication will tend to be more receptive to and cognizant of inward communication from the homes and from the community.

Communication is indeed a very complex and interesting process. Current literature presents a variety of practical procedures or techniques; however, the theory of the process is basic. The communication program should be evaluated according to a theory model. Saying that communication has failed is not enough. Which component caused the difficulty? Saying that communication is successful is not enough if growth and progress are to continue. Each of the component elements must be improved at the local school level.

APPRAISAL, MARKING AND REPORTING OF PUPIL PROGRESS

Pupil appraisal is no simple matter, but neither is the process of reporting the results of appraisal. It is necessary for each school or school system to adopt its own policies concerning pupil appraisal, marking, and reporting the results to parents. These policies should coincide with the philosophy of the school or school system. Great care is needed to make these appraisals and reports reflect the sum total of each individual student's learning process and behavior changes.

There have been numerous forms of appraisals, marking, and reporting experimented with and used throughout the United States. The writers do not believe it is possible to settle on any particular one and say that it is the best one to use. However, it is thought that the following factors should be evaluated: (1) mental ability or academic aptitude, (2) achievement in the various curriculum areas taken by each of the students, (3) personal and social adjustment, (4) physical status of pupils, (5) growth in interest of each pupil, (6) growth in attitudes of each pupil, (7) growth in work-study skills of each pupil, (8) growth in creative self-expression, (9) growth in critical thinking, and (10) the home and community background of each pupil.

An excellent list of guidelines to be followed in improving reporting practices follows:

> (1) The purpose of the reporting to parents is to enlist their cooperation in providing the best educational opportunities possible for the child.
>
> (2) The reporting procedure should include an appraisal of the physical, mental, emotional, and social growth of the child.
>
> (3) The reporting procedure should emphasize the child's progress in terms of his own abilities and past achievements rather than his standing in comparison with other members of the class.
>
> (4) The reporting procedure should emphasize guiding the child rather than judging him.
>
> (5) The reporting procedure should reflect a comprehensive picture of the achievement of the child without requiring too much clerical work on the part of the teacher.

(6) Report cards should be supplemented by letters to parents, samples of the child's work, parent-teacher conferences, and home visits.

(7) The reporting procedure should be consistent with the philosophy of the school.[11]

Reporting procedures have changed over the past 25 years, mostly to the good. There are two important facts to keep in mind which are pertinent to this change. They are (1) differences in reporting practices from level to level and school to school are not easily understood by pupils and their parents, and (2) try as many teachers and parents may to guide learning for learning's sake, there has been far more guidance of learning for the sake of grades and good reports.[12]

There are three major questions which need to be answered concerning reports. They are—"Why report," "What to report," and "How to report." Each of these questions will be considered in the following paragraphs.

Why Report? Teachers report so the parents may know how their children are getting along in school. Reporting systems that fail to convey to parents information they understand about their children's progress invite trouble. Marks could be used to decide on promotion and graduation. Reporting systems have been geared in many communities to their potential for interpreting the school and its needs to parents. One purpose for reporting to parents has been to provide pupils with the incentive to do schoolwork that neither parent nor teacher knew how to supply. In essence then, we must say—(1) parents should have information about their children's progress and standing in school, and (2) it is important that students have the best information available in understandable form about their own progress.

What to Report? The educational philosophy in a school or system and especially in the classrooms concerned would be expected to control the nature of the report. In making these reports the school should make certain that parents understand what their children's reports are intended to tell, and that the reports summarize data which pupils can use.

There is uncertainty concerning the meaning of the various marks or symbols given in school. This is brought about by the fact that some schools use S's and U's, or perhaps E's and O's; others use A's, B's, C's, etc.; while others may use the numerals 1, 2, 3, etc. Not knowing what the school or even what each individual teacher means when a mark, symbol, or numeral is placed on the report also leads to confusion for the student as well as for the parent. It is the responsibility of both the school and the parents, as well as the students, to be acquainted with the meaning of each grade placed on the report.

How to Report? There are many ways to report to parents the progress of their child. The most frequently used are (1) report cards, (2) parent-teacher conferences, (3) written letters, and (4) short notes.

Some results of previous research of reports and appraisal are pertinent. First, a

---

[11] William B. Ragan, *Modern Elementary Curriculum* (New York: Holt, Rinehart and Winston, 3rd edition, 1966), p. 479.

[12] William M. Alexander, "Reporting to Parents, Why? What? How?" *National Education Association Journal*, XLVIII (December, 1959), pp. 15–28.

single symbol is incapable of telling all that was desired. Secondly, teachers' marking procedures are relatively unreliable and finally, it is the teachers who pushed the change in marking rather than the parents.[13]

All persons, no matter what age or occupation, function best in an atmosphere of peace and quiet acceptance. Certainly, then, our teen-agers, so often described as living through an age of stress and strain, need a tension-free climate for school. This is possible only where they are accepted by their teachers who regard them as unique individuals and important parts of our society.

Whatever marking system is used, it should be immediately meaningful both to the learner and his parents. This has usually resulted in the use of written explanations and interpretations to assure that there is some degree of uniformity in the meaning of the symbols. All marking systems should be standardized for all teachers in the system. The standards should be clearly stated on the cards sent home so that both the learner and his parents understand them. Marking systems should be subjected to periodic review, preferably in cooperation with parents. When this is done, we will have more effective home-school-community relations.

EFFECTIVE ADMINISTRATIVE PRACTICES IN SCHOOL-COMMUNITY RELATIONS

On the basis of an exhaustive study of the literature and an analysis of data secured from depth interviews with 42 Indiana Secondary School Principals judged to be highly competent in school-community relations, Baughman[14] reached the following conclusions with respect to effective practices in this aspect of secondary school administration:

1. Certain general administrative practices in the promotion of effective school-community relations are indispensable. They are: (1) cordial relations with the press, (2) upkeep of buildings and grounds, (3) recognition of the importance of community needs in the design of the school program, (4) the acceptance of constructive criticism of the school and its program.

2. Effective media of free communication between the school and its community are: (1) preparation of school news for the public press by the principal, (2) written reports by the principal to the school board, (3) preparation of faculty bulletins by the principal and (4) the utilization of a public address system where parents and other laymen are assembled.

3. Effective techniques for securing citizen participation in the school program are as follows: (1) utilization of lay advisory committees, (2) interviews with patrons and community leaders to determine what they wish the school to do for their children, (3) utilization of educational committees of community organizations.

---

[13] William A. Yauch, "School Marks and Their Reporting," *National Education Association Journal*, L (May, 1961), p. 504.

[14] M. Dale Baughman, *Effective Techniques of Administering School-Community Relations and Means of Professional Growth in These Relations Utilized by Indiana Public Secondary School Principals,* Doctoral Dissertation, Indiana University, 1956, pp. 293–300.

4. Effectual techniques for bringing the community into the school include: (1) unscheduled adult visitors to the school, (2) adult education classes in school buildings, (3) exhibits of school work at school for community groups, (4) special visiting days or nights with regular classes in session.

5. Techniques of considerable value in extending the school into the community are: (1) principal participates actively in church functions, (2) principal participates actively in community projects, (3) principal attends meetings of community civic and service organizations, and (4) teachers speak for public groups away from school.

6. Special techniques of substantial value in the development of harmonious relations between the school and community are the following: (1) maintenance of a record of officers of local organizations, (2) inclusion of units on community study in some courses, (3) continuous study of occupations involving lay participation, (4) maintenance of a systematic work experience program, (5) maintenance of a list of special talents and hobbies of teachers, and (6) a commencement program centered around student speakers.

7. There appears to be no typical organization of personnel for administering the public relations function; however, it is likely that in most cases it is a cooperative effort, involving the participation of the superintendent, the principal, the teachers, and the students.

8. The beginning principal who knows the importance of school-community cooperation would be wise to (1) proceed slowly in making changes and in developing a program of school-community relations, (2) make the faculty conscious of the value of school-community relations, (3) become active in community life, and (4) encourage his staff to become active in community life.

9. "Contacts with others" and "study on the job" seem to be the major sources of professional growth of most principals. About the only area of professional growth in which principals rely mainly on study in the colleges and universities of Indiana is that of using consultants in improving the school program.

10. Both large and small city school principals should find these means of in-service growth helpful in the enterprise of coordinating school and community: (1) attending state conventions for educational administrators, (2) independent reading, (3) attending regional conventions for educational administrators, (4) forming self-study committees of local faculty members, (5) participating in regional school-men's clubs, and (6) reading in professional journals.

Secondary school personnel must recognize and accept their responsibility for defining and clarifying the philosophy and functions of junior and senior high schools. The junior high school, as an organizational unit, has come to be accepted. Adequate justification exists for its continuance as a level in the educational structure; however, such justification has not always been formulated clearly in the minds of those involved directly with the junior high school as professional personnel or as community members. The need for effective communication from home to school to community is apparent. Strengthening the home-school-community relations pertaining to this vital social institution will contribute not only to its continuance but also to its growth and development.

SELECTED READINGS

Alexander, William M. "Reporting to Parents, Why? What? How?" *National Education Association Journal.* 48, (December, 1959), pp. 15–28.

Baughman, M. Dale, *Effective Techniques of Administering School-Community Relations and Means of Professional Growth in These Relations Utilized by Indiana Public Secondary School Principals,* Doctoral Dissertation, Indiana University, 1956, p. 360.

Bradford, Leland P., "The Class Is a Group," *The High School,* XLIV (May, 1961).

Chaffee, Steven H., "Salience and Pertinence as Sources of Value Change," *The Journal of Communication,* XVII (March, 1967), pp. 25–38.

DeFleur, Melvin L. *Theories of Mass Communication.* (New York: David McKay Company, Inc., 1966)

The Junior High School Program in Illinois. (Springfield, Illinois: Office of the Superintendent of Public Instruction, 1961)

Likert, Rensis, *New Patterns of Management.* (New York: McGraw-Hill Book Company, Inc., 1961)

Lindvall, C. M., *Measuring Pupil Achievement and Aptitude.* (New York: Harcourt, Brace and World, Inc., 1967), p. 5.

Miller, Gerald R., "On Defining Communication: Another Staff," *The Journal of Communication,* XVI (June, 1966), pp. 88–98.

Ragan, William B., *Modern Elementary Curriculum.* (New York: Holt, Rinehart and Winston, third edition, 1966)

Robinson, Edward J., *Communication and Public Relations.* (Columbus, Ohio: Charles E. Merrill Books, Inc., 1966)

The Winston Dictionary. (Philadelphia: The John C. Winston Company, 1947)

Yauch, William A., "School Marks and Their Reporting," *National Education Association Journal,* 50 (May, 1961), p. 50.

# Index

A

A Guide to Collective Negotiations in Education, 4
"A New Concept of Staff Relations," 15n
A New Design for High School Education, 86n, 108n, 113n, 115n
"A Guide to Evaluating Self-Instructional Programs," 122n
A Practical Application of the Trump Plan, 64n
"A Sharp Upturn in Teacher Demand," 53n
"A Statement of Policy Concerning the Nation's Human Resource Problem," 165n
A Study of the Competencies Needed for Junior High Principles, 34n
A Study of the Effectiveness of Language Laboratories, 123n
Aaron, J.E., 153
Acceleration and enrichment, 105–106
Accommodations for pupil personnel services, 163–164
Activities, pupil, 185–201
Adaptive programming, 122
Administration, components of, 12–13
Administration of the Changing Secondary School, 135n
Administration of the School Building Program, 137n
Administrative areas, consideration of in planning educational facilities, 142
Administrative practices, effective, in school-community relations, 227–229
Administrative staff in modern secondary school, 3–45
  leadership, educational, nature and challenge of, 3–20
  principles of administration and supervision, 21–36
  self-improvement program, principal's, 37–45
Administrative Theory in Education, 14n, 15
Administrators' Notebook, 15n
Adolescent, characteristics of, 174–176
Advanced placement program, 106
Alexander, William M., 226n
Allen, Dwight, W., 86n, 108n, 113n, 115n
Alternatives for resolution of teacher-principal conflict, 9
American Association for Health, Physical Education, and Recreation, 182n
American Association of School Administrators, 4, 13, 21, 21n, 40, 88n, 103n, 134n, 136n, 137n, 144, 153n

American High School Administration: Policy and Practice, 13n
American Institute of Architects, 146–147
American Library Association, 131, 144
American Personnel and Guidance Association, 165, 165n
American School Board Journal, 144
American Social Health Association, 182n
American Telephone and Telegraph Company, 207
An Analysis of Lay and Professional Attitudes Toward the High School Principalship, 18n
An Analysis and Summary of the Significant Research Findings Concerning Some Problems and Issues of School-Community Relations, 205n
Application form, sample of, 55, 56–57
Appraisal of pupil progress, 225–227
Appreciation vital for good morale, 76
Architect, role of in planning educational innovations, 137
  communicating educational needs to, 143–144
Area zoning, 148
Arrangement second phase of administration, 12–13
Art and music, guidance in course selection for, 92–93
A.S.C.D., 8, 8n, 22n, 31n
Assemblies, student, another form of extra-class activities, 189
Assessment of teacher performance, 28
Association for Supervision and Curriculum Development, 8, 8n, 22n, 31n, 109n
Athletics, interscholastic, 193–195
Auditorium, consideration of in planning educational facilities, 142
Austin, O., 13n
Authority, four concepts of, 22–23
Autocratic leadership approach, 16–17
Automated schedule, 113–115
Auxiliary areas, consideration of in planning educational innovations, 142–143

B

Baden, Walter, 112n
Baden Maurer Letter Number Two, 112n
"Balanced judgment" approach to educational administration, 14
Barrington Middle School, 64, 66, 147
Barrington Middle School: A Report 1966/Barrington, Illinois, 64n

INDEX

Bartels, Dr. Martin H., 53, 53n
Baughman, M. Dale, 227n
Bayham, D., 10n
Beggs, David W. III, 64n, 109n
Bennett, Margaret E., 163n
Bent, R.K., 23, 23n
Bestor, 62
Bird, J.B., 122n
Block of time programs, 102–103
Boardman, C.W., 23, 23n
Borosage, Larry, 223–224
Bossing, Nelson L., 102n
Bradford, Leland P., 220, 220n
Branched programming, 122
Brickell, Henry M., 10n, 80, 80n
Broudy, Harry S., 39
Brown, Bartley Frank, 64n, 109n
Brown, Harry L., 18, 18n
Brown, Ray E., 39
Bruner, Jerome, 39
Brunstetter, Max R., 21n
Budget for instructional materials, 125–126
Buffie, Edward G., 109n
Bulletin of the National Association of Secondary School Principals, 9n, 10n, 34n, 40, 63n, 111n, 115n, 190n
Burck, Gilbert, 40
Burke, A.J., 137n, 138n
Burnett, Joe R., 39
Burnham, R.M., 22, 22n
Burrup, Percy E., 186n
Bush, Robert N., 86n, 108n, 111n, 113n, 115n
Business education, guidance in course selection for, 94
Business Management, 76n

C

Campbell, M.V., 7n
Carioti, Frank, 121n
Carlson, Reynold E., 107n
Carnegie Commission on Educational Television, 119
Carnegie Corporation of New York, 75n
CASSA, 85
Categories to be assessed in screening of teacher-candidates, 55
Caution about use of innovative learning materials, 126–127
Censorship constant problem of school newspaper, 191
Certification in pupil personnel services, 169
Chaffee, Steven H., 224
Change, challenge of, 9–11
Chapman, Dave, 121n
Characteristics of adolescent, 174–176
Checklists hindrance to proper classroom visitation, 69–70
Citizen Participation in Local Policy Making for Public Education, 50n
Citizenship, responsibilities of, benefit of extra-class activities, 187
Civic responsibilities, learning of, benefit of extra-class activities, 187

Clark, R.S., 18, 18n
Clubs, 190
Coleman, James S., 39
Collective negotiations, 4
Columbia Scholastic Press Association, 191
Columbia University, 18n, 30n, 123n
Combines, educational, 124–125
Combs, A.W., 31n
Commission on the Experimental Study of the Utilization of the Staff in the Secondary School, 62–63
Communicable diseases, checking on, 168
Communication, effective, essential to successful professional relationships, 75–76
Communication, principles of, 222–227
Communication and Public Relations, 223n
"Communications," school administration viewed as, 14
Community, role of school in, 206
Community activities, participation in for personal growth, 43
Community school, 211–215
Competencies needed by junior high school principals, 33–35
Competitive sports, arguments for and against, 193–194
Compromise vital in effecting maximum goal achievement between principals and teachers, 8
Conant, J.B., 18, 18n, 39, 86, 86n, 105, 164n, 165n
Conditions of Work for Quality Teaching, 12n
Conflict situations and morale, 74–75
Connell, Charles F., 59, 59n
Conner, Forrest E., 88n
Conrad, Lawrence H., 106n, 107n
Considerations, major, in planning innovations, 138–143
"Constants" in curriculum, 86
Consultant, educational, role of in planning educational innovations, 137
Conventions and conferences, attending, as part of professional growth, 40–41
Cooperative approach, objectives of, 211–215
Cooperative Program in Educational Administration, 13
Coordination second phase of administration, 12–13
Core program, 102–103
Cornell University, 85
"Corporal Punishment, Considerably Less Than Seldom," 184, 184n
"Corporal Punishment, Sometimes Yes," 183n
Corporate image of education in junior high school, 206–209
Council for Administrative Leadership in New York State, 6n, 18, 18n
Council of Chief State School Officers, 13, 160
Counseling, relation of to total program, 162–164
Counselors in personnel, qualifications for, 165
Creative supervision, 29–30
Creighton Junior High School, 11
Criner, Jane, 99n
Crowder, William W., 89n
Cumulative records in organizing personnel services, 160–162

Curriculum design, types of, 101–116
Curriculum Handbook for School Administrators, 88, 88*n*
Curriculum Report, 108, 108*n*

D

Davies, I.K., 122*n*
Daydreaming common activity of adolescents, 175
"Decision for the Principal: Hand or Computer Scheduling?" 111*n*
DeFleur, Melvin L., 223*n*
Democracy and Excellence in American Secondary Education, 39
Democratic leadership approach, 16–17
Democratic Supervision, 23, 23*n*
Demonstrations, reacting to, 5
Design first step of administration, 12
Design for Leadership, 24, 24*n*
Desired program consideration in planning educational innovation, 138
Developing the Core Curriculum, 102*n*
Developmental reading program, need for attention to, 88
Dewey, John, 186–187
Dining facilities, consideration of in planning educational facilities, 142
Disciplinary procedures, developing and maintaining, 173–184
Donaldson, George W., 107*n*
Dope, problems of, 181–183
Douglass, H., 23, 23*n*
Driver and Traffic Safety Education, 153
Driver education, equipment for, 152–153
Drucker, Peter F., 25–26
Drug Abuse: A Call for Action, 182*n*
Drug Abuse: Escape to Nowhere, 182*n*
Drugs, 181–183
"Dynamics of Change," 10*n*
"Dynamics of interaction" as technique of interviewing, 59

E

Economic Opportunities Act, 64
"Education and Community," 210*n*
Education and Public Understanding, 210*n*
Education in the Junior High School Years, 18*n*, 105
Education USA, 40
Educational Administration, 101*n*
Educational Facilities Laboratories, Inc., 66*n*, 121, 121*n*, 130, 144, 146*n*, 147, 147*n*, 148, 148*n*
Educational Forum, The, 53*n*
Educational Leadership, 22*n*, 29*n*
Educational plaza, 147
Educational television, 119–121
Effective Techniques of Administering School-Community Relations and Means of Professional Growth in These Relations Utilized by Indiana Public Secondary School Principals, 227*n*
"Electives" in curriculum, 87
Electronic laboratories, 123

Elementary and Secondary Education Act, 64
Elements of change, 10
Ellena, William J., 88*n*
Ellsworth, R.E., 130, 142*n*
Elmott, Dr. Charlotte, 99
Elmtown's Youth, 200*n*
Emerson, Ralph Waldo, 11
English course, guidance for selection of, 87–88
Engstrom, Y., 209*n*, 222*n*
Enriching the Social Studies, 106
Enrollment, proposed, consideration in planning educational innovation, 138–139
Environment for Learning, 144, 144*n*
Epstein, Benjamin, 4
Equality of Educational Opportunity, 39
Equipment, innovations in, 144–145, 152
E.T.V. Facilities Act of 1962, 120
Evanston, Illinois Township High School, 166
Existing program consideration in planning educational innovation, 138
Expectations of administrative leadership, 5–8
  incongruence in perceptions, 6–8
  leader and led, relationship between, 5–6
"Exploring Improved Teaching Patterns: Second Report on Staff Utilization Studies," 63*n*
Extended school day as type of curriculum design, 104–105

F

Fabub, Don, 159*n*
Factors, five, for composing staff into functioning team, 17
Family Life and Sex Education, 181*n*
Faunce, Roland C., 102
Films, filmstrips and slides, 118
Finance constant problem of school newspaper, 191
Financing extra-class activities, 195–197
First aid in school, 168
Flexible scheduling, 111–113
Focus on Change—Guide to Better Schools, 10, 10*n*
Food preparation facilities, consideration of in planning educational facilities, 142
Ford Foundation, 63, 64*n*, 65*n*, 66*n*, 114
Foreign languages, selection of courses in, 92
Formula for computing teaching stations for particular subject, 139
Fortune, 40
Free-rein leadership approach, 16–17
French, W., 13*n*
Fretwell, E.K., 186
From School Program to School Plant, 139
Fulfillment third stage of administration, 12–13
Fuller, 62
Functions, new, of secondary school principal, 3–5
Functions, traditional, of administrators, 12–16
  administration, components of, 12–13
  considering, ways of, 13–16
  theories, administrative, prior, 14–16
  theory, four sources of, 14
Fund for the Advancement of Education, 63
Fused subject areas program, 102–103
Future Teachers of America, 52

INDEX

G

Gage, N.L., 39, 96n
Gardner, John W., 75, 75n
German Township decision, Pennsylvania, 197
Getzels, J.W., 14n
Gifted, special programs for in curriculum, 95–98
Golden, L.L., 207n
Graduate work as form of professional growth, 38
Gran, John M., 175n
Graybeal, William S., 53
Greer, Edith S., 85, 96n
Griffith Junior-Senior High School, Indiana, 149–150
Griffiths, Daniel E., 12n, 15n
Grouping, serious discussion about, 96–98
Growth of staff, professional, 37–40, 77–82
Guba, E.G., 14n
Guidance, relation of to total program, 162–164
Guidance areas, consideration of in planning educational facilities, 142
Guide to Collective Negotiations in Education, A, 4
Guide for Planning School Plants, 135n, 144n
"Guidelines for an Adequate Investment in Instructional Materials, 1967," 129n
Guidelines for interviewing, 59
Guidelines for reporting pupil progress, 225–226
Guilford, Dr. J.P., 29
Gunn, H.M., 24, 24n
Gwynn, J.M., 23, 23n, 28n, 30n

H

Halpin, Andrew W., 14n
Hamlin, Herbert M., 50, 50n
Handbook, student, 192
Handbook of Research on Teaching, 96, 96n
Handbook for the Study of Administrative Staff Organization, 51n
Handicapped children, special program for, 95
Harris, Ben M., 25, 25n
Harris, Chester W., 32n, 39
Harvard Educational Review, 210n
Harvard Physics Program, 90
Hatfield Township decision, Pennsylvania, 197
Health services, 167–168
  areas, consideration of in planning educational facilities, 142
Hencley, Stephen P., 120n, 186n
Herrick, J.H., 139n
"Higher Horizons" program, 99
Hills, R.J., 15n
Hollingshead, August B., 200, 200n
Home economics courses, guidance in selection of, 91–92
Home room, role of in pupil personnel services, 162–163
Home-school-community, 209–211
  community school, 211–215
  cooperative approach, objectives of, 211–215
  principles, four, 209
Hook, J.N., 88n
"How to Avoid Four Failures When You Talk to Workers," 76n
How to Prepare a Research Proposal, 4
How Teachers View School Administration, 6n
How to Tell the School Story, 211n
How to Understand and Teach Teenagers, 175n
Hull, J.D., 13n
"Human relations," administration as, 14
  principles of, 219–221
Human relationships and morale, 72–75
Human skills in supervision, 25–27

I

Ideas in use, innovative, 146–151
Idiographic style of principal, 8
Illinois Education, LIII, 88n
Illinois High School Association, 195n, 196n
Illinois Journal of Education, 111n
Image of self, satisfactory, vital for successful supervisory and administrative leadership, 30–31
Images of the Future: A New Approach to the Secondary School, 65n
Imperatives in Education, 40
Implications for Education of Prospective Changes in Society, 40
In Search of Self, 30n
In-service appraisal, 80–81
Incongruence in perceptions of administration between principals and teachers, 6–8
Independent study, 108–109
"Independent Study," 108n, 109n
Index of teacher demand, 53, 54
"Index of Teacher Demand Through 1964," 53n
Indiana University, 109n, 134n, 227n
Individual, increasing need for stress on, 159–160
Industrial arts courses, guidance in selection of, 91
Information for planners, sources of, 144
Ingredients, ten, of change, 10
Inlow, Gail M., 106n
"Inner Direction and the Decision Maker," 16n
Inner strength and personal control vital to administrator's decision-making process, 16
"Innovation Study of Nation's High Schools Reveals Important Changes in Recent Years," 126n
Innovations in educational facilities, planning, 134–155
Institutes, attending, as part of professional growth, 40–41
Instruction, reorganization of after staff utilization studies, 63–64
Instruction supervision, design for, 68–70
Instructional area meeting, 78
Instructional leaders meetings, 78
"Instructional leadership" theory of school administration, 14
Instructional Materials Center, 65–66
Instructional Media and Creativity, 40
  consideration of in planning educational facilities, 142
Instructional method and teaching aids, 65–66
"Instructional Revolution," 64n
Instructional teams, theory of, 30
Integrated learnings program, 102–103
Interscholastic athletics, 193–195

"Interscholastics—A Discussion of Interscholastic Contests," 195n
Interviewing prospective teachers, 55–59
Intramural instructional area meeting, 78
Intrinsic programming, 122
Introduction to Secondary Education, 186n, 201n
Investigations into teacher-principal views of administration, 6–8
ITV Newsletter, 119n

J

Jacobs, Paul I., 122n
Jenkins, Russell L., 76, 76n
Jersild, A.T., 30n
"Job Analysis—Junior High School Principals," 34n
Johns, Roe L., 101n
Johnson, Mauritz, Jr., 115n
Jones, J.J., 205n
Journal of Communication, 222n, 224n
Journal of Secondary Education, 98n
Judgment in Administration, 39
"Jun-Hi Teach Corps," formation of, 53
Junior High School Association of Illinois, 53
Junior high school principals, competencies needed by, 33–35
  five areas of work for, 18
Junior High School Staff Personnel, 53n

K

Kahn, Robert L., 59, 59n
Kaplan, Louis, 176n, 178, 178n
Keating, Raymond F., 123n
Kelley, E., 31n
Kellogg, W.K., Foundation, 13
Killian, James R. Jr., 119n
Kindred, L., 211n
King, M.L., 22, 22n
Knowledge, extension of, benefit of extra-class activities, 187
Krathwohl, David R., 4
Krebs, Alfred H., 78, 78n

L

Lakeview Junior-Senior High School, 64
Lamphere Public School District, Michigan, 148
Language laboratories, 123
Lapchick, Joseph D., 51n
Lawson, Herbert G., 106n
Lay citizens, role of in planning educational innovations, 137
Leader and led, relationship between, 5–6
Leadership, educational, nature and challenge of, 3–20
Leadership benefit of extra-class activities, 187
Leadership Styles and Administrator Perceptions, 8n
Learning by doing, benefit of extra-class activities, 186–187
Learning materials, selection and organization of, 117–133
Legal status of school activity funds, 197
Leonhard, Charles, 93, 93n

Liba, Marie R., 39
Library, 129–132
  librarian, 130–131
  location, 130
  staff, 131–132
Likert, Rensis, 27, 27n, 222n
Linder, I.H., 24, 24n
Linear programming, 122
Linscott, N.N., 30n
Literature, professional, 39–40
Lockers, problem of, 149
"Locus of Change: Fifth Report on Staff Utilization Studies," 63n
Longer school year as type of curriculum design, 103–104
Lucio, W.H., 24, 24n, 27, 27n, 28, 28n
Lynd, 62

M

Mackenzie, G.N., 22, 22n
McCleary, Lloyd, 120n
McCleary, Lloyd E., 186n
McCloskey, G., 210n
McClurkin, W.D., 135n
McKown, Harry C., 186
McNeil, J.D., 24, 24n, 27, 27n, 28, 28n
Magazine, student, 192
Maier, Milton H., 122n
Maine Township High School North, 166
March, J.G., 17n
Markus, Frank W., 4
Marking and reporting pupil progress, 225–227
Masters, Hugh B., 107n
Mastery of People, 16n, 17
Materials for learning, selection and organization of, 117–133
Mathematics course, guidance in selection of, 90
Maul, Ray D., 53
Maurer, David, 112n
Melbourne High School, 64
Melby, Ernest O., 74, 74n
Mental Health and Human Relations in Education, 176n
Michigan State University, 4
Middle school concept, 147–148
Midwest Program of Airborne Television Instruction, 120
Miller, Gerald R., 222, 222n
Miller, P.V., 16, 16n
M.I.T., 29
Mitchell, Anne, 80n
Modern Elementary Curriculum, 226n
Modern High School Administration, 186n
Modern Music Masters, 190
Modes of influence, four, for change, 9
Modular scheduling, 110–111
Morale and professional growth of staff, 72–82
  morale, 72–77
  professional growth of staff, 77–81
Morphet, Edgar L., 40, 101n
"Motivating the Under-Achieving Gifted Pupil in Junior High School," 98n
Motivation of reluctant learners, 98–99

M.P.A.T.I., 120
Mueller, Richard J., 63, 63n
Music courses, guidance in selection of, 92–93

N

Narcotics, 181–183
NASSP *Bulletin*, 63n, 111n, 115n, 190n
NASSP Curriculum Report, 90
NASSP Spotlight, 104n
Nation's Schools, 40, 144, 148n, 149n
National Association of Independent Schools, 181n
National Association of Secondary School Principals, 4, 9n, 24n, 25, 29, 34n, 62–63, 63n, 104, 108n, 190
National Conference of County and Rural Area Superintendents, 13
National Conference of Professors of Educational Administration, 13
National Council on Schoolhouse Construction, 135, 136n, 137n, 139n–142n, 144
National Council of Teachers of Mathematics, 106
National Defense Education Acts, 64, 80
National Educational Television, 121
National Inventory of Secondary School Innovations 1967, 63n
National Science Foundation, 80, 90
National Science Teachers Association, 144
National Society for the Study of Education, 163n, 206n, 212, 212n
Nature and extent of pupil personnel services, 164–165
NEA, 12, 12n, 53n, 63n, 89, 129n, 182n
NEA Journal, 93n, 124, 183n, 184n, 226n, 227n
NEA Research Bulletin, 53n
Nebraska Educational Television Commission, 120, 121n
"Needed: A New Concept of Educational Administration," 74n
NEEDS, 114
Negotiations, collective, 4
Negotiations Bibliography, 4
NESDEC, 114
New Directions to Quality Education: The Secondary School Tomorrow, 63n
New England School Development Council, 114, 114n
"New Horizons in Staff Utilization," 63n
New Patterns of Management, 27n, 222n
New Schools for New Education, 66n
New York Times, 40, 43
New York University, 25
Newman, F.M., 210n
News and Views, 44n
Newspaper, school, 191
Newsweek, 40
Noar, Gertrude, 40
Nomination of professional personnel, 60
Nomothetic style of principal, 8
Non-graded school, 109–110
Non-professional personnel, role of in planning educational innovations, 136–137
North Central Association, 126, 126n, 131

North Central Today, 126n
Northern Illinois University, 63n, 106n
Nova High School, Fort Lauderdale, Florida, 104, 110, 120, 130

O

Objective acceptance of others key to principal's authority and influence, 26
"Off to College at 15—Is It a Good Idea?" 106n
Ohmann, O.A., 6n
Oliver, D.W., 210n
On Defining Communication: Another Stab, 222, 222n
Opaque projector, 124
Openshaw, D., 122n
Operation third phase of administration, 12
Organization, 17n
Organization, definition of, 12
Organization first stage of administration, 12
Organizations, professional, as part of growth program, 41
Organizing and Working with Departmental Advisory Councils in the Public Schools, 78n
Organizing New York State for Educational Change, 10n, 80n
Organizing Schools for Effective Education, 12n
Osborn, Alex, 29
Outdoor education, 107–108, 149
Outdoor Education, 107n
Outdoor Teacher Education, 106n, 107n
Ovard, Glen, 135, 135n
Overhead projector, use of, 123–124

P

Page, Ray, 111n
Parker, Hyman, 4
Participation of teacher essential for morale, 76–77
Partners in Junior High School Education, Inc., 207, 209
Pay schedules for extra-class activities, 199
Perceiving, Behaving, Becoming, 8n, 31n
"Perceptual field," definition of, 31
Performance review, 28
Performing arts, 192
  courses, guidance in selection of, 93–94
Permanent records and organization of personnel services, 162
Personal growth, 42–45
Personal interest of principal vital for teacher morale, 73–74
"Personality trait" approach to educational administration, 14
Personnel and Guidance Journal, 165n
Personnel Magazine, 6n
Personnel requirements and selection, 49–61
"Personnel Services in Education," 163n
Phenix, Philip H., 39
Phi Delta Kappan, 40, 41, 124
Physical education, guidance in course selection for, 89
Planning America's School Buildings, 134n, 153n
Planning a Program of Sex Education, 181n

"Planning for Schools with Television," 121n
Plant, innovations in, 144–145
Plath, Dr. Karl, 85n
Policies, study of for professional growth of staff, 79–80
Polner, Murray, 106
"Preparing Junior High Teachers: A Prof's Eye View," 53n
Principal, role of in planning educational innovations, 136
Principal, supervisory function of, 67–68
Principal and pupil personnel services, 171
Principal of secondary school, role of, 16–18
    factors, five, for composing staff into functioning team, 17
    junior high school principal, five work areas of, 18
    "team member" concept vital for success, 16–17
Principal's Role in Collective Negotiations, The, 4
Principles, four, of effective home-school-community cooperation, 209
Principles, guiding, for effective administration and supervision by principal, 32
Principles of administration and supervision, 21–36
"Principles of Democratic Supervision," 21n
Problems, new, for modern secondary school principal, 3
Professional growth, 37–42
Professional staff meeting, 77–79
Profiles of Significant Schools: Schools for Team Teaching, 148n
Profiles of Significant Schools: Two Middle Schools, Saginaw Township, Michigan, 147n
Program of studies, 83–155
    curriculum design, types of, 101–116
    innovations in educational facilities, planning, 134–155
    learning materials, selection and organization of, 117–133
    requirements and optional subjects, 85–100
Programmed learning, 121–124
    advantages, 122
    electronic laboratories, 123
    other, 123–124
    three types, 122
Programmed Learning in Perspective, 122n
"Progressing Toward Better Schools: Third Report on Staff Utilization Studies," 63n
Project English, 88
"Project English: A Concentrated Attack on Old Problems," 88n
Proposal writing, 3–4
Protests, reacting to, 5
Psychological services in personnel services to pupil, 167
Public Law 85–864, 165
"Public Relations," 207n
Public relations and junior high school, 206–209
Public Television: A Program for Action, 119n
Punitive discipline and counseling, relationship between, 166
Pupil activity areas, consideration of in planning educational facilities, 143
Pupil personnel services, 159–172
Pupils, role of in planning educational innovations, 136
Purdue University, 224n

Q

Qualifications for personnel services counselors, 165
Qualitative requirements for personnel, 49–50
Qualities of teacher-candidates to be assessed in screening, 55
Quantitative requirements for personnel, 50–51
Quill & Scroll, 191

R

Race relations, 181–183
Ragan, William B., 226n
Rationale for innovations in school design for early adolescents, 151–152
Reacting to protests, demonstrations and possible walkouts, 5
Reading for personal growth, 42–43
Realms of Meaning, 39
Recruitment activity by principals, 52–53
Reid, John Lyon, 145
Relative process, supervision as, 27
Relaxation, time for essential for personal growth, 44–45
Reller, Theodore L., 101n
Reluctant learners, special programs for, 98–99
Reorganization of instruction after staff utilization studies, 63–64
Repas, Bob, 4
"Reporting to Parents, Why? What? How?" 226n
Reporting pupil progress, 225–227
Requirements and optional subjects, 85–100
Requirements for personnel, 49–51
    qualitative, 49–50
    quantitative, 50–51
Research methodology, 28–29
Research proposal, preparation of, 4
"R/Ingredients of Change," 9n
Richards, J.A., 29n
Rickover, 62
Riots, 181–183
Robinson, Edward J., 223n
"Role of the Supervisor," 22n
Roles, new, of secondary school principal, 3–5
    negotiations, collective, 4
    proposal writing, 3–4
    reacting to protests, demonstrations and walkouts, 5
Roles, theory of, 8
Roles in planning educational innovations, 135–137
Rollins, Sidney P., 186n, 201, 201n
Romine, Stephen, 44n
Rose, H.C., 34n
Ryan, Charles, 40

S

"Salience and Pertinence as Sources of Value Change," 224n

INDEX

Saturday Review, 40
Saturday sessions as method of curriculum design, 105
Saturday Review, 80n
Saunders, Juliet, 34n
Schmidt, Charles T. Jr., 4
School Activities Magazine, 195n
School Administrator and Negotiation, The, 4
School board, role of in planning educational innovations, 135–136
School Building Planning, 135n
School-community relations, 205–229
School-Community Relations, 212n
School-Community Relations: A New Approach, 209n, 222n
School Construction Systems Development project, 147
School day, extended, as form of curriculum design, 104–105
School Executive, 16n
School Management, 51n, 144, 147n, 181n
"School Marks and Their Reporting," 227n
School Personnel Administration, 73
School Review, 14n
Schoolmasters Club of Cincinnati, 215
Schools for America, 137n
Science course, guidance in selection of, 90
Screening process of personnel, 55
Search for competent personnel, 52–55
Secondary school, modern, administrative staff in, 3–45
Secondary School Administration, 24, 24n, 120n
Secondary School Education, 186n
Secondary School Plant Planning, 144
Security, feeling of benefit of extra-class activities, 187
"Seeking Improved Learning Opportunities: Fourth Report on Staff Utilization Studies," 63n
Selection of personnel, 51–55
  professional positions, 52
  search, 52–55
Self-discipline by students important goal of secondary school, 174
Self-improvement program, principal's, 37–45
Self-realization for principal, 30–35
Sex, 181–183
Seyfort, Warren C., 108n
Simon, H.A., 17n
Site consideration in planning educational innovations, 139
"Situational" approach to educational administration, 14
S-M-C-R as essential components in communication theory model, 224
Smith, B. Othanel, 9n, 39
Smith, Julian W., 107n
Smith, Kline and French Laboratories, 182n
Smith, Mark, 98n
"Social Behavior and the Administrative Process," 14n
Social Education, 89n
"Social process" concept of educational administration, 14–15

Social studies courses, guidance in selection of, 89–90
Social values, satisfactory, benefit of extra-class activities, 187
Social worker, 166–167
"Some Trends in Elementary School Social Studies," 89n
Space relationships, consideration of in planning educational facilities, 143
Speaking as form of professional growth, 41–42
Spears, Harold, 186
Special programs in curriculum, 94–99
  gifted, 95–98
  handicapped children, 95
  reluctant learners, 98–99
  troublesome ten percent, 99
Spinning, James M., 184n
Staff, professional, 49–82
  morale and professional growth of staff, 72–82
  personnel requirement and selection, 49–61
  role of in planning educational innovations, 136
  staff utilization and supervision, 62–71
Staff effort, discipline policy as, 179–180
Staff meetings, 77–79
Staff utilization and supervision, 62–71
Staffing personnel services, 166
State-wide adoption of textbooks, 128
Stein, J., 30n
Stolurow, Laurence M., 122n
"Straight Talk About the Drug Problem," 181n
Strasser, M.K., 153
Strevell, W.H., 137n, 138n
Strong, H.R., 18, 18n
Student, 159–201
  activities, pupil, 185–201
  discipline procedures, developing and maintaining, 173–184
  pupil personnel services, 159–172
Student council oldest student organization, 188–189
Students, involvement of in formulation of discipline policies, 180
Study, areas for in encouraging staff growth, 79–80
Subject areas, guidance and, 87–94
  art and music, 92–93
  business education, 94
  English, 87–88
  foreign languages, 92
  home economics, 91–92
  industrial arts, 91
  mathematics, 90
  performing arts, 93–94
  physical education, 89
  science, 90
  social studies, 89–90
Suggestions for innovations in building design, 145–146
"Summer School vs. The Year-Round School," 104n
Sumption, M., 209n, 222n
Superintendent of schools, role of in planning educational innovations, 136
Supervision, 24n
Supervision in Action, 22n
Supervision and administration, principles of, 21–36

INDEX

Supervisory Behavior in Education, 25n
Supervisory visits by principal, 68–70
Syracuse University, 4

T

"Take Time to Think," 44n
Tape recording, use of to open interview, 58
Taylor, Calvin W., 40
Teacher performance review, 28
Teacher-Principal Agreement on the Teacher Role, 7n
Teachers, helping with disciplinary problems, 178
Teachers College Record, 21n
Teaching staff facilities, consideration of in planning educational facilities, 143
Teaching stations consideration in planning educational innovations, 139–141
"Team-member" concept vital to successfully-functioning principal, 16–17
Technical skills in supervision, 28
Technology, growing importance of, 118–121
 educational television, 119–121
 films, filmstrips and slides, 118
Technology and curriculum, 110–115
 automated schedule, 113–115
 flexible scheduling, 111–113
 modular scheduling, 110–111
Tenets, basic, for administrative and supervisory leadership, 30–35
Textbooks, 127–129
The Administrative Organization of the Modern Junior High School, 18n
The American High School Today, 86n, 105
The Anatomy of Change, 9n
"The Antileadership Vaccine," 75n
"The Art of Creative Supervision," 29n
The Bulletin of the NASSP, 9n, 10n, 34n, 40, 63n, 111n, 115n, 190n
"The Class Is a Group," 220n
The Community School, 206n
The Community School and Its Administration, 74n
The Comprehensive High School, 39, 164n
The Computer Age, 40
The Cost of a Schoolhouse, 146, 146n, 147n, 148n
"The Crux of the Matter," 80n
"The Dynamic Junior High School," 115n
The Dynamics of Change, 159n
The Dynamics of Interviewing—Theory, Techniques and Cases, 59n
"The Education Plaza—Death Knell for the Neighborhood School?" 147n
The Educational Forum, 53n
The Emergent in Curriculum, 106n
The Encyclopedia of Educational Research, 39
The Gifted Child in Portland, 96n
The Handbook of Research on Teaching, 39
The High School in a Changing World, 21n
The High School Journal, 220n
"The Illinois Interscholastic," 196n
The Intellectual Responsibility of the Junior High School, 85
The Journal of Communication, 222n, 224n
The Junior High School, 85, 96n
The Junior High School We Need, 109n
The Junior High Schools of California, 85
The Junior High School in Illinois, 206n, 218n
"The Leader and the Led," 6n
The Nongraded High School, 64n, 109n
"The Place of Music in Our Elementary and Secondary Schools," 93n
The Political World of the High School Teacher, 40
The Principal's Role in Collective Negotiations, 4
The Process of Education, 39
The School Administrator and Negotiation, 4
The School Library, 130, 142n
The School Review, 14n
The Schoolmaster and His Publics, 215n
The Teacher and Integration, 40
The Troublesome Ten Percent, 99n
The Wall Street Journal, 106n
The Year-Round School, 103n
Theories of Mass Communication, 223n
Theory, administrative, four sources of, 14
Theory and Practice of Supervision, 23n, 28n
Theory of roles, 8
Thomas, C.A., 122n
Thomas, Myra H., 181n
Three-pronged leadership approach to administration, 16–17
Time, 40
Time, Talent and Teachers, 65n
Times, 40, 43
"Trait" approach to educational administration, 14
Treasurers, student, 198
Troublesome ten percent, special program for, 99
Truant officer, 166–167
Trump, Dr. J. Lloyd, 9n, 10n, 63, 63n, 65n
Typing courses, 94

U

Underground schools, 150
University Council on Educational Administration, 13
University of Chicago, 14n, 15n
University of Colorado, 44n
University of Illinois, 50n
University of Missouri, 4
University of Nebraska, 120
University of North Dakota, 34n
University of Oregon, 40
Unruh, Adolph, 186n, 201n
Uris, Auren, 16n, 17
U.S. Office of Education, 181

V

Vacillation common characteristic of adolescent, 175
Van Zwoll, James A., 73, 73n
"Variables" in curriculum, 87
Vars, Dr. Gordon F., 53, 53n
Video tapes, 119–120
"Vitalizing Student Activities in the Secondary Schools," 190

INDEX

Vocational Education Act of 1963, 64, 91, 94
Vrentas, 33

W

Wagener, H.D., 130, 142*n*
Wagner, Ralph, 99*n*
Walkouts, possible, reacting to, 5
Wall Street Journal, 106*n*
Waterloo, Dr. Glenn, 169–170
Watt, Lois B., 181*n*
Werner, W.G., 215*n*
Whitten, Charles W., 195*n*
"Who Should Hire Elementary Teachers," 51*n*
Why You Do What You Do, 30*n*
Wilkerson, William R., 134*n*
Williams, Clifford W., 96
Williams, Frank E., 40
Willower, D.J., 8, 8*n*
Wilson, John A.R., 183*n*

Windowless schools, 150–151
Winston Dictionary, The, 222*n*
W.K. Kellogg Foundation, 13
Workshops, attending, as part of professional growth, 40–41
Wright, Grace S., 85, 96*n*
Writing and speaking as form of professional growth, 41–42

Y

Yauch, William A., 227*n*
Yeager, William A., 212*n*
Yearbook, 191–192
YMCA and guidance functions, 164
"Youthquake," 5

Z

Zeigler, Harmon, 40